The Poetry Handbook

The Poetry Handbook

A Guide to Reading Poetry for Pleasure and Practical Criticism

JOHN LENNARD

OXFORD UNIVERSITY PRESS

Oxford University Press, Great Clarendon Street, Oxford OX2 6DP
Oxford New York
Athens Auckland Bangkok Bogota Bombay
Buenos Aires Calcutta Cape Town Dar es Salaam
Delhi Florence Hong Kong Istanbul Karachi
Kuala Lumpur Madras Madrid Melbourne
Mexico City Nairobi Paris Singapore
Taipei Tokyo Toronto
and associated companies in
Berlin Ibadan

Oxford is a trade mark of Oxford University Press

Published in the United States
by Oxford University Press Inc., New York

Text © John Lennard 1996
Essays on pp. 188–93 © Adam Barnes, Andrew Miller, Simon Oastler 1996
First published 1996
Paperback edition reprinted with corrections 1996

All rights reserved. No part of this publication may be reproduced, stored in a retrieval system, or transmitted, in any form or by any means, without the prior permission in writing of Oxford University Press. Within the UK, exceptions are allowed in respect of any fair dealing for the purpose of research or private study, or criticism or review, as permitted under the Copyright, Designs and Patents Act, 1988, or in the case of reprographic reproduction in accordance with the terms of the licences issued by the Copyright Licensing Agency. Enquiries concerning reproduction outside these terms and in other countries should be sent to the Rights Department, Oxford University Press, at the address above

This book is sold subject to the condition that it shall not, by way of trade or otherwise, be lent, re-sold, hired out or otherwise circulated without the publisher's prior consent in any form of binding or cover other than that in which it is published and without a similar condition including this condition being imposed on the subsequent purchaser

British Library Cataloguing in Publication Data
Data available

Library of Congress Cataloging in Publication Data
Lennard, John.
The poetry handbook / John Lennard.
Includes bibliographical references.
1. English poety—History and criticism—Theory, etc.—Handbooks, manuals, etc. 2. Criticism—Authorship—Handbooks, manuals, etc. 3. Poetry—Explication—Handbooks, manuals, etc. 4. Books and reading—Handbooks, manuals, etc. 5. Poetics—Handbooks, manuals, etc. I. Title.
PR502.L38 1996 808.1—dc20 96–5461

ISBN 0–19–871149–2 (pbk.)
ISBN 0–19–871154–9

Printed in Great Britain by
Biddles Ltd
Guildford & King's Lynn

For

ANNE BOWLER AND ANNE BARTON

who taught me far more than these basics

and for

JEREMY MAULE

who told me to write them down.

Cricket is an art. Like all arts
it has a technical foundation. To enjoy it
does not require technical knowledge, but
analysis that is not technically based is mere impressionism.

C. L. R. JAMES, *Beyond a Boundary*

Acknowledgements

Beyond the debts acknowledged in the dedication I would like to thank those students who have harassed me into clarity, especially Dan Fugallo, Tess Grant, Rob Morris, Penny Taylor, Nicky White; and those brave students, Adam Barnes, Andy Miller, and Simon Oastler, who have allowed their timed work to appear in the last chapter. My warmest thanks also to Jonathan Lloyd for reading many first drafts, and to Ljubica Dimitrijevic for putting up with me while he did so; to the anonymous first reader at OUP for the most helpful report I have ever had; to Jonathan Steinberg for boundless encouragement; to John Creaser for valuable commentary on the entire manuscript; to William Clocksin for help with the mathematical formula; to John Lyons for help with the Greek; to Gabriel Gbadamosi for a persuasive argument about phrasing; to Francis Ingledew for help with Walcott's West Indian experience; to Hugh Stevens for suggestions about Walcott and gender; and to Mary Luckhurst for everything.

'Nearing Forty' is reproduced from Derek Walcott's *Collected Poems 1948–84* (New York: Farrar, Straus & Giroux, 1986). Reprinted by permission of Farrar, Straus & Giroux, Inc. and Faber and Faber Ltd.

J. C. L.
Trinity Hall, Cambridge
August 1995

Contents

Introduction

This book is for anyone who wants to read poetry with a better understanding of its craft and technique, but it is also a textbook and crib for school and undergraduate students of English who have to sit exams in practical criticism. Teaching the practical criticism of poetry at several universities, and talking to students about how they have previously been taught, has made me sharply aware of how little consensus there is about the subject. Some teachers make no distinction between practical criticism and critical theory, or regard practical criticism as a critical theory, to be taught alongside psychoanalytical, feminist, Marxist, and structuralist theories; others seem to do very little except invite discussion of 'how it feels' to read poem x. And as practical criticism (though not always called that) remains a compulsory paper in most English Literature A-levels and Scottish Highers, and most undergraduate English courses, this is an unwelcome state of affairs.

For students there are many consequences. Their teachers at school and (if they go on to read English) at university may contradict one another, and too rarely seem to put the problem of differing viewpoints and frameworks for analysis in perspective; important aspects of the subject are often omitted in the confusion; and as a result many students who are otherwise more than competent have little or no idea of what they are being asked to do. The problem is how this may be remedied without losing the richness and diversity of thought which, at its best, practical criticism can foster; or, to put it another way, what are the basics? and how may they be taught?

My own answer, as this book makes clear, is that the basics are an understanding of, and an ability to judge, the elements of a poet's craft. Profoundly different as they are, Chaucer, Shakespeare, Pope, Emily Dickinson, Eliot, Derek Walcott, and Sylvia Plath could readily talk with one another about the techniques of which they are common masters; but few undergraduates that I have encountered know much about metre beyond the terms 'blank verse' and 'iambic pentameter', much about form beyond 'couplet' and 'sonnet', or anything about rhyme more complicated than the assertion that two words do or don't. The commonest fault of their own writing is an inability to use any punctuation beyond full-stops and commas (parentheses, colons, semi-colons, dashes, and hyphens might as well not exist) and a consequent tendency to connect endless clauses in parallel—which gains little clarity at the cost of all subtlety. Yet it is exactly these techniques of ordering to which, as to the other elements of craft—the layout and lineation, the diction and syntax, the deployments of biography and history—close reading must attend.

To name and define the elements of poetic craft is, of course, in part a set of ideological decisions, but the influence of ideology on metre or rhyme is very much slower than its influence on what is put into metre or made to rhyme. I do not believe that a craft-based practical criticism is either incompatible with or opposed to theoretical approaches; but rather, that it is a helpful precursor of them all, a foundation course in reading. To interpret a given use of form, or a rhyme, or some metrical device may involve, for any particular reader, reference to Freud, or Marx, or Derrida; but the form, rhyme, or metrical device must first be noticed by the reader, and it is much easier to notice things of which you have some knowledge. And while theoretical criticisms may seek to account for a text without detailed reference to its technique, to how it has achieved its texture, practical criticism—if the term means anything at all—cannot avoid that engagement with technique we call close reading. Close reading is itself only a beginning, to be followed by more distant readings; but for the teacher it is a sensible place to start.

What is to be taught, then, is the value and uses of the tools of the poet's trade: and knowing that makes it clear that the method must be their itemization, description, and demonstration. The basic list of those tools represented by my chapter titles is not in dispute—metre, form, lineation, rhyme and so on are fundamental constituents of almost all Western poetry—but there are certainly some issues, notably layout and punctuation, to which I give more attention than is now usual because I have found it helpful in practice to do so; and equally some issues, notably class- and gender-conscious analysis, to which I attend somewhat less than is usual because I have little to clarify in, or to add to, what others have said. These personal choices are balanced out in the suggestions for further reading, and I have in general tried to describe and explain with an even hand.

The examples use (wherever possible) material available either in the two volumes of *The Oxford Anthology of English Literature* (1973) or in the fourth edition of *The Norton Anthology of Poetry* (1996) which, despite some blemishes, remains the fullest one-volume anthology. To avoid crippling copyright fees without simply ignoring all modern poetry, and to keep the book reasonably short, possession of either the *Oxford* or the *Norton* anthologies is assumed, and the reader is intended to have one or other by them as they read.

ALL REFERENCES OF THE FORM (O1.999) AND (N999) ARE TO PAGES IN THE *OXFORD* AND *NORTON* ANTHOLOGIES; 'O1.999' AND 'O2.999' DISTINGUISH VOLUMES ONE AND TWO OF THE *OXFORD ANTHOLOGY*.

All readers are strongly advised to consult any poem which is referred to but not quoted, for unless you look up these poems, and look carefully at how the particular tool is used in an individual poem, seeing how my generalizations about its use relate to the specifics of its use, your understanding of it can only be partial. As a result of the need regularly to consult poems it is probably best to treat this book as a short guided tour, to be taken at no more than a chapter a day—and only that fast if you are in a hurry. My own advice would be to take a month or more, working through each chapter in short but regular sessions, and going on to the next only when you are happy that you have absorbed the last. In teaching face-to-face I would normally spread out the chapters over at least a whole term as one among several subjects (a practice which candidates for exams are particularly advised to follow); and between this first course and exams there would be other courses to deepen the students' knowledge and develop their confidence. In short, any student who tries to read this book cover-to-cover in a sitting (except as revision) will be wasting their time. I also require my own students to write a timed (1-hour) answer every week, so that they are wholly familiar with the contours of that hour, and the timing of examination answers becomes quite automatic. This seems to me only sensible, and has proven benefits; but if you are facing an exam you and your teachers must decide how much practice you need.

At the end of each chapter I look at the topic of the chapter at work in the same poem, Derek Walcott's 'Nearing Forty', so that a fairly complete technical reading is built up chapter by chapter. It is not a complete reading, for there are many aspects of the poem as a whole which I do not cover: but any reading which did claim to be complete would have to include most (if not all) of what I do say. It may seem odd to choose a poem about a mid-life crisis for students, the majority of whom will not be nearing forty; I have done so partly because I think it a very fine poem, but more importantly because I have found it to work well in both class and individual teaching, and the growing enthusiasm of students working on the poem seems to me a valuable proof of practical criticism. It is not only that familiar and accessible poems can be read more deeply with a knowledge of their craft, but also that such knowledge makes accessible to any reader poems which may at first seem obscure or unrewarding. 'Nearing Forty' is printed in full on pages 14–15, as it appears in Walcott's *Collected Poems 1948–84*.

One of my purposes is to introduce students to the technical vocabulary of criticism. That vocabulary, though it may seem off-putting, is essential if technical knowledge is to be usable in exams, and to make accurate argument about poetic techniques possible, between students as well as with teachers. Without it practical criticism becomes inevitably long-winded and inexact—imagine trying to discuss music without the names of the notes, the keys, and the instruments—so the matter must be tackled; but at the same time it is true that there are some disputes about what things should be called, some terms that are ambiguous or duplicated, and some that are missing. Where there are alternatives to my own choice, or where (in a very few instances) I offer *coinages* (terms of my own invention), my decisions are explained in a footnote. As with any professional *lexicon* (the vocabulary of a specific trade or activity) these technical terms are mutually supporting: the more of them that you know, the easier it is to learn a new one; and, conversely, the first few that you encounter are often awkward, or defined by other words that you do not yet know. I have tried to introduce technical vocabulary in a helpful order, and where I have had to introduce a term before the chapter which deals with it properly I have provided a short definition in the text or a footnote, with a reference to the pages where it is dealt with in full. All technical terms are *italicized* (set in slanting or *italic* letters) on their first appearance,[1] and to avoid confusion I have therefore not used italics for non-technical words which I simply want to stress, but have underlined them instead. (Titles and foreign words, though, are italicized in the usual way.) The commonest and most useful technical terms introduced in each chapter are grouped and defined in a sub-glossary at the end of each chapter, and all the terms I use may be found, defined and with a reference to the pages on which they are used, in the glossary at the back.

[1] The names of the marks of punctuation, at pp. 60–9, are (for reasons of layout) given in bold.

One word which I might be expected to have used in a technical sense I have deliberately avoided. An *image*, according to the *Shorter Oxford English Dictionary* (definition 4), is 'A counterpart, copy M[iddle] E[nglish].; a symbol, emblem, representation 1566; a type, typical example, embodiment 1548'; and the word has been used by critics of poetry in all these and many other ways. So inconsistent has the use been, covering everything from the meaning of a single word to a meaning arising from a whole poem, that 'image' does not seem to me truly a 'technical' term, and I have not found it difficult to avoid. It remains the case, though, that almost all the poetic techniques I discuss (metrical, formal, syntactical, or whatever) will probably first be apprehended by the reader as components or substructures of an 'image' (of one or another kind) which the poem (or the poet) has communicated to them.

There is also one word which I probably use too much, but which does not readily fit into any particular chapter: *irony*. It is a word notoriously hard to define exactly, but common to most definitions is a contrast between what is, or is said or done, and what might be expected to be, or to be said or done; and the difficulty of definition arises because the word always invokes this double state of being and perceiving. The Japanese character for 'irony' literally means 'skin-and-muscle', the surface that you see and the power hidden beneath it; and my own rule-of-thumb definition is that irony is 'the preservation of distance'—the corollary of which is that whenever you use the word you should be able to specify between what and what the distance is being preserved. I have found this definition helpful in teaching, and would recommend it—but one other word of warning is necessary, for many critics seem to assume that this preserved distance is necessarily undermining, antagonistic to one or other pole of the irony, as if the ironic were always a sarcastic response to disappointed expectation. In modern writing, this is often (though by no means always) the case, but that is far less true in writing pre-dating *c.*1650. A Renaissance writer such as John Donne may be acutely aware of the distance between himself and God, and may use irony to figure that distance: but to characterize this agonized relationship as 'undermining' is reductive, and it certainly has nothing whatever to do with sarcasm. Donne knew very well that God was behind him in both senses, albeit sometimes at a distance—and in using the word you should remember that the modern sense is specific to the modern period.

Finally, please remember to appreciate and enjoy the poetry as you learn to see and hear at work within it the techniques with which it is written. Mark Twain once remarked that humour is like a frog—you can dissect it but it tends to die in the process—and some people have felt the same to be true of poetry, that analysis spoils the pleasure. I have never found that true, but quite the opposite, that understanding redoubles pleasure and admiration; and if you don't enjoy what you are studying, the learning will be much slower.

Metre

"... to a poet there is no more important element of a poem."

JON STALLWORTHY (Nlxii)

Rhythm is basic. Hearing our hearts beat, feeling our lungs breathe, walking, dancing, sex, and sport, all create and require a sense of rhythm. In all speech there are rhythmic patterns which we use to pick out meaning and phrase from the strings of syllables which we hear, the syllabic beat. To create and shape these rhythms, and to manipulate readers with words underpinned by them, is part of a poet's job: all poets use rhythm, and all readers of poetry hear rhythm, whether or not they are conscious of doing so. But to describe and analyse these poetic rhythms, which is called *prosody*, can be complicated, as musical notation is: and different languages require different sorts of prosody..

In the Slavic languages, like Russian, words can be very long, because they are *synthetic* languages which build a lot of meaning into one word by adding prefixes and inflected endings. But there is also a rule which allows only one stress per word however long it is, so it doesn't always make sense to analyse Russian poetry through patterns of stress. Instead, it can also be analysed through the patterns of long and short vowels, which are much more flexible, as they are in Latin. In French the rules of stress are more flexible than in Russian, but still more rigid than in English, and French poetry is usually analysed according to the number of syllables in each line.

English is a very *analytical* language, one which distributes the meaning among many words, and has a grammar dependent on prepositions and word order rather than on inflected endings.[1] The main system of prosody in English is called the *accentual-syllabic*, and is concerned with patterns of *stressed* and *unstressed beats*, the syllables on which emphasis (or *accent*) is and is not placed. Syllables do matter,

[1] In Latin the sentences *Nero interfecit Agrippinam* and *Aggripinam interfecit Nero* mean the same thing; but in English 'Nero killed Agrippina' and 'Agrippina killed Nero' don't mean the same thing at all! See pp. 120–1 below.

because each beat will be pronounced as one syllable, but it is possible to conflate or multiply syllables: "thickening", for example, could have two syllables (thicke-ning) or three syllables (thick-en-ing); and some words can be shortened by substituting an *apostrophe* (') for one or more letters, as "cannot" → "can't", "of" → "o' ", or "never" → "ne'er". This is called *elision*, and the missing letters are said to be *elided*, but you can't usually compress stresses in the same way.

Accentual-syllabic prosody isn't perfect, but has proven the most popular and useful system. It is a *neoclassical* system, one derived from Greek and/or Roman writings, which accounts for many of its strengths, its flexibility and widespread acceptance; but some recent scholars have argued forcefully that some aspects of the system are ill-adapted to English, and that alternatives must be considered.[2] Scholars often disagree when analysing prosody, but that is partly because it is a genuinely complicated subject. It's something like the drum- and bass-lines in a song, but poetic rhythm is created by the words, not played behind them. As with music there is a technical vocabulary which puts many people off; but without knowing the words you can't talk about the rhythms usefully, or write about them compactly. So the technical vocabulary is essential, especially in timed work, but your real guide must always be your own ears. Don't hesitate to read a poem aloud as you work (or mouth it silently in an exam), and if I ask you to read something aloud please do so: rhythm is much easier to demonstrate (to hear) than to describe, and reading lines of poetry out loud—making your mouth say what your eyes see—will help you think about them.

In accentual-syllabic prosody the basic unit of poetry is the *line*, which is clearly visible when you look at poetry and may be defined as 'a single sequence of characters read from left to right'. Lines are analysed by breaking the *metre*,[3] the rhythmic pattern, down into the repetition of a basic unit, called a *foot*, and saying how many *feet* make up a line. For example, this line of Shakespeare's, from Sonnet 12 (O1.927/N235):

When I do count the clock that tells the time

would usually be spoken like this (the stressed beats are printed in CAPITAL LETTERS):

[2] See especially the works by Derek Attridge in the 'Further Reading'.

[3] This word can be confusing: in the USA it is always spelled 'meter', but in the UK 'meter' and 'metre' are not the same. Used on its own to mean the rhythmic pattern in general it is spelled 'metre', but used as the end of another word to mean a measurement it is spelled 'meter', as in 'pentameter'.

When I do COUNT the CLOCK that TELLS the TIME

This is analysed as five feet, each foot consisting of an unstressed beat following by a stressed beat; I have separated the feet with a vertical slash:

When I | do COUNT | the CLOCK | that TELLS | the TIME

This kind of foot is called an *iamb* (pronounced e-AMB) and there are five of them, so the line is an *iambic pentameter* (from the Greek word πέντε [pente], meaning 'five'). If there were only four iambs, as there are in this line from *The Winter's Tale* (O1.943/N248):

When DAF- | foDILS | beGIN | to PEER,

then the line is said to be an *iambic tetrameter* (from the Greek τέτταρα [tettara], meaning 'four'); and so on.

The basic feet and line-lengths which you need to know[4] are these; "u" indicates an unstressed beat and "x" a stressed beat:[5]

u x : *iamb*, from which the adjective is *iambic*
x u : *trochee, trochaic*
x x : *spondee, spondaic*
u u : *pyrrhic, pyrrhic*

u u x : *anapæst, anapæstic*
x u u : *dactyl, dactylic*

one foot per line	:	*monometer*, adjective	*monometric*
two feet per line	:	*dimeter,*	*dimetric*
three feet per line	:	*trimeter,*	*trimetric*
four feet per line	:	*tetrameter,*	*tetrametric*
five feet per line	:	*pentameter,*	*pentametric*
six feet per line	:	*hexameter,*	*hexametric*
seven feet per line	:	*heptameter,*	*heptametric*
eight feet per line	:	*octameter,*	*octametric*

[4] The named triple and quadruple feet, most uncommon and some very rare, are in full these:

triple feet: *tribrach* (uuu); *dactyl* (xuu); *amphibrach* (uxu); *anapæst* (uux); *antibacchius* (xxu); *amphimacer* (xux); *bacchius* (uxx); *molossus* (xxx);

quadruple feet: *proceleusmatic* (uuuu); *first* (xuuu), *second* (uxuu), *third* (uuxu), and *fourth paeon* (uuux); *ionic (a) majore* (xxuu); *ditrochee* (xuxu); *choriamb* (xuux); *antispast* (uxxu); *diamb* (uxux); *ionic (a) minore* (uuxx); *first* (uxxx), *second* (xuxx), *third* (xxux), and *fourth epitrite* (xxxu); *dispondee* (xxxx).

[5] In other books a different notation may be used, such as "x" for an unstressed beat and "/" for a stressed one. Always check what system a particular author is using.

There is an easy way of remembering which foot is which, by pronouncing the name of each so that it embodies its rhythm. The word *i-AMB* is an iamb, an unstressed beat followed by a stressed beat; the word *TRO-chee* (TRO-key) is a trochee, a stressed beat followed by an unstressed beat; *SPON-DEE* is a spondee, two equally stressed beats; *pyrrhic* (pih-rick) is really a spondee (no word has no stress) but is pronounced so quickly that it is as near a pyrrhic as any word can be; and *an-a-PÆST* (anna-PEEST) is an anapæst. For dactyls you need to use the adjective *DAC-tyl-ic*, or you can remember that it comes from the Greek word δάκτυλος [daktilos], 'a finger', and is long-short-short (stress-unstress-unstress) like the joints of a finger.[6]

A full description of a line must identify the foot and the number of feet, and immediately tells you what the basic pattern is: a trochaic trimeter will be three trochees, 'xu | xu | xu'; an anapæstic dimeter (like lines three and four of a limerick) will be two anapæsts, 'uux | uux'; and so on. That is the basic pattern, but not every line described as an iambic pentameter (or whatever) will exactly follow that pattern: a sequence of lines that were all completely regular would sound monotonous and artificial. So to describe a poem as 'in iambic pentameter' means that the pattern of five iambs is the template which the poet has used as the basis of each line, and therefore a template which the reader can use to identify the variations, the effects at work in that particular line. There is an analogy with the time-signature and syncopation in music, or if you are familiar with word processors you might think of the template as default settings which the poet will then modify.

Many combinations of feet and line-lengths are possible, but iambic

---

[6] Another mnemonic you may like is Coleridge's little poem 'Metrical Feet', which he wrote for his sons; each line is written in the foot that it names. As a classicist Coleridge refers to 'longs' and 'shorts' rather than to stressed and unstressed beats (because Greek and Latin prosody depend on vowel length), and he includes two more complicated feet, the *amphibrach(ys)* (uxu) and the *amphimacer* (xux):

> Trochee trips from long to short;
> From long to long in solemn sort
> Slow Spondee stalks; strong foot! yet ill able
> Ever to come up with Dactyl trisyllable.
> Iambics march from short to long;—
> With a leap and a bound the swift Anapæsts throng;
> One syllable long, with one short at each side,
> Amphibrachys hastes with a stately stride;—
> First and last being long, middle short, Amphimacer
> Strikes his thundering hoofs like a proud high-bred Racer.

There are also some remarkable verses exemplifying complex metres by Tennyson, usually called 'Experiments' or 'In Quantity'.

pentameter, the line of five iambs, and iambic tetrameter, with four iambs, are much the commonest. Spondees and pyrrhics are never used as basic metres, because lines made up from them would be all stressed beats, which would be very dull (and sound like a dalek), or all unstressed beats, which is impossible. Instead spondees and pyrrhics are used within iambic and trochaic lines to vary the rhythm, and to act as a *distinguishing foot* to the ear, just as SMALL CAPITALS or *italic* are distinguishing *faces*[7] of type to the eye. An iamb in an otherwise trochaic line, or a trochee in an iambic line,[8] is called an *inverted foot,* and will also act as a distinguishing foot to the ear. Both distinguishing and inverted feet are varieties of *substitute feet,* those which replace a regular foot.

Lines made up of iambic and anapæstic feet produce a *rising rhythm,* because the stressed beats, for which the voice tends to be pitched slightly higher, come after the unstressed beats, when the voice is pitched lower. If you read aloud these lines from Marlowe's *Hero and Leander* (O1.900/N216), which are in iambic pentameter, you will hear your voice rise with each stress and drop down to rise again with the next:

> Her veil was artificial flowers and leaves,
> Whose workmanship both man and beast deceives;
> Her VEIL | was ART- | iFI- | cial FLOWERS | and LEAVES,
> Whose WORK- | manSHIP | both MAN | and BEAST | deCEIVES;

It sounds silly when it's exaggerated, but rising rhythm is the basic pattern of sound in most English speech. We all talk in iambs and anapæsts, and as you listen to others you will often | be A- | ble EA- | siLY | to HEAR | the RIS- | ing RHY- | thm IN | their WORDS. This is how most native speakers of English would normally speak those words; and it is also a natural sequence of eight iambs. This explains why the iambic metres are most popular with poets, because they sound most like ordinary speech (like ORdinARy SPEECH, in FACT).

---

[7] A *fount* (or *font* in the USA) of type is a design for a complete printer's set of all the letters and numbers. The fount in which this book is printed is Stone Serif; this is Helvetica; this is Palatino; and this is Times. Each of these founts has designs for all lower-case and UPPER-CASE letters and for numerals,in roman, *italic* and SMALL CAPITALS, each of which is a *type-face* of that fount. Each type-face can also come in different sizes, called points; the main text of the book is printed in 9-point: it could be 12-point, or 14-point, or even 18-point, but it would waste a lot of paper.

[8] An anapæst in a dactylic line, or a dactyl in an anapæstic, would also be inverted feet.

Lines made up of trochaic and dactylic feet produce a *falling rhythm*, with the voice pitched highest on the first beat, the stress, and falling away on the unstressed beat. It is rare to hear anyone talk in trochees, and sounds strange; but in poetry the strangeness can be harnessed to good use. Longfellow's *The Song of Hiawatha* (1855) is famous partly for its trochaic tetrameter; this is from book III, 'Hiawatha's Childhood' (I haven't indicated the stressed beats because every line is regular; if you read the lines aloud you will hear your voice create the falling rhythm):

By the shore of Gitche Gumee,
By the shining Big-Sea-Water,
Stood the wigwam of Nokomis,
Daughter of the Moon, Nokomis.
Dark behind it rose the forest,
Rose the black and gloomy pine-trees,
Rose the firs with cones upon them;
Bright before it beat the water,
Beat the clear and sunny water,
Beat the shining Big-Sea-Water.

As you can hear the falling rhythm becomes a chant, helped along by the repetition of phrases. It doesn't sound natural—but there's no reason why it should, and since Longfellow was writing about Hiawatha and his wife Minnehaha, both strongly trochaic names, it made sense for him to choose a trochaic metre.[9] A very different quality was sought by Browning in 'Soliloquy of the Spanish Cloister' (O2.1286/N913), one of the great hate poems in English. The metre is again trochaic tetrameter:

There's a great text in Galatians,
  Once you trip on it, entails
Twenty-nine distinct damnations,
  One sure if another fails:

THERE'S a | GREAT text | IN Ga- | LAtians,
  ONCE you | TRIP on | IT, en- | TAILS
TWENty- | NINE dis- | TINCT dam- | NAtions,
  ONE sure | IF a- | NOTHer | FAILS:

[9] Longfellow was also strongly influenced by the Finnish epic *Kalevala*; I am informed by one OUP reader that "In trochaic tetrameter, both alliterative and repetitive in phrasing, it was the last oral epic tradition to be collected in Europe, by Lönnrot in the early nineteenth century, and therefore of great interest to philologists of the time and Longfellow's model." In Finnish the first syllable of words is always stressed, and falling rhythms are therefore closest to common speech; but things are otherwise in English, as Longfellow found out.

It sounds more natural than *Hiawatha* (Browning was a better poet) though still odd; but the whole poem shows that the monk who speaks the lines is also odd, and the metrical oddity suggests his mental oddity, the unusual stresses as much as the actual words betraying the monk's obsessions. Trochaic effects vary, but it's always worth noting a falling rhythm, and asking what use the poet is making of it.

You'll notice that the second and fourth lines in Browning's stanza are missing their last unstressed beat (or have an incomplete fourth trochee). You could argue therefore that the poem isn't all in trochaic tetrameter, because every other line is *trochaic sesquitrimeter* (with three-and-a-half trochees);[10] but as it's common to miss off a final unstressed beat people mostly don't bother. In the same way, iambic and anapæstic lines can be missing their first unstressed beat. These short lines are *catalectic* lines (from the Greek *καταληκτικός* [catalektikos], meaning 'to leave off'), and are common; it is almost always unstressed beats at the beginning or end of the line that are missing.

It is also possible for lines to be *hypermetric* (from the Greek *'υπέρ* [hyper], meaning 'over-', + 'meter'), with an extra beat. Shakespeare's famous line from *Hamlet* is an example:

> To be or not to be: that is the question
> To BE | or NOT | to BE: | THAT is | the QUES- | tion

"THAT is", the fourth foot, is inverted, a trochee; but the first, second, third, and fifth feet are regular iambs, and the line works as an iambic pentameter despite the fact that "-tion" is the eleventh beat. An additional beat like this used to be called a *feminine* ending if it was unstressed, and a *masculine* ending if stressed. These needlessly sexist terms may easily be replaced by *stressed* and *unstressed hyperbeats*.

Feet with two beats (iambs and trochees) create *duple* metres, where the basic pattern is the alternation of stressed and unstressed beats; similarly, feet with three beats (mainly anapæsts and dactyls) create *triple* metres; and in English rising triple metre tends to be comic, because of the tripping rhythm produced by consecutive unstressed beats. Limericks, for example, are in anapæstic trimeter (lines 1, 2, and 5) and dimeter (lines 3 and 4): read aloud this limerick by Edward Lear (N942) and you'll hear the triple rhythm (all five lines are catalectic, with the first unstressed beat missing, which is very common in limericks):

---

[10] You can add *sesqui-* (from Latin, *semisque,* meaning 'and-a-half') to any line-length: sesquimonometers, lines of one-and-a-half feet; sesquidimeters, two-and-a-half feet, and so on: but do so only when it really helps.

There WAS | an Old MAN | with a BEARD,
Who SAID, | "It is JUST | as I FEARED!—
 Two OWLS | and a HEN,
 Four LARKS | and a WREN,
Have ALL | built their NESTS | in my BEARD!"

The connection between triple rhythm and comedy is strong, but not unbreakable, and it's possible to write serious limericks, or ones about such a bitter subject that they aren't funny at all, however they might trip off the tongue. As an example here is one about Sir Walter Ralegh, who famously laid his cloak over a puddle for Queen Elizabeth I, and popularized coffee and tobacco in Britain (lines 1, 2, and 5 are catalectic; lines 3 and 4 have unstressed hyperbeats):

Sir Walter was handy with cloaks,
And caffeine, and packets of smokes:
 Such a mighty romancer
 Of insomniac cancer—
I thank him: and hope that he chokes.

It's not great poetry, but it <u>is</u> a limerick. It's a good exercise to try to write some limericks, with the correct pattern of stressed and unstressed beats, perhaps one funny and one serious. Limericks are notoriously often obscene, so the exercise needn't be boring. After that try iambic pentameter and tetrameter, and then some trochaic lines. You'll find it challenging to do well; but the experience of writing even a few metrically accurate lines will teach you and your ears more about the business of prosody than anything else.

These technical terms will make it possible for you to write about the rhythms you hear, but only in a very boring poem will all the lines conform exactly to the pattern prescribed by the metre. For one thing, writing an exactly iambic line means that all the words in the line must have alternating stressed and unstressed syllables, as "AL-ter-NAT-ing" itself has. This leaves a wide choice, but the available vocabulary is nevertheless restricted (and "vo-CAB-u-la-ry" would be out). It would <u>not</u> mean, though, that every word would have to be iambic, because a trochaic <u>word</u> could be split across two <u>feet</u>, as "unctuous" and "vapor" are in this line from *Paradise Lost* (IX.635; N395):

ComPACT | of UNC- | tuous VA- | por, WHICH | the NIGHT

Both "unctuous" and "vapor" must be pronounced trochaically, as 'UNCtuous' and 'VApor'—you cannot naturally say them iambically, as 'uncTUOUS' or 'vaPOR'—but by putting the stressed syllable of each word in one foot and the unstressed in the next, Milton has fitted both words into a regular iambic line. This is one way of making regular lines more interesting, because in reading you hear simultaneously the *cadence* (from Latin, *cadere*, to fall) of the trochaic words, the falling rhythm they try to generate (which slows you down), and the rising rhythm of the iambic metre (which keeps you going). In this way it is possible to fit iambic words into trochaic lines, and vice-versa, but anapæstic and dactylic words are a different problem; and it is common for poets in one way or another to distort the prescribed rhythm.

This variability and irregularity can sometimes make it difficult to decide what the basic metre is. For example, "Hoping for love, longing for change", 'HOping for LOVE, LONGing for CHANGE', could be described as an iambic tetrameter with trochees substituted for the first and third feet ('xu ux xu ux'), or as a trochaic tetrameter with iambs substituted for the second and fourth feet ('xu ux xu ux'). Both descriptions are accurate, and there is nothing in the line itself to indicate that one is better than another; what will usually make one description clearly more helpful than the other is the context, for if the line appears in a sequence of lines which are predominantly iambic (or predominantly trochaic), there is usually little point in supposing that for this one line the poet changed the basic foot. You should therefore never try to identify a metre on the basis of one line—and especially not the first line, which is often irregular precisely because it is the first—but instead read a dozen or so lines and decide which template best fits what you are hearing. The vast majority of poems written before 1900 do have a consistent template which it is not difficult to identify in this way, and once you have identified it, you can begin to spot the variations on the template.

Much twentieth-century poetry, however, has been written in *free verse*, with variable or less strictly observed metre. If the template seems to be changing with every line any complete metrical analysis is likely to be a lengthy and complex business, and (especially in exams) you are probably best off confining yourself to the straightforward observation that the metre is highly irregular, and to pointing out any particularly striking or pleasing local effects—but if you are confronted with a poem like that, don't turn your ears off completely. Sometimes there will be groups of lines in a regular metre: in T. S. Eliot's 'The Love Song of J. Alfred Prufrock' (O2.1971/N1230), for example, the lines vary between three (line 45) and twenty syllables (l. 102) in length; but lines 112–18, where Prufrock is talking about *Hamlet*, and ll. 125–31, the last seven lines, are blocks of regular iambic pentameter. As the metre in which much of *Hamlet* is written it is appropriate (or ironic, as Prufrock is explaining how he isn't like Prince Hamlet) for lines about *Hamlet* to be in iambic pentameter; and the regularity and commonness of iambic pentameter help Prufrock to find a place where he can stop, just as the irregularity of many of the earlier lines reflects the way in which Prufrock rambles on because he is uncertain and worried.

Once you have identified the basic foot and the line-length, you confront three aspects of the metre. The first is the prescribed pattern of stress, as "u x | u x | u x | u x | u x" for iambic pentameter, which is the template (or in the computer analogy, a default setting). The second is the way you would speak the words of the line if they were a part of an everyday conversation, the normal pronunciation of the words (in computer terms, the settings you superimpose on some or all of the default settings). And the third is whatever is created by the interaction of the first two, the rhythm of that particular line described prosodically. Working out this third aspect is called *scanning* the line, and the final pattern that you decide on is called the *scansion*.

Sometimes the prescribed pattern of stress and the normal pronunciation will be identical, in which case there is no problem. Sometimes they will differ, and the normal pronunciation will usually overturn the prescribed pattern to create a substitute foot of some kind. This must be so. You cannot easily mispronounce words to make them fit, because, for example, "VOC-a-BU-la-RY" is at first incomprehensible as a sound, and then irritating or stupid. It is possible, though, especially in song-lyrics, hymns, and strongly oral poems such as ballads (where pitch and stress may be very stylized in performance), to force slight changes of pronunciation, usually for the sake of rhyme. In verse 19 of 'The Twa Sisters'—"The miller quickly drew the dam, / And there he found a drowned woman."—the last word would normally be a trochee (WOman), but the rhyme with "dam" prods a reader towards an iamb (woMAN); the same thing happens in the last verse which rhymes "then" with the name "Ellen", forcing it from 'ELLen' to 'EllEN'. An accent forced in this way to move along by one (or more) beats is called a *wrenched* accent: they rarely sound good, but occasionally can prove useful, or even necessary, in a particular poem. Scanning a line therefore involves identifying first the pattern of the metre, and then which feet (if any) are altered from their prescribed value by the actual words (or, in the computer analogy, identifying what the default settings are, and which of them have been altered).

As an example, here is the last line of a poem by John N. Morris called '*Hamlet* at Sea', describing a performance of Shakespeare's play which took place on the *Dragon*, sailing in convoy with another ship to the East Indies in 1607.[11] For the performance most sailors from both ships went on board the *Dragon*, but some sailors had to stay on the other ship to man it, and couldn't attend the play; but they could see lights and hear noise from the *Dragon*. The poet comments, as these sailors strain to hear *Hamlet* across the water:

It sounds like happiness at a distance.

The poem is in free verse, so the metre is variable; but many lines, including this one, are in iambic pentameter—as one might expect in a poem about *Hamlet*. The prescribed pattern of stresses is therefore five iambs, like this:

It SOUNDS | like HAP- | piNESS | at A | disTANCE.

but in ordinary speech the line would usually be spoken like this:

It SOUNDS | like HAP- | piness | at a | DIStance.

As you can see, the prescription and the ordinary speech are identical in the first two feet, "It SOUNDS | like HAP-", so there is no problem, and the result is two iambs. But in the third foot, the prescribed iamb is not matched by the ordinary speech: "happiness" is usually pronounced 'HAP-pi-ness', with only one stress, on the first syllable (i.e. the word is a dactyl), so that '-pi-ness', which is here the foot, is a pyrrhic, two unstressed beats. Morris's line wants to make that pyrrhic into an iamb by putting a stress on "-ness", so giving 'HAPpiNESS' two stresses, on the first and last syllables. This is not usual, but neither is it obviously wrong: it is a possible pronunciation, which can be understood and doesn't offend the ear unless grossly exaggerated. You could insist that it be scanned as a pyrrhic, but I would allow it as a weak iamb, one with a relatively light stress (HAPpiNESS rather than HAPpiNESS, as it were).

The clash between prescription and speech is stronger in the fourth foot. An iamb is prescribed, to make the foot "at A", but in speech it would be another pyrrhic, without a stress on either word, and the words would be pronounced quite quickly, as short, unstressed words tend to be. Making the foot into an iamb with a stress on "A" would slow the line (which might or might not be acceptable); and would also

[11] The poem may be found in John N. Morris, *A Schedule of Benefits* (New York: Atheneum, 1987); the performance on the *Dragon* is the earliest known performance of *Hamlet* outside Britain.

affect the meaning, insisting that this distance was 'a distance', not 'the distance', or 'two distances': but this would not make anything clearer, and would disturb the usual rhythm of the phrase 'at a DIStance'. Because it is common the way that phrase is normally spoken carries a lot of weight: so this foot does have to be scanned as a pyrrhic, and the prescribed stress of the iamb is missing. (If you decided to scan the third foot as a pyrrhic, you might consider whether you want to have two pyrrhics, four unstressed beats, in a row.)

In the fifth foot the clash between prescription and speech is absolute. The prescription wants an iamb, "disTANCE", but the word is usually pronounced as a trochee. "DIStance", and cannot acceptably be pronounced as an iamb. So the foot has to be a trochee, i.e. in this iambic line it is an inverted foot. This means that the line ends with an unstressed beat, not the stressed beat one would expect with iambs; and as this is the last line of the poem, for it to trail off in the unstressed sibillance of "-tance" sounds rather wistful, in keeping with the fact that the sailors to whom *Hamlet* sounds like happiness would like to be on the *Dragon* watching the performance, not keeping watch on their own ship. The line as a whole has also deviated increasingly from the prescribed pattern—iamb, iamb, weak iamb, pyrrhic, trochee, or:

u x | u x | u x | u u | x u
It SOUNDS like HAPpiNESS at a DIStance.

The loss of the rising rhythm in the weak third foot, unstressed fourth foot, and inverted fifth foot, also makes the line sound wistful, rather than assertively regular. Scanned in this way the line sounds alright and makes good sense; and the relation between sound and sense is coherently expressed in the scansion.

Prosody is now for many students an unfamiliar subject, and some of the things you can describe with prosody (such as dactylic octameter) are very rare; but equally some of them (particularly iambic tetrameter and pentameter, spondees, pyrrhics, and inverted feet) are things which every reader of English poetry will frequently encounter. In writing practical criticism you won't always need prosodic terminology, but when you do, nothing else can be a substitute.

'Nearing Forty'

I shall now turn to Derek Walcott's 'Nearing Forty', but before I say anything at all about it please read the poem carefully for yourself. It is printed on the next two facing pages as it appears in Walcott's *Collected Poems 1948–84*.[12]

[12] I quote from the American edition (New York: Farrar, Straus & Giroux, 1986), 136–7, and have preserved as far as possible the hierarchy of founts, though the actual fount is not the same; I have added line numbers. One misprint, the transposition of a semi-colon and a comma in ll. 14–15, has been corrected by collation with the first British edition in *The Gulf and other poems* (London: Jonathan Cape, 1969, reissued 1974), 67–8.

Nearing Forty

[for *John Figueroa*]

The irregular combination of fanciful invention may delight awhile by that novelty of which the common satiety of life sends us all in quest. But the pleasures of sudden wonder are soon exhausted and the mind can only repose on the stability of truth . . .
— SAMUEL JOHNSON

Insomniac since four, hearing this narrow,
rigidly metred, early-rising rain
recounting, as its coolness numbs the marrow,
that I am nearing forty, nearer the weak
vision thickening to a frosted pane,
nearer the day when I may judge my work
by the bleak modesty of middle age
as a false dawn, fireless and average,
which would be just, because your life bled for
the household truth, the style past metaphor
that finds its parallel however wretched
in simple, shining lines, in pages stretched
plain as a bleaching bedsheet under a gutter-
ing rainspout; glad for the sputter
of occasional insight, you who foresaw
ambition as a searing meteor

will fumble a damp match and, smiling, settle
for the dry wheezing of a dented kettle,
for vision narrower than a louvre's gap,
then, watching your leaves thin, recall how deep
prodigious cynicism plants its seed,
gauges our seasons by this year's end rain
which, as greenhorns at school, we'd
call conventional for convectional;
or you will rise and set your lines to work
with sadder joy but steadier elation,
until the night when you can really sleep,
measuring how imagination
ebbs, conventional as any water clerk
who weighs the force of lightly falling rain,
which, as the new moon moves it, does its work
even when it seems to weep.

'Nearing Forty' is in free verse, but has a strong tendency to iambic pentameter. On the opposite page the poem is printed and scanned in a way I have found helpful when working intensively on metre. Instead of dividing the words up into feet with vertical slashes the stressed and unstressed beats are grouped to reproduce the pattern of the words, so that you can easily see my scansion of each word. Thus the first word, "Insomniac", becomes "uxuu" ('In-SOM-ni-ac'), representing two feet, an iamb ('In-SOM-') and a pyrrhic ('-ni-ac'). As the basic rhythm is duple, with no triple feet substituted, to see what feet make up each line you simply divide the beats into pairs: thus the third line, "recounting, as its coolness numbs the marrow," is scanned as "uxu, x u xu x u xu,"; put in the foot divisions: "ux | u, x | u x|u x | u x|u,": and the line is shown (despite the trochaic "coolness" and "marrow") as five iambs, with an unstressed hyperbeat. The punctuation marks are included with the scansion to help you see where you are in the line; and the numbers on the far right give the number of beats in each line. (In line 19 there is a choice about how to pronounce "narrower", so the number for that line could be one higher.)

The lines vary in length from seven to twelve beats, but more than half (18/32) have ten beats. Another nine lines have eleven beats, of which seven can be scanned as hypermetric iambic pentameters with unstressed (1, 3, 11, 17, 18), or stressed (15, 26) hyperbeats. 25/32 lines, therefore, are scannable as iambic pentameters, and that is clearly the dominant metre among the variations. Working all the numbers out exactly takes a long time, but realizing what the answer is going to be takes only as much time as is needed to read the poem aloud as far as line 7—because (with practice) your ear will by then have heard the rising iambic rhythm, and every line except line 4 will have scanned as a pentameter.

Once this basic metre has been identified, the first thing to notice is that a further four lines (13–14 and 28–29) deviate from the iambic pentameter in the same, striking way. Line 13, with twelve beats, is the longest line, and is immediately followed by a line with only eight beats. Between them the two lines have twenty beats: which is what two pentameters would usually have. In other words, although the lines as they actually are are irregular:

> plain as a bleaching bedsheet under a gutter- 12
> ing rainspout; glad for the sputter 8

they could easily be made more regular, like this:

Nearing Forty

[*for John Figueroa*]

The irregular combination of fanciful invention may delight awhile by that novelty of which the common satiety of life sends us all in quest. But the pleasures of sudden wonder are soon exhausted and the mind can only repose on the stability of truth . . .

— SAMUEL JOHNSON

Insomniac since four, hearing this narrow,	uxuu u x, xu u xu,	11
rigidly metred, early-rising rain	xxx xu, xu-xu x	10
recounting, as its coolness numbs the marrow,	uxu, u u xu x u xu,	11
that I am nearing forty, nearer the weak	u x u xu xu, xu u x	11
vision thickening to a frosted pane,	xu xux u u xu x,	10
nearer the day when I may judge my work	xu u x u x u x u x	10
by the bleak modesty of middle age	u u x xuu u xu x	10
as a false dawn, fireless and average,	u u x x, xu u xuu	10
which would be just, because your life bled for	u x x x, ux u x x u	10
the household truth, the style past metaphor	u xu x, u x x xuu	10
that finds its parallel however wretched	u x u xuu uxu xu	11
in simple, shining lines, in pages stretched	u xu, xu x, u xu x	10
plain as a bleaching bedsheet under a gutter-	x u u xu xu xu u xu-	12
ing rainspout; glad for the sputter	u xu; x u u xu	8
of occasional insight, you who foresaw	u uxuu xu, x u xx	11
ambition as a searing meteor	uxu u u xu xuu	10
will fumble a damp match and, smiling, settle	u xu u x x u, xu, xu	11
for the dry wheezing of a dented kettle,	u u x xu u u xu xu,	11
for vision narrower than a louvre's gap,	u xu xu u u xu x,	10
then, watching your leaves thin, recall how deep	x, xu u x x, ux x x	10
prodigious cynicism plants its seed,	uxu xuxu x u x,	10
gauges our seasons by this year's end rain	xu u xu u u x x x	10
which, as greenhorns at school, we'd	x, u xu u x, x	7
call conventional for convectional;	x uxuu x uxuu;	10
or you will rise and set your lines to work	u x u x u x u x u x	10
with sadder joy but steadier elation,	u xu x u xxx xxx,	11
until the night when you can really sleep,	ux u x u x u xu x,	10
measuring how imagination	xuu x uxuxu	9
ebbs, conventional as any water clerk	x, uxuu u xu xu x	11
who weighs the force of lightly falling rain,	u x u x u xu xu x,	10
which, as the new moon moves it, does its work	x, x u x x x u, x u x	10
even when it seems to weep.	xu x x x u x.	7

plain as a bleaching bedsheet under a 10
guttering rainspout; glad for the sputter 10

Of course, the rhyme is misplaced; and it is an unusual rhyme, one which requires "guttering" to be split between lines, as "gutter- / ing",[13] so that in the middle of the word there is a half-pause, perhaps as air-bubbles make when waste water flows away down piping. The effect is accentuated by the many trochees and trochaic words in lines 12–14 (compare lines 25 and 27, which are notably regular). I suspect this is the effect Walcott wanted, and it is made more noticeable and accurate as an imitation of how rainwater flows out of a gutterspout by being embodied in two lines of unequal length.

There is some confirmation of this effect in the second example, lines 28–29, which repeats it in a different way:

measuring how imagination 9
ebbs, conventional as any water clerk 11

Again, although neither line has the right number of beats, they have between them the right number for two lines. You might be alerted to what is going on here by trying to scan line 29: if you start at the beginning it is awkward, and the result is a very irregular line of two trochees, a pyrrhic, two more trochees, and a stressed hyperbeat:

EBBS, con- | VENTion- | al as | ANy | WAter | CLERK

If, however, you begin after the comma, and so shift all the foot-divisions along by one beat, the line becomes an iambic pentameter with one pyrrhic and an initial stressed hyperbeat:

EBBS, | conVENT- | ional | as AN- | y WA- | ter CLERK

This makes more sense; and the previous line is readily scanned as a catalectic iambic pentameter, with the first foot inverted and the stressed beat of the last iamb missing:

MEASur- | ing HOW | iMAG- | iNA- | tion

The stressed hyperbeat beginning line 29, "EBBS", would complete the truncated iamb at the end of line 28: both lines would then be pentameters, and the comma would coincide with the line-break:

MEASur- | ing HOW | iMAG- | iNA- | tion EBBS, 10
conVENT- | ional | as AN- | y WA- | ter CLERK 10

13 A line-break is usually represented by a *solidus* or *slash* (/): see p. 75 below.

So when Walcott wrote the lines as they actually are, with one foot split between the two lines:

MEASur- | ing HOW | iMAG- | iNA- | tion 9
EBBS, | conVENT- | ional | as AN- | y WA- | ter CLERK 11

he allowed the last stressed beat of line 28 to ebb down to the beginning of line 29, and left the unstressed beat, "-tion" trailing, as if the strongly iambic word "imagination" itself ebbed away. In this way the foot split between two lines is a rhythmic illustration of the meaning of the lines; but it is itself rather an imaginative thing to do, and so contradicts the idea that it is the poet's imagination that is ebbing.

There is a different sort of metrical device in line 2. "rigidly" would normally be pronounced as a dactyl, "RIG-id-ly", but I have scanned it as three consecutive stresses, so that the line begins with two spondees:

RIGID- | LY ME- | tred EAR- | ly-RIS- | ing RAIN

You could scan the first foot as a trochee and the second as an iamb, "RIGid- | ly ME-", which would preserve the normal pronunciation. But "rigid-" is not strongly trochaic, weaker, for example, than "metred" or "rising"; and so scanning it as a spondee, which sounds all right, seems a better compromise between the normal trochaic pronunciation and the prescribed iamb. But once you have scanned it as a spondee, it sounds odd to scan "-ly" as an unstressed beat, and so pronounce "rigidly" as "RIG-ID-ly"; more odd, in fact, than scanning it as three lightly stressed beats, as "RIG-ID-LY". It's debatable, and questions of pitch are as important as the weight of the stresses: but what persuades me to scan the line as two spondees followed by three iambs is that such a scansion shows "rigidly metred" as itself rigidly metred, and the rising rhythm then returns with "early-rising rain". Because the poem is partly about writing poetry, such metrical self-reference seems satisfying. (Both "early-" and "-rising" are trochaic words, but both are divided between feet, so the rising rhythm is preserved, as happened in the line from *Paradise Lost*.)

There is again some confirmation when Walcott uses a similar technique in line 26:

with sadder joy but steadier elation,

I have scanned this as three iambs, two spondees and a stressed hyperbeat:

with SAD- | der JOY | but STEAD- | IER | ELA | TION,

"steadier" is normally pronounced as a dactyl, "STEAD-i-er"; and "elation" is normally pronounced with only one stress, on the middle syllable,[14] "e-LA-tion"; so you could argue that the line should actually be scanned with the fourth foot pyrrhic, and an unstressed hyperbeat:

with SAD- | der JOY | but STEAD- | ier | eLA | tion,

This is possible, but I don't like it. The pyrrhic "-ier" is a very weak foot, and "eLAtion" falls away dismally, so that the metre is doing nothing to help the meaning, and everything to defeat it. But if, as with "rigidly metred", you let your voice pick up the iambic stress on "stead-" and carry it on as two light spondees and a stressed hyperbeat, the scansion of the whole line moves from the trochaic cadence of "sadder" lying across two iambs to a steadier beat in keeping with the note of general resolution which begins at line 25.

Finally, there is a problem with "narrower" in line 19, "for vision narrower than a louvre's gap". It is another word that would normally be pronounced as a dactyl, "NAR-row-er"; but if you allow it to be a trisyllable, occupying three beats, the scansion of the rest of line 19 becomes very awkward. If instead it is compressed into two syllables, as the trochaic 'NARR-'wer', the line can readily be scanned with the third foot as a pyrrhic:

for VIS- | ion NARR- | ower than | a LOU- | vre's GAP,

The elision which compresses "narrower" is awkward but not impossible to say, and the metrical result is satisfying because "narrower" is compressed into a narrower space than it would like to have. It is metrically the opposite of "thickening" in line 5 ("vision thickening to a frosted pane"), which could have two syllables, 'thicke-ning', but here has to be pronounced as three, 'thick-en-ing', to help thicken the line up to its proper metrical size.

There are many more things that could be said about the metre. The poem has 322 beats, and a lot is going on metrically in that space. In later chapters metre will again be relevant—in considering, for example, what happens in the rhymes 'middle age / average' and 'foresaw / meteor'— but I hope I have said enough here to persuade you that, despite the off-putting technical words, it is worth understanding what is going on metrically in a poem, and being able accurately and compactly to describe what you can hear.

---

[14] i.e. as an *amphibrach* (uxu): see p. 3, n. 4 above.

Chapter Glossary

Accent: the emphasis or stress placed on a beat.

Accentual-Syllabic: the kind of prosody principally used in English.

Analytical: of a language, dependent on prepositions and word order, having no inflections etc.

Anapæst, Anapæstic: a foot of three beats, two unstressed and the last stressed (uux); the metre produced by such feet.

Beat: a word or syllable(s) bearing one stress (x) or unstress (u).

Cadence: a fall, in tone, pitch etc.

Catalectic: of a line, missing one or more beats.

Dimeter: a line of two feet.

Distinguishing: of a foot, type-face, or fount, different from that normally used.

Duple: of a foot, having two beats; the rhythm produced by such feet.

Elision: the omission of one or more letters from a word, usually indicated with an apostrophe.

Face: of a type, a particular appearance of the letters and numbers, as roman or *italic*; thus any given fount of type will have many faces.

Fount: (or in the USA, 'font') of type, a particular design of the letters and numbers; each fount will comprise designs for each character in a number of faces.

Falling rhythm: that produced by feet with unstressed beats following stressed beats.

Feminine: of an ending, with one or more unstressed hypermetrical beats.

Font: the standard US spelling of 'fount'.

Foot: a prosodic unit of stressed and/or unstressed beats, the component of a line.

Free verse: poetry in which the metre varies.

Heptameter: a line of seven feet.

Hexameter: a line of six feet.

Hyperbeats: those beats in a line which are surplus to the beats allowed by the metre; *stressed* and *unstressed* hyperbeats are politically corrected *masculine* and *feminine* endings.

Hypermetric: of a line in a given metre, with one or more hyperbeats.

Iamb, iambic: a foot of two beats, an unstressed followed by a stressed (ux); the metre produced by such feet.

Inverted: of a foot, the reverse of that normally used in a given line.

Italic: of a fount, with angled characters (such as *these*).

Line: a single sequence of characters read from left to right.

Metre

Line-break: the turn of one line into the next; notated as '/'.

Masculine: of an ending, with one or more stressed hypermetical beats.

Metre: the rhythmic pattern of beats.

Neoclassical: Of prosody, etc., derived from Greek and/or Latin writings.

Pentameter: a line of five feet.

Prosody: the study and notation of metre.

Pyrrhic: a foot of two unstressed beats (uu).

Rising rhythm: that produced by feet with stressed beats following unstressed beats.

Roman: of a fount, with ordinary upright characters (such as these).

Scansion: the individual metrical pattern of a particular line or poem.

Spondee: a foot of two stressed beats (xx).

Stressed: of a beat, spoken emphatically, often with the voice pitched slightly higher than for an unstressed beat.

Substitute foot: any foot used as a replacement for one of the regular feet in a given line; includes inverted and distinguishing feet.

Synthetic: Of a language, having inflected endings, prefixes etc.

Tetrameter: a line of four feet.

Trimeter: a line of three feet.

Triple: of a foot, having three beats; the rhythm produced by such feet.

Trochee, trochaic: a foot of two beats, a stressed followed by an unstressed (xu); the metre produced by such feet.

u: notation for an unstressed beat.

Unstressed: of a beat, spoken unemphatically, often more rapidly and with the voice pitched slightly lower than for a stressed beat.

Wrenched accent: occurs when the requirements of metrical stress (and/or rhyme) prevail over the natural stress of a word or words.

x: notation for a stressed beat.

Form

To choose a form is to acquire two sets of baggage which are tangled up with one another. The first set exists because a decision about form is also a decision about one or more of structure, metre, rhyme, punctuation, and tone, any or all of which may be prescribed. For example, if you have decided to write a *sonnet* you have decided to write fourteen lines of iambic pentameter, with a choice of *rhyme schemes*[1] which reflect different ways of structuring the fourteen lines; and approximately 140 syllables after you begin you will have to stop. The second set of baggage exists because forms become historically associated with particular kinds of poetry. Sonnets have long been used as love poems and declarations of courtship, from Petrarch's fourteenth-century sonnets in Italian, through the great Elizabethan sonnet sequences by Sidney (O1.630/N192), Spenser (O1.820/N165), and Shakespeare (O1.927/N234), to Elizabeth Barrett's *Sonnets from the Portugese* (N856): so when W. B. Yeats used the sonnet form for a poem about Leda being brutally raped (O2.1704/N1095), there was a tension between the history of the form and the story Yeats used it to tell. His choice of form was ironic, and the form itself comments on the poem.

Much twentieth-century poetry in free verse has also been in *open form*, and, again, this does not mean that there is no form, but that the form is variable. Just as Eliot used iambic pentameter in 'The Love Song of J. Alfred Prufrock', so he used *blank verse* (unrhymed iambic pentameter) in lines 77–102 of *The Waste Land* (O2.1987/N1238–9), to parody a speech from Shakespeare's *Antony and Cleopatra*, and *heroic quatrains* (iambic pentameters rhyming *abab*) in lines 235–46. In *The Waste Land* as a whole Eliot created a complex new form, of five parts with the fourth very short, which he later developed in *Four Quartets*.

[1] The *rhyme scheme* of a poem indicates with letters which lines rhyme with which: the rhyme-word at the end of the first line is always *a*, and all lines that rhyme with it will also be *a*; the second rhyme-word, and all lines that rhyme with it, are *b*; and so on. Thus both the limericks on p. 8 have the rhyme scheme *aabba*, showing that lines 1, 2, and 5 rhyme together, and so do lines 3 and 4; the four lines by Browning on p. 6 have the rhyme scheme *abab*; and the poem by Coleridge in the footnote on p. 4 is *aabbccddee*.

As with free verse and metre, open form doesn't mean you needn't think about forms while you are reading: all lines have a rhythm which can be metrically described, and all poems have a form.

Poems may be *stichic*, a simple sequence of lines, but form is especially important in poems written in *stanzas* (the adjective is *stanzaic*). A stanza is a group of lines printed together with a space above and below them; in Italian the word *stanza* means 'a room, or stopping place', and if the whole poem is a house, stanzas are the rooms into which the house is divided. Spenser only completed half of *The Faerie Queene* (O1.662/N152), but even so it is one of the longest poems in English at *c.*35,000 lines. It is written in the *Spenserian stanza*, eight iambic pentameters and a ninth line in iambic hexameter (called an *alexandrine*), the whole rhyming *ababbcbcc*:

Like as a ship, whom cruell tempest drives
  Upon a rocke with horrible dismay,
  Her shattered ribs in thousand peeces rives,
  And spoyling all her geares and goodly ray°, *array*
  Does make her selfe misfortunes piteous pray.
  So downe the cliffe the wretched Gyant tumbled;
  His battred ballances° in peeces lay, *scales*
  His timbered bones all broken rudely rumbled,
So was the high aspyring with huge ruine humbled.

(v.ii.50)

It may seem a severe constraint to use a stanza form like this, and it certainly affected what Spenser could say as well as how he could say it. The longer final line is a very definite end to the stanza (read it aloud and you'll hear what I mean), and makes it extremely difficult to *enjamb* (i.e. to carry the syntax over) from one stanza to the next—so difficult, in fact, that Spenser never did it: every stanza is heavily *end-stopped* (the opposite of enjambment, punctuation ending the sense with the line), almost always with a full-stop. The 35,000 lines contain more than 400,000 beats; and when Spenser decided to use this stanza form he effectively committed himself to having a full-stop after every ninety-second beat. He could have other full-stops as well, but he couldn't omit that recurring, regular full-stop. Yet the form was also a help and an opportunity. Instead of pages stretching blankly away in front of him, Spenser was confronted, once he had decided on his stanza form, with a well sign-posted road, or a series of empty moulds all capable of being filled with words and internally articulated with punctuation; and so designed that once filled each would have structural integrity and strength. Far from being repetitious or dull, it is one of the pleasures of reading *The Faerie Queene* to see how Spenser manages to vary the internal structure of the stanza, and how one variant or another becomes his favourite at different points in the poem. The *ababbcbcc* rhyme scheme is made up from two interlocking sets of four lines (or *quatrains*), *abab* and *bcbc*, plus the final alexandrine: but in the stanza above there is a full-stop at the end of line 5, so that its individual structure isn't the obvious *abab–bcbc–c*, but the much less obvious *ababb–cbcc*. If you don't notice this structural variation the poem can seem dull, but if you do notice it there is always something interesting going on.

It is easy to think of forms as if they were objects, as if a poet wanting a form looked through the catalogue and picked one out; but it can be very misleading to think in this way. Spenser did not buy in his stanza form: he created it (which is why it is named after him), and in this sense it is not an object but a possibility he discovered.

The range of possible forms is huge, because any of the specified elements of a given form may be varied, creating sub-groups which overlap. A *quatrain*, for instance, will always have four lines: but the metre of any line can be differently prescribed, and the lines made to rhyme in any of fifteen combinations. Even sticking to the four major feet, and to the line lengths between trimeter and pentameter, which are the commonest, there are nearly five thousand possible types of quatrain, from iambic trimeters rhyming *aaaa* to dactylic pentameters rhyming *abcd*. For a stanza of five lines the possible number of rhyme schemes alone rises to 52, and for one of six lines to 203; and with the possible combinations of metres also rising exponentially the number of variant types soon becomes astronomical[2]—so much so that only a tiny fraction of them have ever been used.

This is often forgotten. Sonnets, for example, are sometimes discussed as if the three most popular kinds (the *Petrarchan*, *Shakespearean*, and *Spenserian*: see p. 36 below) were all the kinds there are; but it is possible to arrange 14 iambic pentameters in any one of 190,899,322

---

[2] Students familiar with A-level maths may be interested to know that the number of rhyme schemes *r(n)* for a stanza of *n* lines is:

$$r(n) = \sum_{i=2}^{n} i \left\{ {n-1 \atop i-1} \right\}$$

where $\left\{ {n \atop k} \right\}$ denotes a Stirling Number of the Second Kind.

rhyme schemes, and all are possible variants of the sonnet form. The three major variants are popular, and named, because they have proven particularly useful and influential; but they are as much like small charted areas on a large and mostly blank map as they are like ready-made objects that a poet can simply collect. If you pick any five sonnets by different authors—say, Wyatt, Spenser, Sidney, Shakespeare, and Wordsworth (O1.616, 820, 630, 927; O2.173/N113, 165, 192, 234, 736)—the chances are that you will find five distinct rhyme schemes, and to reduce such variety to the three commonest rhyme schemes is an absurd critical shortcut. Poets know better:

On the Sonnet

If by dull rhymes our English must be chained,
  And, like Andromeda, the Sonnet sweet
Fettered, in spite of painéd loveliness;
Let us find out, if we must be constrained,
  Sandals more interwoven and complete
To fit the naked foot of poesy;
Let us inspect the lyre, and weigh the stress
Of every chord, and see what may be gained
  By ear industrious, and attention meet;
Misers of sound and syllable, no less
Than Midas of his coinage, let us be
  Jealous° of dead leaves in the bay-wreath crown; *intolerant*
So, if we may not let the Muse be free,
  She will be bound with garlands of her own.

John Keats (O2.536/N842)

This has the very unusual rhyme scheme *abcabdcabcdede*, which has no name, and was obviously intended by Keats to be different from any sonnet rhyme scheme which had previously been used; so that his own sonnet 'On the Sonnet' is itself an example of the experimentation it recommends. As readers it reminds us that any particular form is a tiny and temporarily frozen portion of an endlessly fluid medium, and only comes to seem a solid object through its repeated use by different poets. It may seem easier to think of forms as fixed and solid, but to do so will handicap and diminish your reading.

Given this fluidity of forms there is no wholly satisfactory way of cataloguing them; but the easiest way of examining the major forms which have been used is to take as an index the number of lines whose proportions and relations are specified. Line-lengths may vary, as well as rhyme schemes, so it is sometimes necessary in notating stanza forms to record both. This is done by writing the number of beats after the letter denoting the rhyme:

The King sits in Dumferling town,	*a*	8 beats
Drinking the blude-reid wine:	*b*	6
"O whar will I get guid sailor,	*c*	8
To sail this ship of mine?"	*b*	6

This stanza is from 'Sir Patrick Spens' (O1.443/N87), and is an iambic quatrain rhyming *abcb*, with the first and third lines tetrametric, and the second and fourth trimetric; it would be notated as *a8b6c8b6*.

One-line forms

There are no major one-line forms which use trimeters or tetrameters, because these lines are too short to say much in; and one-line forms using hexameters or a longer line are rare (for examples, try Blake [N675] and A. H. Clough [N949]). However, *blank verse*, unrhymed iambic pentameter, is the form used by Marlowe, Shakespeare, Jonson, and many other Elizabethan and Jacobean dramatists for the poetry in their plays. It is close to ordinary speech, and, both strong and flexible, as good for a poem of only a few lines as for an epic of ten thousand. It is also a weighty form, the decasyllabic line (plus hyperbeats) giving enough space for complete clauses and expansive oratory. Blank verse is sometimes called *heroic verse*,[3] and since it developed as a dramatic form in the late sixteenth century, and was influentially chosen by Milton (somewhat against the contemporary odds) for his Christian epic *Paradise Lost*, has been in fairly continuous use: notably, Wordsworth used it for his meditative verse autobiography *The Prelude*, Tennyson for his long Arthurian cycle *Idylls of the King*, and Browning for many of his *dramatic monologues* (poems spoken by an 'I' who is not the poet), including the *c*.21,000 lines of *The Ring and the Book*. It has remained a common form in the twentieth century, but the decision to use it now is often seen by critics as consciously alluding to a better and statelier past, as if to use blank verse were a kind of nostalgia (which is nonsense, as—most recently—Jim Powell has shown in three striking blank-verse letters).[4] By definition, blank verse is not stanzaic, but long poems in blank verse are often divided into *verse paragraphs*, just as novels and short stories are divided into prose paragraphs.

[3] The adjective 'heroic', applied to any form (as 'heroic couplets' or 'heroic quatrains') means the line of that form is iambic pentameter.

[4] They may be found in *It was Fever that Made the World* (Chicago: Chicago University Press, 1989).

Two-line forms

The basic two-line form is the *couplet*, a rhyming pair of lines which may be *open*, when the syntax runs on from couplet to couplet, as in Chaucer's 'Prologue' to *The Canterbury Tales* (O1.130/N17), but increasingly became *closed*, units of syntax as well as form, as in the major poems of Dryden (O1.1602/N458) and Pope (O1.1857/N539). Closed couplets (where there may be *internal enjambment*, between the first and second lines, but not *external* or *couplet enjambment*, between successive couplets) tend to sound assertive and epigrammatic: Shakespeare often used them on stage to end blank verse speeches, and as the last two lines of the Shakespearean sonnet. A dominant form in the later seventeenth and eighteenth centuries, couplets went out when Romanticism came in. More recently the open couplet has returned to favour, but often with less than full-rhyme[5] and persistent enjambment, both internal and external, producing a rippling effect rather than the clear point-by-point sequence of closed couplets.

Chaucer, Shakespeare, Dryden, and Pope all tended to use the *heroic couplet*, where two iambic pentameters give the space to say a lot, and to accommodate polysyllables without bursting. But couplets in iambic tetrameter are also popular, and were used to perfection by Marvell, who wrote of lying in a garden in summer (O1.1156/N442) that it had the effect of:

> Annihilating all that's made
> To a green thought in a green shade.

The full-rhyme and completed syntax give a strong sense of closure, but the scale of the thought that the couplet has managed so elegantly to capture seems too big for its tetrameters; and in the eighteenth century the tetrametric couplet tended to be used comically or satirically, while the heroic couplet was regarded as epic and serious (but could therefore be made fun of in a *mock-epic*, such as Pope's 'The Rape of the Lock', O1.1867/N547). Swift was fond of the tetrametric couplet, and gravely explained that he <u>had</u> to be comic:

> For Pope can in one couplet fix
> More sense than I can get in six.

[5] A *full-* or *perfect* rhyme is one in which the last stressed vowel and all following sounds are identical in two or more words—most obviously in such pairs as bat/cat or hiss/miss, but equally in longer word pairs such as imperium/delirium and frantic/Atlantic. A *half-rhyme* is one in which either the last stressed vowel (as lust/lost) or the following sounds (as bite/fire) differ: see pp. 87–91 below.

More recently Eliot and Tony Harrison have rescued the tetrametric line from comedy: Eliot used it mainly in quatrains, but Harrison, especially in his most recent film/poems,[6] has fully restored the tetrametric couplet as a serious form.

Couplets using trimeters or shorter lines are rare in their own right, but occur as components of other forms. In 'An Horatian Ode' (O1.1162/N444) Marvell alternated couplets in iambic tetrameter and trimeter, the extreme brevity of the trimetric couplets making even the tetrametric couplets seem spacious. Something of the same effect can be heard in the third and fourth lines of a limerick, a couplet in anapæstic dimeter, where the syntactical proximity of the rhyme-words combines with the triple rhythm to accelerate the form into its punch line. The fifth and sixth lines of the stanza of Donne's 'A Valediction: Of Weeping' (O1.1033/N270) form a couplet in iambic dimeter.

Couplets using a longer line, however, have been used, particularly those in iambic heptameter (sometimes called *fourteeners*). The length of heptametric lines tends to make their rhythm sound rather galumphing, as in Golding's sixteenth-century translation of Ovid (O1.521); but they can be very effective. The stanza of Kipling's 'Tommy' (N1076) is made from four couplets in iambic heptameter (with lines 5, 6, and 8 hypermetric), and the long lines give space for the colloquial idiom of the soldier who speaks the poem. Long trochaic couplets are rarer, but Tennyson used couplets in trochaic heptameter (with a stressed hyperbeat) for his 'Locksley Hall' poems (O2.1213).

It is also possible to make couplets from lines of unequal length. Any combination is possible, and the effect must be judged on its merits in a particular poem. It is uncommon for the lines to differ by more than one foot, but Ogden Nash, in 'Columbus' (N1329), rhymes a line of 17 beats with one of 55:

> And, just as he thought, her disposition was very malleable,
> And she said, Here are my jewels, and she wasn't penurious like Cornelia the mother of the Gracchi, she wasn't referring to her children, no, she was referring to her jewels, which were very valuable,

And there is one excellent form which constantly produces unequal couplets, the *clerihew*, named after its inventor, Edmund Clerihew Bentley. It is a quatrain of two couplets, and the first line is always

[6] See Tony Harrison, *The Shadow of Hiroshima and other film/poems* (London: Faber and Faber, 1995).

someone's name, to comment on whom is the purpose. Among the best is Bentley's own about Nell Gwynne, the mistress of Charles II:

Nell
fell
when Charles the Second
beckoned.

Three line-forms

There are two basic three-line forms, the *triplet*, where all the lines rhyme (*aaa*), and the *tercet*, where one or more lines do not rhyme (*aab, aba, abb, abc*). They are worth distinguishing because the effect of triple rhyme is very different from any effect of tercets.

Heroic triplets are commonest as a variation in longer poems in heroic couplets; see, for example, Pope's 'Epistle to Dr Arbuthnot', ll. 323–5 (O1.1920/N572; in the *Norton* the triplet is indicated by a brace). The triple rhyme will usually sound very emphatic, but can easily go over the top and sound insistent-because-uncertain. Mixed-metre triplets occur often in the stanza forms invented by Donne: in 'The Canonization' (O1.1026/N266) lines 5–7 of each stanza form a triplet, with the first two lines in iambic tetrameter and the third heroic (*a8a8a10*); and in 'A Valediction: Of Weeping' (O1.1033/N270) the last three lines of each stanza form a triplet of the type *a10a10a14*. Such variation of line-lengths, especially when it slightly delays the third rhyme by having a longer last line, can lessen the thumping insistence of the triplet; but even so, Donne's fondness for triplets is in keeping with the aggressive and imperious qualities of his work. A falling rhythm can also diminish the clang of the rhyme, and Browning managed to use triplets in catalectic trochaic octameter (eight trochees missing the final unstressed beat) for 'A Toccata of Galuppi's' (O2.1304/N926). At the other extreme is Herrick's 'Upon His Departure Hence' (Nlxiv), which amplifies and exploits the clanging rhyme: it consists of five triplets in iambic monometer.

Tercets often occur in iambic pentameter, for example as part of the *sestet* (the last six lines) of a Petrarchan sonnet (where the pattern depends on the rhyme scheme of the whole sestet), or as the stanza form for the body of a *villanelle*[7] (where they will rhyme *aba*). Most importantly, linked tercets rhyming *aba bcb cdc* are called *terza rima*, and were used by Dante for *The Divine Comedy*. (In Italian the metre is not iambic pentameter, but in English tends to be.) The rippling effect

[7] See p. 39 below.

of *terza rima* is stronger than that of open couplets, and persists even when rhyme is replaced by a pattern of stressed and unstressed hyperbeats (as in part II of Eliot's *Little Gidding*, ll. 80–151: O2.2006–8/Nlxxii, and see pp. 89–90 below). Mixed-metre tercets of the type *a8a8b6* (or equivalent) may be paired to make a six-line stanza, as in Sir John Suckling's 'A Ballad upon a Wedding' (N409); and Auden created a rather unstable stanza, approximately *a12b12c7d14e14c7*, for 'At the Grave of Henry James'. The effects obtained by using tercets are very variable, and must be judged poem by poem.

There is also the Japanese *haiku*, a *syllabic* form specifying three lines of five, seven, and five syllables (no prescribed feet or beats), with a *turn*, a moment of disjunction from which a new or redirected sense develops, between the first and second, or second and third, lines:

Helpful little book:
includes even Japanese
three-line form of verse.

Four-line forms

The four-line form is the *quatrain*: it is the commonest form, both in its own right, as in many hymns and ballads, and as a component of larger forms. Like other structures based on the number 4 (such as the square), the quatrain is both strong and pleasing. The enormous variety of quatrains has been explored more widely than any other form, and to follow that exploration you need an anthology; but the major variants of rhyme provide a useful set of subdivisions.

Monorhymed quatrains, with one rhyme throughout (*aaaa*), are rare, though Donne used them in lines 7–10 of 'The Anniversary' stanza (O1.1031/N268), and D. G. Rossetti in 'The Woodspurge' (O2.1409/N1004). Quatrains in which only two lines rhyme (*abac* or *abcb*[8]) have no agreed name, but may be called *single-rhymed*. In any regular metre they are easy to construct, and to use for narrative; the type *a8b6c8b6* (alternating lines of iambic tetrameter and trimeter, as in the stanza from 'Sir Patrick Spens' at p. 27 above) is the staple form used for ballads and hymns, and is known as the *ballad stanza* or *common metre*. Making the first line a trimeter (*a6b6c8b6*) produces *short metre*; and making all the lines iambic tetrameter produces *long metre*, brilliantly used (and made very disturbing) by Eliot in such poems as 'Whispers of Immortality' and 'Sweeney Among the Nightingales' (N1234).

[8] A quatrain rhyming *abca* would also be single-rhymed, but it is very uncommon.

Emily Dickinson (N1010) was an inventive user of many of these quatrains.

Cross-rhymed quatrains, *abab*, are harder to write well: unless the metre is very long, or the poet skilled, the tick-tock rhyme will soon become very obvious and insistent. It will also tend to drag, because the third line, as well as advancing the poem, looks back in rhyme to the first, and the fourth line to the second: so the poem is always looking back over its shoulder (and is likely to fall over). The modern master is again Eliot, who made the difficulty work for him in the lines from part III of *The Waste Land* (235–48) describing the joyless copulation between a young man and a typist (O2.1991–2/N1243):

> The time is now propitious, as he guesses,
> The meal is ended, she is bored and tired,
> Endeavours to engage her in caresses
> Which still are unreproved, if undesired.
> Flushed and decided, he assaults at once;
> Exploring hands encounter no defence;
> His vanity requires no response,
> And makes a welcome of indifference.

The lines are metrically regular, and in the first quatrain are chimed along by the stressed polysyllabic rhymes, their rhythm as remorseless as the man and as tired as the typist. Matching the man's rising excitement (but hardly passion) the second quatrain is metrically a little disturbed and somewhat faster; but it remains remorseless enough to plough through the tolling rhymes, still just *abab* but very close to *aaaa*. The result is a memorable indictment of indifferent lust.

The *couplet-rhymed* quatrain (*aabb*) splits dully into two couplets, and is not often used; but when one couplet is split by the other, so that the fourth line rhymes with the first, and the second and third lines pair in the middle, you have an interesting quatrain, rhyming *abba*. The mirror symmetry of the rhyme would split the quatrain in the middle, *ab–ba*, but the central *–bb–* couplet is fastened across the breaking-point, giving to the lines the tension of an arch and the sense of coming back to the ground (or even coming home, like a return to the tonic key in music) at the end of each stanza. It is sometimes called *chiasmic* rhyme,[9] but I prefer to call such quatrains *arch-rhymed*.[10]

[9] From the Greek χιασμός [chiasmus], 'a diagonal arrangement' (the root is 'chi' [χι], the Greek name for the letter X).

[10] In written work you would need to gloss this term the first time you used it for a particular teacher, or in an exam: 'the arch-rhyme (*abba*) is . . .' would be enough.

Tennyson used arch-rhymed quatrains in iambic tetrameter for *In Memoriam A. H. H.* (O2.1226/N899), and that variant is called the *Tennysonian stanza.*

Longer forms

Stanzas of five or more lines can usually be broken down into *singletons*, couplets, tercets or triplets, and quatrains; and the properties of the stanza will reflect the properties and placing of those components, as a gearbox reflects the ratios of its component cogs. Even the limerick (five anapæstic lines in the form *a9a9b6b6a9*) may be regarded as two couplets and a singleton, or even (when the first and last lines end with the same word) as a triplet interrupted by a couplet. The range of longer forms is so vast that they cannot be surveyed, but few have been much used.

Besides the limerick, five-line stanzas are uncommon. They have no agreed name, but may be called *cinquains* or *pentains* if the need arises.[11] Larkin used a mixed iambic and anapæstic pentain rhyming *abbab* for 'Annus Mirabilis'; and Coleridge varied the ballad metre of 'The Rime of the Ancient Mariner' (O2.238/N744) with (among other variants) an iambic pentain usually of the form *a8b6c8c8b6*. Because so few of the possible pentains (there are at least 50,000) have ever been used there must be good ones still undiscovered. One which I have found useful for myself is an iambic pentain of the form *a8b8a8b8b10*, called a *long five*: it is a cut-down version of the Spenserian stanza, and because it is shorter, and in iambic tetrameter with a final pentameter (rather than heroic with a final hexameter), it is much easier to enjamb between stanzas. It is useful for narrative, and readers who also write verse might experiment with it, or with other pentains of their own invention.

The six-line stanza, or *sestet*, occurs in Petrarchan sonnets, where it usually consists of two tercets; but is also a narrative and lyric stanza (often in a quatrain plus couplet form, *abab–cc*, where the quatrain narrates and the couplet summarizes or comments). The creation of sestets from iambic tercets by Suckling and Auden was mentioned (p. 31 above), and when the third and sixth lines are shorter (called *bobs* or *bob-lines*) this 3 + 3 sestet is an excellent comic stanza. Another fine sestet is one in iambic tetrameter, rhyming *abbcac*, used by Larkin in 'An

[11] 'Cinquain' is the logical form, given 'quatrain . . . sestet', but was used by Adelaide Crapsey (d. 1915) for a five-line syllabic form of her invention; I personally prefer the less logical but more euphonious 'pentain'.

Arundel Tomb' (N1543). What distinguishes it is the long delay before the *a*-rhyme in line 5, which (as with cross-rhymed quatrains) turns the stanza back into itself and slows it down: Larkin used this against the acceleration given by the *-bb*--- couplet to control the pace of his poem, and generate a very mellow and elegiac tone.

The sestet is also the component stanza of the *sestina*, a 39-line form in which the six rhyme-words of the first stanza are used in a different order as the rhyme-words of every subsequent stanza, to produce *abcdef faebdc cfdabe ecbfad deacfb bdfeca eca* (or *ace*).[12] The *b*-, *d*-, and *f*-rhyme-words must also be used in the last three lines. For examples, see Sir Philip Sidney's double sestina 'Ye Goatherd Gods' (O1.627/N188), D. G. Rossetti's 'Sestina (after Dante)' (O2.1410), W. H. Auden's 'Paysage Moralisé' (O2.2097), Elizabeth Bishop's 'Sestina' (N1412), Anthony Hecht's 'Sestina d'Inverno', and John Ashbery's 'The Painter' (N1626). It is a difficult form to compose, highly dependent on the chosen set of end words and on the poet's skill in shaping the syntax grammatically around those fixed points; but used well the form can draw great strength from its fixity, and the echoing repetitions can be both beautiful and (in every sense) telling—as bells tell the hours and the dead. Sidney's virtuoso double sestina, for a long time the best-known instance of the form, perhaps intimidated later poets, and seventeenth- and eighteenth-century sestinas are rare; but as the examples above suggest, the form has enjoyed wide popularity since the later-nineteenth century.

The principal seven-line stanza is *rhyme royal*, heroic and rhyming *ababbcc*, used by Chaucer for *Troilus and Criseyde* (O1.496/N52), by Wyatt (O1.621/N115), by James I of Scotland for 'The Kingis Quair' (hence the name), and by Auden for 'A Letter to Lord Byron' and some of the stanzas in 'The Shield of Achilles' (N1372). At its best rhyme royal can balance readings of it as a tercet and two couplets (*aba–bb–cc*) or as a quatrain and a tercet (*abab–bcc*): in narrative the balance between these readings fuses narration (associated with quatrains) with moral commentary (associated with the summary epigrammatism of couplets) to produce morally charged action.

The principal eight-line stanza is *ottava rima*, heroic and rhyming

[12] Each stanza is generated from the last by rocking in, taking in sequence the last, first, penultimate, second, antepenultimate, and third lines; thus the stanza '123456' is followed by '615243', and that by '364125'. Applying this to the sixth and final full stanza of a sestina, *bdfeca*, would return one to the pattern of the first stanza, *abcdef*: the form (except in the hands of Sidney) stops short when the variations are once complete.

abababcc (which naturally breaks down into a cross-rhymed sestet and a couplet: *ababab–cc*). As the stanza of Byron's *Don Juan* (O2.315/N769), *ottava rima* is now often thought of as comic, and the argument is sometimes advanced that the triple *a-* and *b*-rhymes, acceptable in richly-rhyming Italian, have to be forced—and so inevitably become comic—in English. It is true that Byron's triple rhymes are often funny; but Byron can be altogether serious when he wants to be, and *ottava rima* was used in the sixteenth century for two of the great Elizabethan translations from Italian, Sir John Harrington's translation (1591) of Ariosto's *Orlando Furioso,* which is comic, and Edward Fayrfax's translation (1600) of Tasso's *Il Goffredo,*[13] which isn't comic, and in which the triple rhymes do not prompt comedy. The stanza is not intrinsically comic at all, though it may be that changes in the language (including a substantial increase in vocabulary) between 1600 and 1800 made triple rhyme in some way prone to comedy; or it may be that (as happened to couplets in iambic tetrameter between Marvell and the twentieth century) we have now lost sight of how to use *ottava rima* seriously: for since *Don Juan* (1819–24) it has tended to be used comically (as by James Agee[14]). An honourable exception goes to Yeats, who, with the help of less-than-full rhymes,[15] and at the cost of some dignified pomposity in the couplets, managed serious *ottava rima* in 'Sailing to Byzantium' and 'Among School Children' (O2.1701, 1705/N1094, 1096). Even so, Yeats's choice of *ottava rima* for these sad poems can be read as ironic, like his choice of a sonnet form for 'Leda and the Swan'.

At nine lines there is the Spenserian stanza, *ababbcbcc12,* of *The Faerie Queene* (see p. 24 above), later used by Keats in 'The Eve of St. Agnes' (O2.524/N833), Shelley in 'Adonais' (O2.458/N807), and Tennyson in 'The Lotos-Eaters' (O2.1192/N892). The eight heroic lines form two linked quatrains, *abab–bcbc,* which allows narration, and the stanza is strongly bound together by the central *b*-rhyme couplet and its outlying *b*-rhymes, *-b-bb-b--*. The alexandrine provides variety, and space to finish off or comment on the action of the stanza, but prevents stanza enjambment. Majestic and self-contained, it rolls sonorously along with much decoration and harmony, especially when Keats is at the wheel.

---

[13] The poem is subtitled *Gerusalemma Liberata,* and Fayrfax's translation was published as *Jerusalem Delivered.*

[14] See 'John Carter', in Robert Fitzgerald (ed.), *The Collected Poems of James Agee* (London: Calder & Boyars, 1972).

[15] See p. 28 n. 5 above, and pp. 87–91 below.

Keats also invented a range of ten- and eleven-line stanzas for his major odes. All are heroic, the 'Ode on Melancholy' (O2.542/N847) rhyming *ababcdecde*, the 'Ode on a Grecian Urn' (O2.541/N848) *ababcdedce*, the ode 'To Autumn' (O2.556/N849) *ababcdedcce*, and (with line eight reduced to a trimeter) the 'Ode to a Nightingale' (O2.538/N845) *ababcdec6de*. The narrative (such as it is) tends to be dealt with in the initial cross-rhymed quatrain, and an emotional commentary supplied in the tercets (the absence of which toughens the longer 'To Autumn' stanza). The 'Ode to Psyche' (O2.537/N843) runs through five forms of between eleven and eighteen lines in as many stanzas, and any explanation of what Keats might be doing would take pages.

Three major forms remain: with fourteen lines, sonnets and *Onegin stanzas*, and with nineteen lines the *villanelle*. All are iambic, the sonnet and villanelle heroic, the Onegin stanza tetrametric.

The word sonnet comes from the Italian *sonetto*, 'a little sound', and until the early-seventeenth century meant any short lyric poem; but the particular form used by Petrarch—fourteen lines divided into an *octave* (or *octet*) of two quatrains linked by rhyme, *abbaabba*, and a sestet usually of two tercets linked by rhyme, such as *cdecde* or *cdedce* or *cdeedc*—slowly became a restrictive norm, the *Petrarchan sonnet*. It was (and is) normal to have a turn between octave and sestet, producing a tangential relationship between the parts or giving a degree of spin to the whole; and the asymmetric 8–6 form proved flexible and satisfying, as did the internal structure of each part, the octave readable as two quatrains (*abba–abba*) or three couplets with binding rhymes fore-and-aft (*a–bb–aa–bb–a*), and the sestet variable at need.

The great vogue for sonneteering in England between 1580 and *c.*1610 produced two major variants named after their inventors or most famous practitioners, of which the better known is the *Shakespearean* sonnet:[16] three quatrains and a terminal couplet, *ababcdcdefefgg*. The couplet (which in Shakespeare's own sonnets is almost always closed) has its usual tendency to summarize or comment on the quatrains, and hence to moralize; the turn (the developmental break or pivot in the sense) usually comes between lines 12 and 13. It is easy to think the 4–4–4–2 form a greater break from the Petrarchan 8–6 than it really is for many Shakespearean sonnets reproduce the 8–6 division with a heavy stop and a slight, secondary but more central turn at the

[16] It was first used by Henry Howard, Earl of Surrey (1517–47), and popularized by the publication of his sonnets in *Tottel's Miscellany* (1557), a very influential anthology. See O1.622/N123.

eighth line, allowing the third quatrain to develop away from the first two.

In the second variant, the *Spenserian* sonnet, the quatrains are interlocked by rhyme, *ababbcbccdcdee*: this does tend to undermine any 8–6 division, and so makes the end of line 12 the most probable place for the turn; but it partly restores, in lines 4–5 and 8–9, the medial couplets of the Petrarchan octave. Used as the stanza form for a sequence (Spenser's original sequence was the *Amoretti*: O1.820/N165) the Spenserian sonnet is more fluid (or nimble) than the Shakespearean, but pays in lessened authority and clarity.

Many other variants are possible (see pp. 25–6 above). Sidney began *Astrophel and Stella* (O1.630/N192) with an 'alexandrine sonnet', using iambic hexameters; Gerard Manley Hopkins produced what he called 'curtal sonnets', such as 'Pied Beauty' (O2.1469/N1063), ten lines dividing 6–4½ and reproducing in miniature the structure of a sonnet; George Meredith challenged the limitation to 14 lines with 16-line sonnets, constructed as four arch-rhymed quatrains and now known as *Meredithean* sonnets (O2.1423/N1007); and Robert Lowell wrote unrhymed sonnets. All three major variants have continued to be used respectfully; but in the hands of poets like Seamus Heaney (N1792), Michael O'Siadhail, or Tony Harrison (N1764),[17] whose poetry demands attention to the relations between regional poet and classical form, the choice and variety of the sonnet can acquire a degree of irony (as in 'Leda and the Swan', but more delicate); strong ironies also attend the sonnets of Geoffrey Hill (N1724) and Wole Soyinka.[18]

One other interesting point about the sonnet offers a lesson in notation. If the variant forms are notated as 8–6 and 4–4–4–2, or with the more usual comma (8,6 and 4,4,4,2), the punctuation is serving only to separate, because '8 , 6' is clearer than '86', and '4 , 4 , 4 , 2' clearer than '4442'. It isn't indicating the relationship between the parts, and doesn't indicate where (if anywhere) there is a turn: which it could

[17] See particularly O'Siadhail's 'Perspectives', in *Hail! Madam Jazz: New and Selected Poems* (Newcastle-upon-Tyne: Bloodaxe, 1992), and the poems comprising 'Filtered Light', the first section of *A Fragile City* (Newcastle-upon-Tyne: Bloodaxe, 1995). Harrison's continuing sequence *The School of Eloquence*, in his *Selected Poems* (Harmondsworth: Penguin, 1985) and elsewhere, is in Meredithean sonnets.

[18] See especially Soyinka's 'Apollodorus on the Niger', in *Mandela's Earth and other poems* (London: Methuen, 1990); Hill is an astonishing sonneteer, writing individual and paired sonnets as well as longer sequences. See especially 'Asmodeus', 'Requiem for the Plantaganet Kings', 'Two Formal Elegies', 'Annunciations', 'Funeral Music', 'Lachrimae', and 'An Apology for the Revival of Christian Architecture in England', all in Hill's *Collected Poems* (Harmondsworth: Penguin, 1985) and *New & Collected Poems 1952–1992* (Boston & New York: Houghton Mifflin, 1994).

easily do. In both cases the mark that is needed is the semi-colon: the notation '8 ; 6' accurately records the Petrarchan turn of octave into sestet; and the notation '4 ; 4 ; 4 : 2' records the itemization of quatrains as on a list, while the colon records the summary relationship of the terminal couplet to the quatrains. The variation of a particular sonnet can also be recorded: for example, a Shakespearean sonnet with a heavy turn between the second and third quatrains, and the third quatrain and couplet acting as a sestet (so mixing the Petrarchan and Shakespearean forms) could be notated as '4 , 4 ; 4 , 2'. Whenever you use numbers to notate form, and need to separate the numbers with punctuation, it's worth asking which mark would be most accurate and helpful: and the fuller notation is both an aid to clear thinking, and potentially a valuable time-saver in exams.

The Onegin stanza, invented by the Russian poet Alexander Pushkin in *Eugene Onegin*, can be regarded as a sonnet in iambic tetrameter. It has a cross-rhymed quatrain, a couplet-rhymed quatrain, an arch-rhymed quatrain, and a couplet, in that order, *ababccddeffegg*; and in its strictest form specifies that three of the rhymes will be *unstressed* (or *feminine*) and the rest *stressed* (or *masculine*).[19] This may be written using vowels (*a*, *e*, *i*) for the unstressed rhymes, and consonants (*b*, *c*, *d*, *f*) for the stressed ones, producing *ababeecciddiff*; it is to this rhyme scheme that Nabokov refers in his fine account of the Onegin stanza. His terminology is different, but he makes compact sense:

> The *abab* and the *ff* part are usually very conspicuous in the meaning, melody, and intonation of any given stanza. This opening pattern (a clean-cut sonorous elegiac quatrain) and the terminal one (a couplet resembling the code of an octave or that of a Shakespearean sonnet) can be compared to patterns on a painted ball or top that are visible at the beginning and at the end of the spin. The main spinning process involves *eecciddi*, where a fluent and variable phrasing blurs the contours of the lines so that they are seldom seen as clearly consisting of two couplets and a closed quatrain. The *iddiff* part is more or less distinctly seen as consisting of two tercets in only one third of the entire number of stanzas in the eight cantos, but even in these cases the closing couplet often stands out so prominently as to cause the Italian form to intergrade with the English one.[20]

[19] See p. 87 below.

[20] *Eugene Onegin: A Novel in Verse by Aleksandr Pushkin: Translated from the Russian, with a Commentary, by Vladimir Nabokov* (revised edition, in 4 vols; London: Routledge & Kegan Paul, 1975), i. 10.

Nabokov is writing about Pushkin, but what he says is applicable to two recent uses of Onegin stanzas in English, by Vikram Seth in *The Golden Gate* (1986), and by Jon Stallworthy in 'The Nutcracker' (1987).[21]

The villanelle is the oddest of all, nineteen heroic lines in five tercets and a quatrain, the first line repeated as lines 6, 12, and 18 (written here as a^1) and the third line repeated as lines 9, 15, and 19 (a^2), to produce a^1ba^2 aba^1 aba^2 aba^1 aba^2 aba^1a^2. Minor variation is allowed in the repeating lines, called *burdens* or *refrains*, but only minor, and the double pattern of repetitions can produce effects between the tolling of a bell, the insistence of anger or fear, and wry meditation. Originally the villanelle was a folk form associated with dancing; but as a written form it is extremely difficult, and depends utterly on the lines used as refrains. Among the best recent examples are Empson's 'Missing Dates' (O2.2121/N1360), Roethke's 'The Waking' (N1391), and Dylan Thomas's 'Do Not Go Gentle into That Good Night' (O2.2127/N1465).

Beyond these relatively strict stanza forms are a number of looser terms which usually refer to whole poems, and are variably defined. The most important is the *ode* (from the Greek ʼαοιδή [aoide], 'a song'), usually a formal, stately, or grand poem of some length: public odes (for ceremonial occasions) and private odes (for meditation and reflection) may be distinguished; but the stricter differences are between the *Sapphic, Alcaic, Pindaric,* and *Horatian* odes. Sapphic and Alcaic odes, named after the poets Sappho (flourished *c.*600 BCE)[22] and Alcaeus (flourished *c.*611–580 BCE), are both in highly prescribed and mostly dactylic quatrains: neither adapts well to English, but Sidney, Watts (N533), Tennyson, and Pound (in *Apparuit*) have attempted English Sapphics; and Tennyson and R. L. Stevenson Alcaics. The Pindaric ode, named after Pindar (522–442 BCE), of three complex stanzas (the metrically identical *strophe* and *antistrophe,* followed by a metrically distinct *epode*),[23] has been more successfully adapted, as has the Horatian ode, named after Horace (65–8 BCE), a longer form with a less complex and repeating stanzaic pattern. The great English Pindaric and Horatian odes are those of Jonson (O1.1067/N305), Marvell (O1.1162/N444), Dryden (O1.1641/N480), Gray (O1.2202/N606), Wordsworth (O2.175/N728), Coleridge (O2.275/N760), and Keats (O2.537/N843).

21 Vikram Seth, *The Golden Gate* (London: Faber and Faber, 1986). 'The Nutcracker' appeared in the *London Review of Books*, 9:16 (17 Sept. 1987), 12, and does not seem yet to have been collected.

22 The non-denominational terms BCE (Before Common Era) and CE (Common Era) are now replacing the Christian BC (Before Christ) and AD (Anno Domini).

23 The strophe, antistrophe, and epode are sometimes referred to as the *turn, counterturn*, and *stand.*

The *ballad* (from Latin *ballare,* to dance) was originally a narrative song, usually straightforward, often unhappy, and with a refrain; but the *folk ballad* may now be distinguished from the *literary ballad,* the consciously written form which tends to be more complex and clever. Even the most literary ballads can retain much of the form's power, however, as Blake Morrison demonstrated in *The Ballad of the Yorkshire Ripper* (1985).[24] The 'Ripper', Peter Sutcliffe, was a serial killer who between 1975 and 1981 killed thirteen women with DIY tools; he was later attacked in prison, and badly slashed, for tearing the daily pictures of topless women out of the tabloid newspapers. While he was still horribly at large, and during the trial, many people had said or thought, 'If I could get my hands on him I'd . . .'; but when someone did give Sutcliffe 'a taste of his own medicine', it was for ripping paper women, not for what he had done to human female flesh and blood. It may not have been poetic justice, but it was a kind of justice to the irony of which only poetry could do justice. Morrison's problem, though, was that the relatives of the victims were still very much alive, and to treat such a subject in poetry is to run terrible risks—risks in handling which the choice of form is crucial. The villanelle of the Yorkshire Ripper? the limericks? the sonnets? All would court hideous offence; but the ballad, simple, public, and with a track-record of accommodating tragedies and crimes, is the one form that could be used, and Morrison seized on it to strong and moral effect.

The *dramatic monologue,* used particularly by Browning and Eliot, has a single speaker throughout, who is not the poet, and whose character is revealed by what he or she says (or, latterly, thinks); the form often privileges the printed mimesis of speech, and while there can be by definition only one speaker, there may be also a specific listener, named or implied, as well as the general audience of readers—so it is often productive to ask why this person is speaking, and perhaps why they are not being interrupted. There are also such 'forms' as the *effusion,* usually an indication by Romantic poets that they are feeling inspired and intend to do whatever they feel like: but component structures will be visible or audible.

Forms may themselves be grouped into *genres* (from French *genre,* a type or kind; cf. 'gender'). Classically five genres were distinguished, the *epic, tragic, lyric, comic,* and *satiric,* and each of these terms has a long and complex history, beginning (mostly) in classical Greek drama,

[24] The poem first appeared in the *London Review of Books,* and was collected in Blake Morrison, *The Ballad of the Yorkshire Ripper and other poems* (London: Chatto & Windus, 1987).

continuing through Roman adaptation and development of Greek practice and theory, and descending to the present day in a continuous and pan-European tradition subject to constant challenge and revision. 'Lyric', for example, is the adjective from 'lyre', a stringed musical instrument, and lyrics—like those of modern songs—would in Greece normally have been musically accompanied; but in contemporary modern use 'lyric poetry' covers most shorter poems, and seems to be defined only by a process of exclusion (not any of the other genres, not narrative, not martial . . .). 'Epic' (from Greek 'επικός [epikos], narrative or song) refers both to long narratives collected from oral tradition and to literary imitations of them, and the process of imitation, in different cultures at different times, has created tremendous diversity. 'Satire' (from late Latin *satira,* a medley) was until 1605 believed to derive from the Greek *satyr,* a wood-dwelling half-man-half-goat: the mistake still causes confusion, but the modern sense of the word is loose, and covers almost any composition that ridicules someone or something.

Such complex (and sometimes inconsistent) ideas as these may not be readily summarized, but, broadly speaking, until the Romantic period each of the five genres comprized a number of conventions regarding subject-matter, style, tone, audience, forms, etc., which poets and dramatists more-or-less obeyed (though sometimes with reservations). In the baldest possible terms, epics were long and usually martial; tragedies ended in death and comedies in marriage; lyrics expressed personal emotion; and satires attacked vice or folly. Since about 1800 the meanings have become confused, and artists more rebelliously inclined to compound and distort generic proprieties, while technological developments (especially film, TV, and mass-market paperbacks) have strained generic distinctions. Two new prose genres, the *novel* and *short story,* have become clearly recognizable, though both are hard to define: novels may certainly also be tragic or comic, and hybrids, such as the *novella* and *long short story,* abound. Thus the attempt to classify works—trying to insist, for example, that something is either comic or tragic—may inhibit understanding, and if you do decide that 'x is a comedy' or 'y is a tragedy' it may not get you anywhere. But the genres have not lost all their power: one classical distinction between tragedy and comedy was social, tragedy dealing with the lives and deaths of great individuals, rulers and warriors, while comedy dealt with the lives and marriages of those 'ordinary' people who form society: tragedy was thus a nobler form than comedy, outranking it in the hierarchy of genres: and the weight of both distinction and hierarchy continue to be felt in many ways. It is, for example, widely agreed that westerns can be a modern form of tragedy; but it would be far more tendentious to argue that any soap opera could 'achieve' the stature of tragedy; and what is at stake is not simply what most people might call 'tragic' but also beliefs about what qualifies as 'art'. It is therefore worth being familiar with the hierarchical view of literature implicit in the classical distinction of genres: its assumptions and influence have been challenged, but not done away with; and in dealing with poets who shared and used that view it is a handicap to be ignorant of it. Equally, however, it is worth consulting several different definitions of each genre, the *OED* and a dictionary of literary terms, for example, because for genres there is no exactly 'correct' definition, only the accumulation of knowledge and experience.

'Nearing Forty'

We already know that 'Nearing Forty' is (mostly) heroic, in iambic pentameter. It cannot be blank verse because it is rhymed; but it is printed as a continuous sequence of thirty-two lines, and is not stanzaic. The first thing therefore is to work out the rhyme scheme: which is:

abacbcddeeffgghhiijjkbklcmjmcbcj

Some of these are less than full rhymes—for example the sequence gap/deep/seed, *jjk*, in ll. 19–21 are half-rhymes: but it is sensible at this stage to be fairly ruthless in working out the basic pattern of rhyme to see if any underlying structure emerges. For that reason I am prepared to call the gap/deep rhyme (19–20) a couplet, *jj*, and consider the next half-rhyme, "seed" (21), as a new rhyme, *k*, picked up two lines later with "we'd" (23).

Obviously this complicated rhyme scheme could be broken down in different ways; but what would be of most use is a principle that repeats in the different parts: and in 'Nearing Forty' that principle, outside the central sequence of couplets, is overlapping single-rhymed quatrains. This can be shown if the rhyme scheme is written out with each internal structure on a new line, but progressing across the page, so that rhyme letters repeated in vertical column denote the same line:

5	10	15	20	25	30	
abac						
acb	c					
cb	cd					
	ddee	ffggh	hiijj			
			j	kbk		
				kbkl		
				c	mjm	
					mjmc	
					mcb	c
					cb	cj
5	10	15	20	25	30	

The quatrains leading into and out of the central sequence of couplets, *cbcd* and *jkbk*, are weaker than the others, because the *d*- and *j*-rhymes tend to be subsumed by their couplets; but it is worth insisting on them, because if you do it becomes clear that there is only one point in the poem, the break at line 24 between *kbkl* and *cmjm*, where there is no over-lapping between the internal structures. This is interesting: numerically line 24 is exactly three-quarters of the way through the poem (24/32); it is the only line which does not rhyme with any other (though it has a strong *internal* rhyme, conventional/convectional); and it is heavily end-stopped with the second semi-colon (the first is in line 14, the second *g*-rhyme, at roughly the mid-point of the sequence of couplets), and so syntactically marks a point two-thirds of the way through. It is also followed by a strong resolution in tone, line 25 beginning "or you will rise . . .", which distinguishes the last eight lines.

An analysis like this flattens some features of the poem, but makes others clearer. After an initial sequence which edges forward, the poet takes a deep breath and drives through the central sequence of couplets, which are all open (except the first, *dd*, ll. 7–8, and the sixth, *ii*, ll. 17–18) and so progress rapidly, finally spilling out through half-rhymes into the *jjkbkl* sequence (ll. 19–24), marked by the return of the *b*-rhyme (rain) and the overlapping single-rhymed quatrains, and ended by the unrhymed line 24. The last eight lines then return to the structure of the opening sequence, tying themselves into the poem by using the *b*-, *c*-, and *j*-rhymes (rain, work, sleep) as well as the new *m*-rhyme (elation/imagination). The overlapping quatrains and the late return to the *b*- and *c*-rhymes help to explain the cohesion and unity of the poem; the sequence of open couplets helps to explain the central momentum; and that the quatrains are always single-rhymed, two lines in any quatrain rhyming with lines outside that quatrain, helps to explain the internal fluidity, which becomes a quality of searching progression, an inability to come to any easy rest or certain conclusion (cf. the heavy certainty of Eliot's cross-rhymed heroic quatrains in *The Waste Land*, at p. 32 above). This in turn helps to explain why Walcott made the last line very short (only seven beats), which helps to mark the ending without betraying the characteristic structure and dominant tone by using a cross- or arch-rhymed quatrain (which would also have been possible ways of ending).

This form is Walcott's invention in this poem, and has no name; but he created it from elements which do have names, and from whose combined properties the properties of this form are created. Such formal analysis is not always as useful as it is here, but knowledge of the forms, their natures and histories, is something that writers, readers, and practical critics cannot afford to be without.

Chapter Glossary

Alexandrine: an iambic hexameter.

Arch-rhyme: a rhyme scheme with mirror symmetry, as *abba*.

Ballad: a narrative poem, commonly of traditional origin, often in quatrains with refrain; *literary* and *folk* ballads are now distinguished; of a stanza, or of metre, an iambic quatrain of the form *a8b6a8b6* (also called *common metre*).

Blank verse: unrhymed iambic pentameter.

Burden: an alternative term for a *refrain*, a line or lines that are repeated.

Closed: of a couplet, with the second line end-stopped; of form, prescribed.

Comedy, comic: one of the five classical genres, comedies dealt with ordinary people, social life, and marriage; applied to poetry, 'comic' has tended to the much broader meaning of 'humorous'.

Common metre: also *ballad metre* or *ballad stanza*, an iambic quatrain of the form *a8b6c8b6*.

Couplet: a unit of two lines, usually rhyming, often used terminally to summarize or moralize; a very popular form in the eighteenth century.

Cross-rhyme: a rhyme scheme with alternating rhymes, as *abab*.

Dramatic monologue: a poem cast as a speech by a particular (historical or imaginary) person, usually to a specific auditor. The form is particularly associated with Browning and Tennyson, and has remained popular in the twentieth century.

End-stopped: of a line or stanza, having a terminal mark of punctuation.

Enjamb(+ed/ment): of lines, couplets, or stanzas, not end-stopped, with the sense (and/or syntax) continuing into the next line, couplet, or stanza.

Epic: one of the five classical genres, epics are long narrative poems usually dealing with the heroic or martial exploits of a person or race.

Fourteeners: couplets in iambic heptameter.

Genre: a classical method of distinguishing and grouping literary forms; the sets of conventional expectations readers learn to have.

Heroic: of a form, in iambic pentameter.

Lyric: one of the five classical genres, lyrics were at first musically accompanied; the term now covers most short, non-narrative, non-dramatic verse.

Mock-epic: a poem comically or satirically dressed in epic conventions for which its subject and/or manner are inappropriate.

Octave: (or *octet*) a unit of eight lines, usually the first eight of a sonnet.

Ode: a formal poem of some dignity or length; *Alcaic*, *Sapphic*, *Pindaric*, and *Horatian* odes are formally distinguished.

Open: of form, variable; of couplets, with the second line enjambed to the first line of the next couplet (or other component unit of form).

Ottava rima: a stanza of eight lines, in iambic pentameter, having the rhyme scheme *abababcc*.

Pentain: a unit of five lines.

Petrarchan: of a sonnet, having the octave rhyme scheme *abbaabba*, and the sestet rhyme scheme *cdecde* (or a variant thereof).

Quatrain: a unit of four lines; often used for narrative.

Refrain: (or *burden*) a line or lines that are repeated.

Rhyme royal: a stanza of seven lines, in iambic pentameter, having the rhyme scheme *ababbcc*.

Rhyme scheme: a method of notating the pattern of rhymes in a stanza or poem using the alphabet. The first line, and all subsequent lines that rhyme with it, are *a*; the next line that does not rhyme, and all subsequent lines that rhyme with it, are *b*; and so on. Line-lengths may also be indicated, by placing the number of beats after the letter denoting the line.

Satire, satiric: one of the five classical genres, satires were (and are) complex forms (or sequences) unified by the intention to ridicule.

Sestet: a unit of six lines.

Shakespearean: of a sonnet, having the rhyme scheme *ababcdcdefefgg*.

Single-rhyme: a rhyme scheme with only one set of rhyming lines, as *abcb* or *abac*.

Singleton: a unit of one line.

Sonnet: until the early seventeenth century, any short lyric poem; thereafter specifically a poem of fourteen lines in iambic pentameter. As a form its traditional use is for poems of (frustrated) love and courtship.

Spenserian: of a sonnet, having the rhyme scheme *ababbcbccdcdee*; of a stanza, in iambic pentameter and having the rhyme scheme *ababbcbcc12*.

Stanza: a group of lines with a specified rhyme scheme, pattern of line-lengths, etc.; used as a unit of form; usually shown on the page by blank lines above and below.

Tercet: a unit of three lines in which one or more does not rhyme with the others.

Terza rima: successive tercets rhyming *aba bcb cdc ded* etc.

Tragedy, tragic: one of the five classical genres, tragedies dealt with the lives and fates of individuals, usually of high social or political rank; long-regarded as the highest or noblest genre.

Turn: a moment of disjunction and/or renewal, creating a shift or development in the sense at a specified point in a form; in relation to the Pindaric ode, another name for the strophe.

Triplet: a unit of three lines which all rhyme together.

Verse paragraphs: the divisions of a long poem in a constant, non-stanzaic form, indicated (like prose paragraphs) by indenting the first line of each.

Layout

Most people do not think about layout as a separate feature of written texts, but it is crucial. If you were shown three printed pages, from a novel, a telephone directory, and a volume of poetry, you would not have to be close enough to read words to tell which was which: the pattern of the black words and white spaces (and the size of the pages) would tell you at first glance.

And if you could not tell—if the novel suddenly began to be printed in columns, or if the telephone directory were printed as continuous prose—then the pages of both would be odd to read, and the telephone directory very awkward and irritating to use. So you can see that readers notice layout even when they aren't thinking about it particularly, and that in consequence layout matters a good deal.

There are many standard layouts with which all readers are familiar: the large, bold headlines and column format used in newspapers; the use of a new line for the name, street, and town in an address; the initial line-by-line itemization of the ingredients in a recipe, followed by the cooking instructions in continuous prose; the use of a separate line for the 'Dear . . .' and 'Yours . . .' at the beginning and end of letters; the space left between each speech of a play; and so on. It is precisely because all these formats are so familiar, registered by your eyes before you begin to read the words, that they tend to be noticed automatically, and not thought about consciously. Usually that is fair enough, for the whole purpose of different formats is to make different kinds of texts equally easy to read, the information set out in a way that helps the reader to analyse the sequence of characters correctly, just as the spaces between words help readers to distinguish one word from another. It is only whenallthespacesorhyphensaremissing, or thelay ou tincorrect, that you realise how helpful spacing and layout is. But in poetry noticing the layout automatically is not good enough, because the various common layouts may be used in uncommon ways.

Layout, especially in poetry, means more than simply where the words go and where the spaces are left. There is also whether any words are printed in lower-case letters, SMALL CAPITALS, or CAPITALS; in roman letters, *italic letters*, **bold letters**, or any other face or fount of type,[1] such as *blackletter* (the old gothic-style fount[2]); whether the fount and size of type are constant; whether different colours of ink are used; whether there is any underlining; whether accents are used; whether the left and right margins are *justified* (straight line) or *ragged*; how the title and *epigraph*,[3] if any, are set; and so on. Decisions about these things were in the past often made by the printer or publisher, not the author, and so are of qualified value to the critic; but in this century authors, and particularly poets, have increasingly taken command of this aspect of their work, and told printers and publishers what they want. The word used for all of these things together is the French term *mise-en-page*, the putting-on-the-page (cf. the *mise-en-scène*, which refers to the material production of a play or film, the provision of actors, costumes, props, and so forth, as distinct from the dialogue and stage-directions which comprise the script). A 'text', considered in abstract, need not have a *mise-en-page*, but a book always does, and most people encounter most texts within the covers of books, laid out on the page.

Poetic layout is intimately bound up with punctuation and rhyme, through the *lineation*, the division into lines, which fundamentally determines layout and the placing (if there are any) of rhyme-words, and is an aspect of punctuation in its own right.

One basic distinction is whether each line simply follows on directly from the previous line, as in blank verse and many poems in couplets, or whether the lines are grouped into stanzas with spaces left between them; and a second basic distinction is whether a line is set hard to the left margin (which is called *ekthesis*, though the word is rarely used) or *indented* by one or more spaces to the right (which is called *eisthesis*). When a poem is set as a continuous sequence of individual lines, and there is no indentation other than to indicate verse paragraphs, the

[1] For definitions of 'face' and 'fount' see the chapter glossary and p. 5, n. 7 above.

[2] Now most popular for band names and places called 'Ye Olde Shoppe', blackletter was the standard fount for all printed books before *c.*1580. Since then it has occasionally been used in poetry as a distinguishing fount: on the title-page of the first edition of Lord Byron's *Childe Harold's Pilgrimage*, for example, the title was in blackletter, in keeping with the terminal -e in "Childe".

[3] An *epigraph* (from the Greek ’ἐπί [epi], 'upon' + γράφειν [graphein], 'write') is a short motto, often a quotation, placed between the title and the beginning of the text. I used the quotation from Jon Stallworthy's essay in the *Norton Anthology* as an epigraph to Chapter 1, and the quotation from Dr Johnson is the epigraph to 'Nearing Forty'. See pp. 55 and 148–9 below.

most interesting question is whether the first word of each line is given a capital letter. Unless the particular word usually has one the only reason for doing this is to emphasize the line as a unit, and so reinforce the lineation: which is helpful when you are first learning to read poetry, and largely redundant thereafter. It used to be a common practice to mark the end of every line as well, usually with a comma, whether or not one was needed syntactically: modern editors almost always remove these commas from older texts, because they now obscure the sense and don't help the reader, but usually keep the capital letters that begin each line. Poets, however, have increasingly tended to use an initial capital letter only for words that usually have one, or that they wish to emphasize.

When a poem is stanzaic it is normal (though not universal) to indicate the rhyme scheme eisthetically, with indentation. In stanzas up to the quatrain it is easy to see what kind of rhyme there is, if any; and it is most common not to use indentation in poems using such short stanzas. But in longer and more complex stanzas the pattern of indentation is a real visual help in working-out and remembering the rhyme scheme. This is how Keats's 'Grecian Urn' stanza (O2.541/N848) is usually printed:

Thou still unravished bride of quietness,
  Thou foster child of silence and slow time,
Sylvan historian, who canst thus express
  A flowery tale more sweetly than our rhyme:
What leaf-fringed legend haunts about thy shape
  Of deities or mortals, or of both,
    In Tempe or the dales of Arcady?
  What men or gods are these? What maidens loath?
What mad pursuit? What struggle to escape?
    What pipes and timbrels? What wild ecstasy?

The *ababcdedce* rhyme scheme is exactly reflected in the pattern of indentation, the *a*- and *c*-lines unindented, the *b*- and *d*-lines indented by two spaces, and the *e*-lines indented by four spaces. You might expect every line with a new rhyme-sound to be more deeply indented than the last: but on an ordinary page even a short poem would soon shuffle across to the other margin, so it is usual to reset the indentation to zero as soon as any substructure is complete. Here that resetting occurs between the cross-rhymed quatrain (1–4) and the two tercets (5–7, 8–10).

Sonnets are a special case, particularly the Shakespearean sonnet. Perhaps because the unlinked cross-rhymed quatrains are in any case easy to see and hear, it is not unusual to print Shakespearean sonnets without indentation or with only the terminal couplet (lines 13–14) indented (as in the *Oxford* and *Norton Anthologies*). On the other hand the *b*-lines of the octave of the Petrarchan sonnet (*abbaabba*) usually are indented, and any variation in the rhyme scheme (such as *abababab*) can often be seen at a glance in the eisthesis, without having laboriously to work out all the *a*'s and *b*'s. It is also possible to go a step further and leave a line blank between the component quatrains and tercets (see, for example, Geoffrey Hill's sonnets in 'Lachrimae': N1724), which emphasizes the substructures at the expense of the complete sonnet form.

Some care is needed, for poets can deliberately use eisthesis which does not coincide with the rhyme scheme. The quatrains of Richard Wilbur's 'A Baroque Wall-Fountain in the Villa Sciarra' (N1529) are arch-rhymed, *abba*, but each stanza is printed like this:

> Under the bronze crown
> Too big for the head of the stone cherub whose feet
> A serpent has begun to eat,
> Sweet water brims a cockle and braids down

The tension between layout and rhyme makes the stanza much more complicated and ornate than it would be if the layout supported the rhyme, sufficiently so to evoke baroque decoration: which is presumably Wilbur's point, his stanza physically echoing the decorative complexity of the wall-fountain his poem describes. It is also the shorter lines that are indented, and indentation may distinguish line-lengths rather than a rhyme scheme (as often in the layout of the Spenserian stanza: see O1.671/N152); or, where the patterns of line lengths and rhyme coincide (as in common metre), both may be simultaneously indicated by the indentation.

A factor which makes a surprising amount of difference is whether the lines are single-spaced or double-spaced, and how much space is left between stanzas (if the poem is stanzaic). These things together, the amount of the page left white, are called the *leading*, because in setting metal type spaces between lines and stanzas were traditionally created by placing bars of lead between the lines of type.[4] Between the early eighteenth century (the first editions of Gay and Pope) and the mid-nineteenth century (the first editions of Browning) there was an age of very great printing in England. Some of the masterpieces of that

[4] Computer setting has made the technique largely obsolete, but the word is still used.

age, the joke pages in Sterne's novel *Tristram Shandy*, and the etched poems of William Blake, are acknowledged, so that when those works are reprinted care is taken to reproduce the *mise-en-page* with some accuracy. But in an age of great printing even ordinary books may be printed very intelligently, and one of the characteristic features of poetry printed during that age is heavy leading, with the lines double (or even more widely) spaced. As a result the pages are very elegant and clear to read; but in modern editions, where there is usually as much text as possible on each page in order to keep down the production costs, and in cheaply-bound paperbacks this elegant *mise-en-page* is sacrificed.

Better an inelegant text than no text, and the cheaper the better: but there is a cost to this cheapness. Byron's *Don Juan*, for example, was originally printed with only two stanzas per page, but the Penguin edition prints four per page, and the *Oxford* and *Norton* anthologies (although they include only a fraction of the poem) print between five and six stanzas per page, and regularly split stanzas between two pages (O2.315–72/N769–92). If you're only looking up a line or two it doesn't make any difference; but if you're reading the whole poem (which has nearly two thousand stanzas) the cumulative difference is considerable. Sitting and reading *Don Juan* in the six volumes of the first edition (smelling the calfskin binding, feeling the thickness of each page, and encountering every stanza spaciously laid out in a way that is pleasing to the eyes) introduces you to a more leisurely and considered poem than reading the busy and cramped Penguin text, or the few stanzas in the anthologies. There the leisure and consideration have been replaced by constriction and economy, which makes the poem seem more rattlingly comic, less capable of being movingly serious.[5] It's much cheaper, so far more people can afford it; but a price has been paid.

Leading and eisthesis are only the beginning of what a poet can do with the *mise-en-page* and the materiality of the text, especially in free verse and open form, where there are no regular patterns of rhyme or line-length to be displayed. T. S. Eliot famously experimented with unusual layouts in *The Waste Land*, especially in the middle section of

[5] In the same way reading the Bible in one of the huge old lectern bibles that are used in churches, and reading it in a modern pocket-paperback, is not the same experience: for the lectern bible you will need a table (or a lectern) to read at, and will handle the pages differently, see some headings strikingly printed in red ink, and so on. To damage such a book would take an effort, but a small paperback Bible may casually be used as a pocket-edition, or maltreated.

part II (O2.1988/N1239–40) and the last section of part III (O2.1992–4/N1243–5); and since then many poets, including David Jones (O2.2060), Charles Olson (N1404–8), Denise Levertov (N1571–2), A. R. Ammons (N1586–90), and Leslie Marmon Silko (N1832), have continued to experiment.[6]

A popular poem to exploit the *mise-en-page* is e. e. cummings's 'r-p-o-p-h-e-s-s-a-g-r', where the letters of 'grasshopper' scramble about the page as "PPEGORHRASS" and "gRrEaPsPhOs" until they finally stop in their proper order when the grasshopper stops jumping. Another interesting example is D. J. Enright's 'The Typewriter Revolution' which must be set in a fount imitating the appearance of typewritten (as opposed to printed) documents. Both go so far beyond the simple use of indentation as to become *shape poems*, where pictorial and verbal representation are fused.

The shape poem dates from classical antiquity, but its more recent history begins with George Herbert's poems 'The Altar' (O1.1167/N329) and 'Easter Wings' (O1.1168/N330–1), from *The Temple* (1633). Herbert thought of his whole book as a material object as well as a set of texts, and (even more than with Byron) aspects of his poems are often lost in reprinting. In the *Oxford Anthology* the two stanzas of 'Easter Wings', which physically represent wings, are printed below one another on the same page, which looks perfectly normal; but in the first edition each stanza had a page to itself, and the lines were printed vertically (so that to read them you have to turn the book sideways: see N331). As a result, when you turn the page of the first edition and come to 'Easter Wings' you see the shape before you can read the words, and between the two stanzas/wings, where the spine of the angel would be, there is the spine of the book. This is not true in most modern editions of Herbert.

What Herbert does with these poems is effectively to take his own metaphors visually and literally. He was a very religious man, and his poems are all in one sense prayers, offered up to God in *The Temple*, his book itself becoming a material metaphor for the building in which he prays; and within the temple/*The Temple* the reader will also find (a poem shaped as) an altar, and (a poem shaped as) wings which can carry prayers to heaven. The visual perception of drawing and painting

[6] These poems are particularly difficult to reproduce accurately, and there is no point in reproducing them inaccurately: so there is more citation and less quotation in this chapter, and looking the references up in the *Norton* is particularly important. The *Oxford Anthology* includes no modern shape poems, partly because it is restricted to English literature.

is mixed with the visual perception of reading, and the poem becomes a picture as well as a text. The picture is only schematic, lacking visual perspective, and is subordinate to the words of the poem $\binom{\text{WORDS}}{\text{picture}}$; but in the first half of the seventeenth century, when Herbert was writing, there was a parallel form, the *emblem*, in which drawing and reading were more evenly balanced[7] $\binom{\text{PICTURE}}{\text{WORDS}}$. Emblems explicitly matched an illustration, usually a small woodcut of a scene, with a poem about the same subject. Picture and poem together were often moral or political, sometimes both; and printed collections of these emblems, *emblem books*, were popular for a time,[8] but they fell out of use after the civil war. At the other extreme, where a very brief text or motto is subordinate to a picture, often symbolic, $\binom{\text{PICTURE}}{\text{words}}$, are coats-of-arms, many sentimentally moral Victorian pictures accompanied by a literary or biblical text, and perhaps some modern forms, including posters, advertisements on hoardings, and charity T-shirts. In about 1910, when Picasso and Braque began to paint or collage words into their paintings many thought it a radical feature of their new Cubist technique, but in this both artists were working in an old tradition. More recently still there has been an intensive development of the graphic novel, drawing on the traditions of comics as well as fine art, notably by Art Spiegelman and Alan Moore.

Shape poetry is now often thought of as comic, probably because the best-known examples, Lewis Carroll's 'Fury Said to a Mouse' and the mirror-stanza from 'Jabberwocky', first appeared in children's books; but 'Easter Wings' is as serious as Herbert's hope for the salvation of his immortal soul. The finest living writer of shape poetry, John Hollander (N1664), is more like Herbert than Carroll; and the poets (such as Eliot) who, without quite going as far as shape poetry, have nevertheless used the *mise-en-page* inventively and intensely, also tend to be perfectly serious about what they are doing. Shape poetry may be a sort of game, and it is fun—but not necessarily funny.[9]

---

7 The Renaissance period as a whole was characterized by an intense interest in the visual, including both major areas of culture (such as widespread changes in the handwriting that people were taught, the development of printing, and the political use of media imagery) and minor but intriguing oddities (such as pictures in false perspective, or that you have to look at in a mirror, and the frequent use in printed books of decorated borders for each page). Interest in the shape poem is part and parcel of this background.

8 The best known was *Emblems* (1635), by Francis Quarles (1592–1644).

9 Shaped layouts can also be used in prose, and one of the most extraordinary recent examples may be seen in Alasdair Gray's novel *1982 Janine* (Harmondsworth: Penguin, 1985), 177–90. The text develops over several pages multiple columns

Shape poems are the extreme of layout, but just as every poem has a form of some kind, so every poem that is written or printed must be organized on the page in one way or another. When the layout is more-or-less standard, it will tend to help in understanding other aspects of the poem rather than to be of real interest in its own right; but layouts of the same poem can vary considerably between editions, affecting your reading more than you realize; and you can never be sure that a layout is standard, even if it looks like it, until you have checked for yourself.

One final suggestion. The best and most enjoyable way to learn the ins and outs of layout is to design and print for yourself. Word-processors offer a great deal, and it is well worth experimenting with different founts and leading; better still is to do some printing on a hand-press, learning with cold-metal type to *compose* (to set the letters and inter-word spaces) and to *impose* (put the pages of type on the press). Various night-schools and university boards of continuing education offer courses in which hand-press printing is an element, and if you ever have the opportunity it is well worth seizing. When you are responsible for every letter and every space, and for the overall balance of the page, the practical importance of layout becomes clearer than any reading or discussion can ever make it.

---

which widen and narrow and eventually collide, representing the fracturing mind of a man attempting suicide by overdose; blank pages represent the mind asleep. Gray designs his own work, and *Poor Things* (Harmondsworth: Penguin, 1993) is (among much else) a wonderful compendium of layouts.

'Nearing Forty'

When you talk about the *mise-en-page* of a given poem you are not talking simply about the 'text', but about a particular printed version of that text. The reprint of 'Nearing Forty' on pages 14–15 reproduces closely (though in a different fount, and with one misprint corrected and line-numbers added) the poem's *mise-en-page* in Walcott's *Collected Poems 1948–84*, the most recent edition seen through the press by the author.

The thirty-two lines of the poem are set ekthetically, and do not have initial capital letters. This reflects the fact that the poem is a single sentence, all the way from the capital letter of "Insomniac" to the full-stop after "weep". There is good leading, as there is throughout the *Collected Poems*, so that each line can be clearly seen, the metrical and rhyme schemes readily worked out, and the syntax (which involves much enjambment) easily followed. If a poet is going to use these devices, and hopes that some readers will appreciate them, it is good to be kind to those readers' eyes.

On the other hand, one could equally argue that this *mise-en-page* does not offer some kinds of help that it might. There is no eisthetic indication of rhyme, no annotation of unfamiliar phrases or literary allusions, and for many readers this single-sentence block of type, marching down its pages, may be far more intimidating than a poem which appears broken-up (into manageable pieces) on the page. It <u>is</u> an elegant setting, achieving visual clarity—but that may equally be a way of enhancing authority.

The title, dedication, and epigraph are set in italics (which are not used anywhere else in the poem), and the dedication and epigraph are indented. This is perfectly standard: yet an epigraph need not be italicized; at five lines this is quite a long epigraph to italicize; it is printed with good leading (whereas an epigraph is often single spaced, even if the lines of the poem are double spaced); and the attribution of the epigraph, "——SAMUEL JOHNSON", is nicely printed, with an initial rule, in spaced small capitals: all of which strongly suggests a conscious decision by someone.

The point of these small touches, as well as of the heavy leading and ekthesis of the main text, is, I suspect, that all these features (as well as being pleasing to the eye) are reminiscent of the first edition of the book from which the epigraph is taken, Dr Johnson's great edition of Shakespeare, published in 1765. This elegant (but for some intimidating) layout may allude to that edition, and so visually reinforce Dr Johnson's authority and certainty, which are very evident in the passage that Walcott quotes. As the poem itself is partly about trying to rediscover some of that authority and certainty in the second half of the twentieth century, and during a spiritual crisis in middle age, the visual reinforcement of the Johnsonian epigraph is a useful preparation for reading the poem, and following Walcott's meditation.

Chapter Glossary

Composition: in hand-press printing the process of assembling the individual pieces of type, including inter-word spaces, in the correct order.

Eisthesis: the indentation of a line or lines by one or more spaces from the left margin.

Ekthesis: the setting of a line or lines hard to the left margin.

Epigraph: a short motto or quotation prefixed to a text.

Face: of a type, a particular appearance of the letters and numbers, as roman or *italic*; thus any given fount of type will have many faces.

Font: the standard US spelling of 'fount'.

Fount: (or in the USA, 'font') of type, a particular design of the letters and numbers; each fount will comprise designs for each character in a number of faces.

Imposition: in hand-press printing the process of arranging the composed type on the bed of the press; decisions about leading, ornaments, running-heads etc. are involved, and two or more pages will have to be imposed together in any book or pamphlet format.

Indentation: the setting of a line or lines in from the left margin by one or more spaces.

Justified: of text and margins, aligned straight up and down.

Leading: the amount of white space left between lines, stanzas, or other units of form, and in the margins.

Lineation: the organization of a poem into lines.

Mise-en-page: the actual layout of a given poem (or prose text) on a given page.

Ragged: of text and margins, not justified.

Shape poems: or *concrete* poems, those whose text is organized on the page to depict a shape, or otherwise to involve pictorial as well as verbal representation.

Punctuation

Pause and Effect
——Title of a history of punctuation by M. B. PARKES

Punctuation is to the written word as cartilage is to bone, permitting articulation and bearing the stress of movement. Like layout, it is another thing that is always there, and matters a great deal, but is not often thought about. Without punctuation words are hard to construe: this is a depunctuated passage from Dickens's *Bleak House*:

> out of the question says the coroner you have heard the boy cant exactly say wont do you know we cant take that in a court of justice gentlemen its terrible depravity put the boy aside

but restore the punctuation and:

> 'Out of the question,' says the Coroner. 'You have heard the boy. "Can't exactly say" won't do, you know. We can't take *that* in a Court of Justice, gentlemen. It's terrible depravity. Put the boy aside.'

The punctuation is shown to be doing a great deal.[1] Lawyers know this, and know how easy it is fraudulently to insert or delete a comma: some legal documents have to be written using capital letters and full-stops but without other punctuation or pronouns. Such documents are circumlocutory, and make dull reading, but they are insured against ambiguity.

In poetry, however, it may be precisely the possible ambiguity, or uncertainty, the opportunity delicately to shade a meaning, that makes a particular way of punctuating attractive. Despite the best efforts of grammarians for five hundred years, no-one has found any hard and fast rules for the punctuation of English: because there aren't any. Like English itself, punctuation in English is an open system, in which any-

[1] For a full commentary see M. B. Parkes, *Pause and Effect: An Introduction to the History of Punctuation in the West* (Aldershot: Scolar Press, 1992), 1—from whence I take this example.

thing is possible but there are conventional ways of doing most things. Such conventions can be ignored, or broken: if you break all the conventions simultaneously the result will be difficult to understand,[2] and take a long time to read, because the whole point of conventions is to make communication easier and quicker; but if you observe most of the conventions, and break only one or two at a time, the results can be very useful. This means that (especially in poetry, where all aspects of language are heightened) there is no such thing as 'correct' or 'incorrect' punctuation, but only conventional, unconventional, and counter-conventional punctuation, where the usual conventions are straightforwardly employed, or in some way exploited. Punctuation can be helpful or unhelpful, elegant or inelegant, economic or fulsome, consistent or inconsistent: and in practical criticism it is more useful to ask these questions than whether it is 'correct'.

The grammarians and rhetoricians of some centuries have argued that all punctuation is *elocutionary*, signalling pauses which guide the voice in reading aloud (like breathing or bowing marks in music); while the grammarians of other centuries have argued that all punctuation is *syntactic*, indicating grammatical sense. Both sorts of grammarian admit that some punctuation is also *deictic* (or *emphatic*), stressing one word or phrase but not others. In point of fact almost all punctuation is <u>both</u> elocutionary <u>and</u> syntactic, working simultaneously for ear and eye: that colon is syntactic, and so is that comma, but if you read this sentence aloud you will naturally pause after "eye" and "syntactic", and quite right too. So (as usual) what grammarians say is largely irrelevant to what poets do.

The current conventional use of a particular mark of punctuation is not necessarily the conventional use of 100 or 300 years ago. Many twentieth-century editors habitually modernize the punctuation of older texts, which can be very damaging. It's supposed to help students, but denies them the author's (or at least a contemporary) construction of the text, which may well have been doing a better job of making the text readable than the modern construction which the editor imposes. Unthinking modernization has become rarer, but not rare enough; and though older punctuation may be unfamiliar at first it is never impossible to understand, and often very helpful.[3]

---

[2] James Joyce's *Finnegans Wake* is an extreme example, but even it follows many basic conventions.

[3] If you are buying a text, and there is a choice of editions, prefer one that is not modernized. This information can usually be found at the end of the introduction, or in a 'Note on the Text'.

The principle forms and marks of punctuation are these.

The **paragraph,** dating from the second century BCE, is the oldest surviving form of punctuation. In non-fictional prose the paragraph is the basic unit of argument; in fictional prose it tends also to be a basic unit of emotion, the tone of the last sentence of any paragraph signalling (as it were) the tonic key of that paragraph, and colouring re-readings. This may be the case with verse paragraphs also, but less commonly so if the verse paragraphs are long. The marks called the *paraph* (¢, ¶, ||) and the *paragraphus* (§) indicate paragraphs or sections, and may replace or accompany initial eisthesis (the indentation of the first line).

The **sentence** (or *period*[4]) is a traditional unit of grammar, "forming the grammatically complete expression of a single thought" (*OED*). The conventional indication of sentences with initial capital and terminal full-stop was not fully developed until the eighth century CE. In printing or typing it is usual to use a double space between sentences, so that the normal indication of a sentence break has three elements: the full-stop, the space, and the capital letter. It follows that there are several intensities (or levels) of sentence break which can be indicated, by using the full-stop and the space but not the capital letter, or the full-stop and the capital letter but not the space, and so on. The American poet e. e. cummings[5] particularly enjoyed this game.

It is often said that a complete sentence must comprise 'subject + intransitive[6] verb', or 'subject + transitive verb + object', which is reasonable: but it is possible to punctuate as a sentence something that isn't. This is often associated with the written imitation of speech, which is commonly ungrammatical and full of incomplete sentences; examples are line 24 of Browning's 'Caliban upon Setebos' (O2.1354), "Setebos, Setebos, and Setebos!", and line 284 (O2.1360), beginning "What, what?".

The **word** is a traditional unit of sense. Word-separation began in Ireland in the later-seventh century CE, before which all writing was in *scriptio continua* (continuous script), astringoflettersrecordingastringof-

[4] Strictly, a *sentence* and a *period* are not identical: periods are rhetorical and aural, sentences syntactical and visual. See pp. 122–5 below.

[5] cummings always had his name printed without any capital letters, though in many books his idiosyncrasy is standardized to E. E. Cummings.

[6] An *intransitive* verb does not take a direct object, but a *transitive* verb does. "The dog exists"—it does not need to exist something, and 'to exist' is intransitive; but if "the dog eats" it must eat something, and 'to eat' is transitive.

sounds, like that. It is unusual to interfere with standard word-separation, but e. e. cummings did, to produce, for example, "deafand-dumb" (N1284) and "firstclassprivates" (N1285). It is much commoner to replace the space separating two words with a hyphen which turns them into one jointed word (see p. 69 below).

● The **full-stop** (or in the USA *period*) is the heaviest of the four *stops*[7] and indicates the end of a sentence, which in reading aloud will normally enforce a substantial pause. Eliot experimented in *The Waste Land* and later poems with the effects of omitting an expected full-stop (see, for example, lines 279–91, O2.1993/N1244), and others, such as A. R. Ammons (N1586) have followed suit. The same mark is used as a *suspension mark*, to indicate a word shortened by the suspension of the last letters, such as 'etc.' for 'et c^{etera}' and 'ed.' for 'ed^{itor}' or 'ed$^{\text{ited by}}$'. Three suspension marks in a row (. . .), called an *ellipsis*, indicate incompletion: that words have been omitted from a quotation, that the speaker has been interrupted, or a trailing off into silence (see O2.1992/N1243, O2.2179, N1588).

●● The **colon** is the second-heaviest stop. When printed in roman letters the term 'colon', plural 'colons', refers only to the mark, but when printed in italic letters the term *colon*, plural *cola*, refers to the part of a sentence separated by colons: so three colons would divide a sentence into four *cola* (1 : 2 : 3 : 4 .), and this sentence has one colon and two *cola*[8] (1 : 2.). The division of a sentence into *cola* dates from classical antiquity, but the practice of marking was a mediæval development. Because this division into *cola* affects the construction and rhythm of the sentence it involves both *rhetoric*, the formal persuasiveness of the argument,[9] and *style*, meaning in this sense 'how the argument is verbally conducted'. The great classical rhetoricians Cicero (106–43 BCE) and Quintilian (*c.*35–*c.*100 CE) suggested that periods (see pp. 122–5 below) had on average four *cola*: during the Renaissance many people took Cicero very seriously, and made his observation a strong

---

[7] The *stops* are the full-stop, the colon, the semi-colon, and the comma (. : ; ,), which indicate the end of various grammatical units.

[8] Since the eighteenth century the classical meaning of *colon/cola* has dropped out of use, and only colon/colons is now common. I find it worthwhile to revive *colon/cola* (and the parallel *comma/commata*: see pp. 63–4 below), but you should gloss them briefly when you first use them in an exam or for a new teacher.

[9] 'Rhetoric' used to mean 'the formal rhetorical devices used in any text', such as rhetorical questions, repetition, and so on, but now (especially in the USA) has the looser sense of 'the persuasiveness of a text'.

recommendation: so (especially in work between *c.*1500 and *c.*1700) it is always worth checking any long period with colons in it to see exactly how many *cola* there are: for if the answer is four (i.e. if there are three colons) it is unlikely to be so by chance. Such Ciceronian sentences are often used to express an argument that its author thinks well-proportioned; and the rhythm of such sentences is (like quatrains and squares) another thing in fours which is intrinsically attractive.

In normal modern use the distinctive feature of the colon is that it implies a logical or dependent relationship, like connecting an electrical circuit in series; whereas the comma, for example, usually connects clauses in parallel. The common example is a list:

There are four seasons: spring, summer, autumn, and winter.

The commas separate each season from the next, but each is referred back by the colon to the clause before the colon, its presence explained as an enumeration of the "four seasons". The same basic function can be seen even in sophisticated exploitations.

; The second lightest stop is the **semi-colon,** the last of the three marks of punctuation invented and disseminated by Italian humanist scholars and printers between 1360 and 1500. (The others are the *exclamation-mark* and *lunulae*). It was invented by Pietro Bembo (whose name is commemorated in *Bembine* type) in Venice in the 1490s, the upper point of the colon placed above the comma expressly to create a stop intermediate between the colon and the comma. In an extension of the Ciceronian analysis of a period (see pp. 122–3 below) as divided into *cola*, some scholars analyse *cola* as subdivided into *semi-cola*, and so distinguish between the semi-colon (plural semi-colons), the mark, and the *semi-colon* (plural *semi-cola*) parts of a sentence indicated by semi-colons. These terms are not commonly used, but they can be very useful—if, for example, you are faced with a bit of *Paradise Lost*. Book IX, lines 13–41 (from "Sad task" to "poem.": N382–3) form a single period, the syntax and argument of which are hard to construe unless you follow the pattern of the major stops (everything above a comma). This pattern can be described as: three *cola*, the first of three *semi-cola*, the second and third of two, with a parenthesis in the first *semi-colon* of the second *colon*, which may be written as:

; ; : ( ) ; : ; .

Read Milton's 28-line sentence (by no means the longest in *Paradise Lost*) with this pattern in your head (obtained by scanning ahead and jotting down before you read), and it will make more sense more easily. Each *semi-colon* within a *colon* builds on the last; and the colons are weightier than the semi-colons, each marking a clear development within the period.[10]

One function of semi-colons is a clearer connection in parallel than can be managed by commas. In the sentence about the seasons, each of the commas could be a semi-colon:

There are four seasons: spring; summer; autumn; and winter.

but in a short list of short components, it is unnecessary for clarity, and looks pedantic. If the list were longer; or if the items varied in length; and especially if, as in this list, some of the items were sufficiently long to have internal commas, not signifying a break between items: then it would be worth using semi-colons.

The more interesting function of the semi-colon is to make a syntactical turn, allowing a clause to move away from the previous clause at a tangent. It is for prose repeatedly using the semi-colon in this way that Henry James is notorious,[11] and it is true that too many turns can leave a reader dizzy: but James at his best was a wonderful punctuator, subtle and steely.[12] In verse the semi-colon is often essential to long sentences in long works, but can be used powerfully in short poems, and within narrative stanzas. Try, for example, Keats's 'Ode to a Nightingale' (O2.538/N845) paying serious attention to his choice of colons and semi-colons. You'll be surprised.

, The **comma** is the lightest of the four stops, but cannot therefore be used carelessly. The effects, of adding commas, or, of omitting them, will vary widely but affect any or all of pace tone logic and clarity. Classical analysis (which didn't have semi-colons or *semi-cola*)

10 To test my argument, try the same passage in the *Oxford Anthology* (O1.1322–3), which 'modernizes' the punctuation by replacing both colons with semi-colons, and demoting the last semi-colon to a comma. The result—; ; ; ( ) ; ; .—is a period of six *semi-cola* which makes rather less syntactical sense than the original.

11 What James often does is to change the grammatical subject across a semi-colon, and the reader goes astray by not changing subject, and effectively reading the semi-colon as a comma. In this (simplistic) example—"The cat curled up on the sofa; old and lumpy as it was it was comfortable."—the mistake would be to think it was the cat that was "old and lumpy", rather than the sofa. The difference is slight, but in a long sentence can be crucial.

12 Other great users of the semi-colon are Proust, in *A la Recherche du temps perdu*, and Paul Scott, in the *Raj Quartet*.

distinguished comma, plural commas, the mark, from *comma*, plural *commata*, into which a *colon* might be divided.[13]

The mark which we now call, and use as, a *slash*, or *solidus* (/), used to be an alternative form of the comma, and as such is properly called a *virgula*, plural *virgulae*[14] (or, even more precisely, a *virgula suspensiva*, or 'raised virgula'). Many Elizabethan poets, including Sir Walter Ralegh, used virgulae rather than commas in their handwriting; and Coleridge habitually used them in his notebooks, though not in his poetry: but they have not been much used in print since the 1520s, and modern editors usually replace virgulae with commas. Almost all the '/ 's you see will be slashes, used to separate alternatives (as in 'he/she'), rather than commas; but if you find one that doesn't make sense as a slash (see N1750) try reading it as a variety of comma.

The commonest modern abuse of the comma is to use it alone where either a semi-colon or another word (usually a conjunction) are needed, so connecting too many clauses in parallel. Poets are rarely guilty, but may (like Eliot) omit commas which prose would require, especially if they would coincide with a line-break. For some first-class commas try Seamus Heaney's 'The Strand at Lough Beg'.[15]

? The first origins of the **question-mark** are unclear, but its modern use began at the court of Charlemagne, in the late eighth century CE. That use, of course, is to mark questions (including rhetorical questions, where no answer is expected); but in English speech questions are usually sounded with a rising tone, and the question-mark is also a tonal indicator in printed texts (as is the exclamation-mark). As a result the question-mark may be doubled or tripled (???), to indicate complete bewilderment or surprise.

Many people think that the lower point always has the value of a full-stop; but while it may have, it need not. Do you see that in consequence the question-mark can be used medially, within a sentence? as well as being used terminally. (See *Paradise Lost* IX.546 [O1.1335/N393], for example.)

In 1754 the Real Academia Española began the practice (still current in Spain) of using two question-marks, one upside-down at the beginning of the sentence, and the other the right way up at the end (as

---

[13] These terms, like *colon/cola*, are also now rare, and should be glossed the first time you use them.

[14] Cf. *virgule*, the modern French for a comma.

[15] In *Field Work* (1979), and *New Selected Poems 1966–1987* (London & Boston: Faber and Faber, 1990), pp. 98–9.

"¿What did you say?". The practice is not used in English, but there has recently been much activity in Spanish literature, and as European integration proceeds the initial inverted question-mark may spread.

! The **exclamation-mark**, another tonal indicator, was the earliest of the three Italian humanist marks. It was invented in the 1360s by Iacopo Alpoleio da Urbisaglia (or so he claimed), and may, exactly like the question-mark! be used medially. As a tonal indicator the double or multiple exclamation-mark (!!) is common in comics and letters, but tends to make things louder rather than refining the sense.

In Spanish initial inverted exclamation-marks are used in the same way as inverted question-marks (as "¡Ouch!").

Brackets (which is a generic term) come in four varieties.

<> **Angled brackets**, useful in maths, are rare in poetry, but are used in editions showing textual variants.

{} **Braces** (or 'curly' brackets) are most often used to indicate a triplet in a poem in couplets: see, for example, N542. They were once used rather inventively to indicate rhyme, as in this twelfth-century copy of a Latin poem,[16] where the middle words of each line of a couplet rhyme with one another as well as with the end-words:

Miles ad arma fre	} mit	vita fraus Hectora d	} emit
Vrbem pugna pre		troia sub hoste tr	

Such layouts disappeared with the Middle Ages, as a clearer *mise-en-page* was developed which made it easier to see rhymes. In a printed text they would now look very obtrusive; but as a mark which may be hand-added to a printed text (as, for instance, during an exam when you are looking at a poem and wondering what to write about it) braces are worth remembering.

[] **Crotchets** (or 'square' brackets) developed during the fifteenth century. Their principal use now is to indicate that something has been changed or inserted, by the editor of a text, so they create a stronger disjunction in the text than other brackets, and of a different kind, signalling not a shade of meaning but a change of author. In poetry this normal function becomes a point of departure: Browning,

[16] I quote from Parkes, *Pause and Effect*, 99; see also plate 45, p. 238.

for example, enclosed the first and last verse paragraphs of 'Caliban upon Setebos' (O2.1354–5, 1360–1) in crotchets, to distinguish lines that Caliban thinks from lines that he speaks aloud.

( ) **Lunulae**, singular **lunula**, the 'little moons', (or 'round' brackets) were the second of the Italian humanist marks.[17] As a rhetorical figure the *parenthesis* (one clause intercluded within another) dates to classical antiquity; but the practice of marking parentheses with lunulae was invented by Colluccio Salutati in the 1390s, and the practices of marking them with commas or dashes are later still. There is therefore a distinction between lunulae, which are only (and), and a parenthesis, which in print is the opening lunula (or dash or comma), the alphanumeric contents, and the closing lunula (or dash or comma). The significance of lunulae is very variable, and must be inferred in context: but they always create a disjunction between one status of the text, as it were the equivalent of the tonic key in music, and another status, parenthetical to that tonic. That is to say, lunulae distinguish their contents, but how they distinguish them depends on context: and it is quite possible for that distinction to be emphatic. Grammarians traditionally argue that parentheses are subordinate, irrelevant, or clumsy; but no poet has ever meant by putting words in parenthesis 'Skip this bit if you like'. What they often do mean is 'Please pay special attention and think about why I am asking you to do so'; and in satire parentheses almost always intensify the attack.

For some examples of what can be done with lunulae consider line 35 of Marvell's 'Bermudas' (N433), where a "(perhaps)" is exquisitely shaded, and made more powerful, by being in parenthesis; lines 11–12 of Coleridge's 'Dejection: An Ode' (O2.276/N760), where lunulae help to figure 'the new moon in the old moon's arms'; and lines 24–30 of *The Waste Land* (O2.1984–5/N1237), a sentence where the main verb is in parenthesis, a grammatical impossibility. In Roethke's 'I Knew a Woman' (N1392) the last line of each stanza is in parenthesis, which effectively incorporates the parentheses into the stanza form: so that the form is not iambic pentameters simply rhyming *ababccc,* but rhyming *ababcc(c)*. And in Hill's 'September Song' (N1721), a poem about a child victim of the Nazis, lunulae around the only lines to include the word "I" crucially preserve Hill from sliding from pity for the victim into self-pity: a moral parenthesis.

[17] They are sometimes called *parentheses*, but this can be confusing, as parentheses are then indicated by parentheses. *Lunula/lunulae*, a term first used by Erasmus in 1531, is gaining modern currency.

“ ”

Inverted commas, like their French equivalent, *guillemets* (« »), developed from a mediæval *nota*, the *diple*. *Notae* are printed in the margin (while punctuation is within the body of the text), and the diple was originally used in theology to indicate a quotation from scripture. (A modern equivalent would be drawing a pencil line in the margin, as you read, to indicate a passage you may wish to find again.) In the later sixteenth century printers began to make the diple a punctuation mark by incorporating it into the text, still to indicate a quotation, but increasingly also for simple emphasis (comparable with putting a word in italics). In the 1570s English printers began a major extension of the use, to indicate direct speech as well as quotations; and in this extended function it came (by the eighteenth century) to be supported by *alinéa*, the convention of beginning each passage of direct speech on a new line. The exact combination of these conventions which is now the normal way of indicating direct speech dates only from 1857; and the multiple functions that inverted commas now have (indicating quotation, qualification, and direct speech) reflect the complicated history of the mark.

Inverted commas may be single or double, and may be composed of simple vertical strokes (',") or of actual commas, which are usually inverted when they open a quotation or speech (‘,“), and the right way up (but still raised) when they close it again(’,”). If two varieties of the mark are used within one text, it is possible to distinguish between exactly what each is doing: the commonest distinction is probably between using double inverted commas for direct speech and accurate quotation, and single inverted commas to show some kind of doubt or hesitation over the ‘truthfulness’, or perhaps ‘validity’ is a better term, of a word or phrase. (In speech this doubt is signalled by tone, but increasingly people simultaneously waggle their fingers in an inverted-comma charade.) Different printers have different house-styles[18] about this, but clarity and consistency (in <u>that</u> order) are more important than what each variety happens to mean in a particular case.

If a whole poem (or a complete stanza) is in direct speech the inverted commas may be omitted, as they are around Browning’s dramatic monologues. But omission can be a technique in its own right, as Eliot showed in lines 111–38 of *The Waste Land* (O2.1988/

[18] The *house* or *in-house* style are the standing orders of a printshop, their habitual ways of doing particular things. Compare the same play in two editions by different publishers, and you will see that many printing conventions—whether stage directions are italicized or bracketed, for instance—will differ.

N1239–40), where a series of questions are in inverted commas (and so presumably spoken aloud), but the answers are not in inverted commas (and are presumably thought in reply, but not spoken). Alter this punctuation and the meaning of the passage, which is to do with the waste land that an unhappy marriage can become, will be completely changed.

’

The **apostrophe** is the same mark as a single closing inverted comma, but is used singly rather than in pairs. Its principal uses are, with or without an ‘s’, to indicate ownership or possession[19] (the ship’s bell; the ships’ bells); and as a mark of elision (it’s = it is). Some poets, when using it to indicate elision, do not now close up the spaces, and so would have not “it’s ten o’clock”, but “it ’s ten o’ clock”: this may affect pronunciation, but does not alter meaning, and is commonest in dialect or regionally accented poetry. (Tony Harrison [N1766] in particular uses what he calls the ‘floating s’ to reconcile classical prosody with his Leeds accent.) The very heavy (and inconsistent) use of elisional apostrophes in printing work in Scots (see the poetry of Burns [O1.2267/N684] and MacDiarmid [O2.2071]) has been condemned for representing Scots as an inferior branch of English, and recent editions of poetry in Scots (including those of Burns and MacDiarmid) have been repunctuated and respelled to avoid “the vile, truckling apostrophe”.[20]

— The **dash** is normally used in script, typescript, and word-processing (though not in print) with a space on either side of it. Its Latin name is the *virgula plana*, the ‘flat virgula’, which distinguished it from the *virgula suspensiva* or ‘raised virgula’ (the modern slash); both are varieties of comma. Like commas, dashes may be used singly, or in pairs to create a parenthesis (which may then be described as *dash’d-off*[21]), or in infinite sequence—one after another—chopping the sentence up—and allowing changes of subject—to anything at all—even zebras—without ever generating a full-stop. This can work well, to suggest breathlessness, or someone who talks in clipped clauses; but it is often simple laziness, the substitution of the dash for every other mark: which is easier to write, but sacrifices so much subtlety and range as to be a worthless bargain. The eighteenth century was quite unreasonably

[19] Grammatically this is the *genitive* case (mine), as opposed to the *nominative* (I), for the subject, and the *accusative* (me), for the object.

[20] An unnamed American, quoted by MacDiarmid in a letter first published in *The Scotsman*, 28 Aug. 1968, and reprinted in *Lines Review*, no. 27 (Nov. 1968).

[21] It is better to write ‘dash’d off’ than ‘dashed off’, to avoid confusion.

fond of the dash used in this careless way, and since then it has been a popular style for letters, probably because it is felt to make writing less formal, and more like speech between friends.

The English master of the dash was Laurence Sterne (O1.2306), and the American mistress Emily Dickinson (N1010). In Sterne's novel *Tristram Shandy* (a stupendous shaggy-dog story) he used four lengths of dash —— the quarter-inch ———— half-inch ———————— three-quarter-inch ———————— and inch—to represent meditative or wool-gathering pauses of different durations and qualities; and sometimes used horizontal *rules* that continue for several lines, or even pages (the narrator pausing when he nods off). Dickinson's poetry is usually printed with the many dashes identical, but the autograph manuscripts suggest that Dickinson herself may have distinguished several varieties of dash. If reproduced in printed editions, this would make a substantial difference to her poetry.

▬ The **hyphen** has no space on either side, and is used either to yoke together two words, or the two halves of a word broken by lineation. The use at line-ends is patently helpful, but not in itself interesting; but the yoking together of words is a fascinating resource which English inherits from its Germanic ancestry. Keats was an obsessive creator of hyphenated compounds: the thirty-three lines of the ode 'To Autumn' alone yield (in the *Norton*: N849) eleven: *bosom-friend, thatch-eaves, cottage-trees, o'er-brimmed, soft-lifted, half-reaped, cider-press, soft-dying, stubble-plains, full-grown,* and *garden-croft*; and in the *Oxford* (O2.556) thirteen (add *Hedge-crickets* and *red-breast*[22]). Some of these could easily be dehyphenated, to become a single word (*overbrimmed*) or two words (*cider press*), as happens in the two cases about which the anthologies disagree. Clearly, some of the first elements are common qualifiers which wouldn't make sense on their own (*half-, over-, full-*); but equally clearly others (*cottage-trees, soft-dying*) can only mean what they do in this hyphenated form. Eliot was another hyphenator (his poem is *Ash-Wednesday*, not 'Ash Wednesday'), and of living poets the best compound-welder is probably Geoffrey Hill (O2.2184/N1720) (*pig-headed, soft-voiced, phantom-bird / stone-wearing, soft-thudding, martyr-laurels*).

Finally, there are ***signes de renvoi***, "any sign used to associate matter in the text with material added in the margin".[23] The commonest

[22] These appear as "Hedge crickets" and "redbreast" in the *Norton*.
[23] Parkes, *Pause and Effect*, 307.

are the arabic numerals printed in superscript and keyed to foot- or end-notes (as in this book); but the *degree-sign* (°), the *asterisk* (*), the *obelus* or *dagger* (†), the *double-obelus* (‡), the paraph (¢, ¶, or ||), the paragraphus (§), and various other *special sorts* of type may also be used as *indices* (the plural of *index*).

The footnote can be regarded as a form of punctuation in its own right, especially if the reader obeys the *signe de renvoi* and reads the footnote before continuing the text proper. In some poems which have notes, such as *The Waste Land*, it seems desirable to keep the notes separate from the text, and they are usually printed as endnotes;[24] but footnotes can be integral to a poem (see, for example, Tony Harrison's 'The Heartless Art': N1771). It is commoner to exploit footnotes in prose, often comically (as in Swift's *A Tale of a Tub*: see O1.1739); and Jacques Derrida has one critical text which consists of the main text and a running footnote which occupies the bottom third of each page, so that one never knows whether to read page by page, or all the main text and then all the footnote. But at that point punctuation can no longer be distinguished from layout.

[24] Both the *Oxford* and *Norton* anthologies incorporate Eliot's notes into their own footnotes; the *Norton* does so wholesale, the *Oxford* very selectively.

'Nearing Forty'

The first oddity is the crotchets around the dedication, "[*for John Figueroa*]". It is not uncommon to place a dedication within lunulae, withdrawing it slightly from the sequence 'title—epigraph (if there is one)—poem'; and when poets read their own poetry aloud dedications are sometimes omitted, or spoken as an aside. But crotchets are stronger and rarer, and so pose a question. There is perhaps a clue in the practice of Robert Lowell, a mentor of Walcott's: his poem 'The Quaker Graveyard in Nantucket' (N1485) is "(FOR WARREN WINSLOW, DEAD AT SEA)", and the poem is partly about such drownings; 'Skunk Hour' (N1493) is "(*For Elizabeth Bishop*)", and is modelled on a poem by Bishop; but 'The March 1' is "[FOR DWIGHT MACDONALD]", and as it is markedly political, about an anti-Vietnam demonstration, I take it that the crotchets dissociate the dedicatee from Lowell's political opinions, perhaps to prevent any embarrassment from accompanying the gift of dedication. In 'Nearing Forty', therefore, Walcott may intend the crotchets to prevent any easy identification of John Figueroa (b. 1920), a distinguished West Indian educator, cricket historian, and commentator, with the "you" whom the poem addresses. If the dedication were unguarded, one might read the poem as saying that Figueroa's "life bled for / the household truth", and so on; but with the crotchets in place that is not so readily possible.

The second oddity is the ellipsis following the epigraph. In the 'Preface to Shakespeare' Johnson's sentence and paragraph end with "truth.", so the apparent meaning of the ellipsis, that words have been omitted, is misleading; and the other value of an ellipsis, to indicate an uncertain trailing away of the voice, produces a cadence false to Johnson's full-stop after "truth", and alien to his elegant eighteenth-century prose and moral certainty. The ellipsis can be read, therefore, as ironising that elegance and certainty, and undermining "the stability of truth".

The poem itself comprises a single 32-line sentence, of three *semi-cola* (semi-colons in l. 14, after "rainspout", and l. 24, after "convectional"); alternatively, working upwards, there are thirty-two *commata* organized into three *semi-cola*. The fact that there are the same number of lines and *commata* (although the two measures otherwise do anything but coincide) is probably coincidental, but interesting given the very balanced feel of the poem. There are also two hyphens: the first creates "early-rising" (2), necessary because 'early rising rain' would be ambiguous; the second allows "gutter- / ing" (13–14) to be split between lines, an effect discussed on page 18.

Each of the semi-colons is clearly performing its 'turn' rather than its 'listing' function. The first comes after water flowing downwards ("rainspout"), the second after water evaporating upwards ("convectional"); so that these turns (like the corners of a wire coat-hanger) are what allows the thought developing away from the initial image of "early-rising rain" (2) to be modulated back towards the terminal image of "lightly falling rain" (30). Both semi-colons also mark emotional resolutions, turns towards the upbeat ("; glad" and "; / or you will rise") mapping the poem's emotional cycle onto the water-cycle of rain, evaporation, and more rain which underlies many of the images Walcott uses.

Each *semi-colon* is shorter than the last (13½ lines, 10½, 8), and the number of commas per *semi-colon* also decreases (13, 10, 6) but decreases more than would be proportional in the last *semi-colon*. This is notable because the number of commas in the first five lines (2, 1, 2, 1, 1):

> Insomniac since four, hearing this narrow,
> rigidly metred, early-rising rain
> recounting, as its coolness numbs the marrow,
> that I am nearing forty, nearer the weak
> vision thickening to a frosted pane,

is markedly more than the number in the last five lines (0, 1, 1, 2, 0):

> measuring how imagination
> ebbs, conventional as any water clerk
> who weighs the force of lightly falling rain,
> which, as the new moon moves it, does its work
> even when it seems to weep.

This reflects the development between the troubled, alert opening and the more accepting and restful close.

The terminal full-stop, wholly conventional as it is, carries weight after such a long sentence (and at the end of such a short last line), and brings the poem to a definite and balanced end at a point of achieved complexity. Walcott's willingness to have a full-stop (by no means compulsory in poetry) can be read against the ellipsis which replaced the full-stop in the epigraph, and undermined the stability of Dr Johnson's "truth".

Chapter Glossary

Apostrophe: used with or without an 's' to indicate possession (the genitive case), or the elision of a letter; in either case marked ' or '.

Braces: curly brackets, marked '{ }'; a single brace is conventionally used to indicate a triplet within couplet-rhyme.

Brackets: a generic term covering braces, crotchets, and lunulæ; all may be used singly, but crotchets and lunulæ are normally used in pairs, to isolate (for subordination <u>or</u> emphasis) a word or phrase.

Colon(s): the second-heaviest stop, marked ':'; conventionally implies a completion of the immediate sense and a logical or dependent relationship between *cola*.

Colon, cola: the part(s) into which a period is divided by colons.

Comma(s): the fourth and lightest stop, marked ','; conventionally implies the completion of a sub-clause or clause, and is used in pairs to create parentheses.

Comma(ta): the part(s) into which a period (or smaller unit of syntax) is divided by commas.

Crotchets: square brackets, marked '[ ]'; conventionally used to distinguish editorial comments and emendations from authorial prose.

Dash: a variety of comma, marked ' — '; conventionally used, in script, typescript, and word-processing (though not in print) with a space on either side, simultaneously to distinguish and link a sequence of clauses, and in pairs to create parentheses.

Deictic: of punctuation, used to emphasize a word or phrase; distinguished from 'elocutionary' and 'syntactic' punctuation.

Ellipsis: the omission of a word or words, and the indication of such omission with three suspension-marks, '. . .'.

Elocutionary: of punctuation, indicating speech-derived pauses; distinguished from 'deictic' and 'syntactic' punctuation.

Exclamation-mark: used (instead of a full-stop) to indicate exclamations, marked '!'; also a tonal indicator, usually of rising pitch and volume; may be used both medially and terminally; invented in the 1360s by Iacopo Alpoleio da Urbisaglia, an Italian humanist.

Full-stop: (or in the USA, *period*) the heaviest stop, marked '.'; conventionally required at the end of each sentence.

Hyphen: used to join two words into a single one, or to join the two parts of a word split between lines, marked '-'.

Intransitive: of a verb, not requiring an object.

Inverted commas: used to indicate direct speech and quotations, marked " and ", or “ and ”; may also be single (' ', ‘ ’), often to indicate a slight suspension of the sense, or a distrust of the word.

Punctuation

Lunula, lunulæ: round brackets, marked '( )'; historically used in many conventions, including the indication of stage directions, attributions of speech, metaphors and similes, quotations, and the cruxes of argument; commonly used to indicate both subordination and emphasis; invented by Colluccio Salutati (1331–1406) in *c.*1399.

Nota, notæ: marks made or printed in the margins of texts; distinguished from 'punctuation', which is within the text.

Paragraph: the basic division of prose or verse into groups or lines, marked by the indentation of the first line; a unit of argument, and of emotion; the oldest form of punctuation in the West.

Parenthesis: in rhetoric, one clause intercluded within another; such clauses may in written texts be marked with paired commas, dashes, or lunulæ. In the criticism of printed texts a parenthesis comprises the opening mark, the alphanumeric contents, and the closing mark.

Period: a classical, rhetorically defined unit of syntax and argument, composed of *cola* and *commata*; closer to the modern paragraph than the modern sentence; latterly, and in the USA, a full-stop.

Punctuation: a variety of marks, spaces, and other signs (such as distinguishing type-faces or founts) placed within the text to indicate pauses, emphases, and the sense.

Question-mark: used (instead of a full-stop) to indicate questions, marked '?'; also a tonal indicator, usually of rising pitch; may be used medially or terminally.

Rhetoric: originally, the formal rhetorical devices used in any text, such as rhetorical questions, repetition, and so on, but the term now (and especially in the USA) usually has the looser sense of 'the persuasiveness of a text'.

Semi-colon(s): the third heaviest stop, marked ';'; conventionally implies completion of the immediate sense, and either a development in the sense between *semi-cola*, or the itemization of each *semi-colon*; invented by Pietro Bembo (1470–1547) in Venice in the 1490s explicitly as a stop intermediate between the colon and the comma.

Semi-colon, semi-cola: the part(s) of a sentence between semi-colons, and/or between a semi-colon and a heavier stop.

Sentence: in modern use, the largest unit of syntax, composed of one or more clauses, and normally containing at least one grammatical subject, one transitive or intransitive verb, and if appropriate an object; typographically, sentences begin with a capital letter and end with a full-stop.

Slash: (or *solidus*) used to indicate alternatives, marked '/', as in 's/he', and to indicate line-breaks (/) and stanza breaks (//) in transcribed verse.

Stops: a collective term once covering all punctuation, but now usually restricted to the four marks (comma, semi-colon, colon, and full stop) which, analysed syntactically, indicate some degree of completion of the sense, or, analysed as elocutionary, require the reader to pause. Though imprecise the term can be particularly useful in the analysis of long verse periods.

Syntactic: of punctuation, indicating the sense; distinguished from 'elocutionary' and 'deictic' punctuation.

Transitive: of a verb, requiring an object.

Lineation

Christopher Ricks once offered the following rule-of-thumb distinction between poetry and prose: that whereas prose has to go to the end of the line, in poetry it's an option. Another way of putting this would be to say that poetry may use one additional form of punctuation, the line-break, a moment of spatial
organization different from every other mark and space. It is a bald way of distinguishing poetry from prose, but the distinction is less obvious than it seems: prose may be metrical, or even rhymed, while poetry may be in unrhymed free verse. Ricks's formulation holds good in cases where stricter definitions fail, even covering the *prose poem*, one which has chosen not to use lineation (or to use it in a very particular way).

It is consequently important to indicate the *lineation*, the division into lines, of any poetry you quote; and in embedded quotations, when each line of poetry is not given a new line on your page, the line-break should be represented by a slash (/) and the stanza break, effectively a blank line, by a double slash(//).

If a poet has chosen a regular metre or a stanza form there are clear constraints on how the line-break can be used (though the division of one line into two half-lines, as in the paragraph above, remains possible; it could be regarded as the use of medial line-breaks). Equally, the freedom of free verse has much to do with being able to use line-breaks at will. But in both cases there is at every line-break a question of what words will be on either side of it, and whether the line will be end-stopped (the line-break reinforced by a mark of punctuation) or enjambed (the line-break used as punctuation in its own right). Both factors will affect the value the line-break has; for (like lunulae) its meaning in any given instance is determined as much by the context as by any absolute value. When there is enjambment across a stanza break (the frequency of which will depend largely on the particular stanza) the stakes will be higher, because the stanza break is heavier.

These lines are from Seamus Heaney's 'The Strand at Lough Beg' (see p. 64, n. 15 above), which is dedicated to, and about, Colum McCartney, a cousin of Heaney's murdered in sectarian violence in Northern Ireland, while driving his car:

> What blazed ahead of you? A faked road block?
> The red lamp swung, the sudden brakes and stalling
> Engine, voices, heads hooded and the cold-nosed gun?

> What BLAZED | aHEAD | of YOU? | a FAKED | ROAD BLOCK?
> The RED | LAMP SWUNG, | the SUD- | den BRAKES | and STAL- | ling
> ENgine, | VOIces, | HEADS HOOD- | ed and | the COLD-| NOSED GUN?

"stalling" is a trochee creating an unstressed hyperbeat, and "Engine, voices," are both trochaic, inversions of the iambic metre: so that after "the sudden brakes" the impetus of the rising rhythm is lost until "the cold-nosed gun". But the metre does not have to do the work alone, for the line-break—"and stalling / Engine"—makes the falling rhythm cough or stutter, miming the treacherous car engine; and this in turn is reinforced by the commas after "Engine" and "voices", making it impossible for the rhythm of the line to get going—as impossible as it was for Heaney's cousin to drive safely away. What Heaney achieves here cannot be described without reference to the lineation which separates "stalling" from "Engine".

As with other forms of punctuation a good way to see how much lineation matters is to do without it. Here is the first verse paragraph of Tennyson's 'Tithonus'[1] (O2.1204/N909) set as prose:

> The woods decay, the woods decay and fall, the vapors weep their burthen to the ground, man comes and tills the field and lies beneath, and after many a summer dies the swan. Me only cruel immortality consumes; I wither slowly in thine arms, here at the quiet limit of the world, a white-haired shadow roaming like a dream the ever-silent spaces of the East, far-folded mists, and gleaming halls of morn.

The poem is in blank verse, and some of the lines are signalled by their metrical integrity. But restore the lineation and much is clearer:

> The woods decay, the woods decay and fall,
> The vapors weep their burthen to the ground,
> Man comes and tills the field and lies beneath,
> And after many a summer dies the swan.

1 Tithonus loved and was loved by Aurora, the Goddess of Dawn. He asked for and was granted immortal life, but forgot to ask for eternal youth: now, hopelessly infirm, he wishes only to die.

Me only cruel immortality
Consumes; I wither slowly in thine arms,
Here at the quiet limit of the world,
A white-haired shadow roaming like a dream
The ever-silent spaces of the East,
Far-folded mists, and gleaming halls of morn.

Each of the first four lines is self-contained, end-stopped, and a complete parallel clause. The full-stop after "swan", coinciding with the line-break, completes both the sentence and an unrhymed quatrain; and is immediately followed, in strong contrast, by the first enjambed line—but the enjambment requires only one word from line 6 before the semi-colon. One's ear has already become adjusted to the complete end-stopped lines, so the sequence "Me only cruel immortality / Consumes;" effectively mimics Tithonus's unending life, forcing readers to carry on when they expected to be able to stop, and giving a strong stress to "Consumes". End-stopping returns for two lines, and enjambment is then used again, more delicately, in lines 8–9, creating between "dream" and "The ever-silent spaces" an odd half-silence as the reading voice wants to stop but is forced to continue. The value of this second enjambed line-break is made more ghostly (or dream-like) because the syntax requires the whole of both lines, and there is no equivalent to the early pause enforced in line 6 by the semi-colon. The last line metrically echoes the first, a comma after the second foot producing a distinctly broken rhythm, to end the verse paragraph audibly and syntactically.

The medial pause created by the semi-colon in line 6, and by the commas in lines 1 and 10, is called a *cæsura*, plural *cæsurae* (from Latin, *cædere*, to cut). Some people argue that all lines have a natural cæsura whether or not it is enforced by punctuation; but I think this true only of lines longer than a tetrameter. Up to eight beats the line can be (though need not be) a whole; but unpunctuated pentameters tend to split 4–6 or 6–4, and unpunctuated longer lines almost always split somewhere in the middle, like a tree-branch grown too long to support itself. The ballad stanza (*a8b6c8b6*) probably originated as a heptametric couplet (*a14a14*), and became a single-rhymed quatrain when the last three feet of each line broke off at an 8–6 cæsura, and were moved down to form the *b*-rhyme trimeters. The cæsurae in unpunctuated lines will naturally occur roughly in the middle, but a poet can force the cæsura towards the beginning or end of the line with punctuation, as Tennyson did with his semi-colon after "Consumes", producing a

2–8 split. Arguably, a line like Heaney's "Engine, voices, heads hooded and the cold-nosed gun?" has two cæsurae, the commas creating a 2–2–6 split; but many critics use 'cæsura' only of a single distinctive break, and would call what Heaney's commas create 'pauses' (or an equivalent word).

In any regular form cæsurae can be delicately manipulated. One of their principal effects, much used in blank verse, is obtained by having the cæsura in the same place in successive lines, so giving, for example, a sequence such as 6–4 / 6–4 / 6–4. If there is punctuation at the cæsurae, but the lines are enjambed, the last two feet of each line, after the cæsura, can be read with the first three feet of the next line, before its cæsura, to create a line of the right length which runs from cæsura to cæsura (6– 4/6– 4/6– 4/6– etc.). Your eyes see the lines that are printed, but your ears begin to hear the cæsura-to-cæsura lines as counterpoint, the sense reading against the layout. Done well this creates a feeling of never reaching a finish, because the end of each line is the middle of a clause, and the end of each clause the middle of a line: this *rocking lineation* becomes a powerful engine driving the verse. You can hear that engine in Shakespeare's blank verse speeches, and the closed couplet that often ends speeches is a way of braking the momentum generated by rocking lineation.

A good example comes in Book I of Wordsworth's *The Prelude*, of which (in its full form) there are two texts: *1805*, the first complete version, and *1850*, the text published after Wordsworth's death. In this passage Wordsworth is remembering how one evening, as a boy, he 'borrowed' a boat and rowed out onto Ullswater (in the English Lake District), where he became frightened by a mountain which, from this new perspective, suddenly loomed over him. This is the 1805 version; the last line of the quotation ends a verse paragraph:

With trembling hands I turned
And through the silent water stole my way
Back to the cavern of the willow-tree.
There, in her mooring-place, I left my bark
And through the meadows homeward went with grave
And serious thoughts; and after I had seen
That spectacle, for many days my brain
Worked with a dim and undetermined sense
Of unknown modes of being. In my thoughts
There was a darkness—call it solitude
Or blank desertion—no familiar shapes

Of hourly objects, images of trees,
Of sea or sky, no colours of green fields,
But huge and mighty forms that do not live
Like living men moved slowly through my mind
By day, and were the trouble of my dreams.

In most good verse there is a swirling relationship between the clause, a grammatical unit, and the line, a poetic unit; and variations produced by clauses shorter or longer than a line are instrumental in preventing dullness. Wordsworth was capable of very great blank verse in this manner, and the first part of this quotation, down to "modes of being." (l. 420), is a fair example of it: read the lines aloud, punching through line-breaks that are enjambed, and pausing appropriately at punctuation within the line, and you will hear (and see) the patterning of clause against line. But after the full-stop in line 420 Wordsworth seizes that patterning by the scruff of its technical neck and begins to do something far more muscular, involving rocking lineation. A medial full-stop creates the heaviest possible cæsura, demanding a substantial pause by splitting line 420 7–3; but line 421, split 5–5, also has a fairly heavy cæsura enforced by the dash: and the counterpoint begins. The first counterpoint line has only eight beats, –3/5– ("In my thoughts / There was a darkness—"), but the cæsurae which isolate it are heavy, and the metrical brevity is appropriate to the meaning. Line 422 is again split 5–5 by a heavy dash, creating a second counterpoint line of full length, –5/5– ("—call it solitude / Or blank desertion—"), and grammatically independent as a dash'd-off parenthesis. Line 423 is also split 5–5, creating a third counterpoint line of full length ("—no familiar shapes / Of hourly objects,"). Because all three counterpoint lines begin and end in the middle of iambs they are not iambic but trochaic pentameters:

IN my | THOUGHTS / there | WAS a | DARKness—
CALL it | SOLi- | TUDE / or | BLANK de- | SERtion—
NO fa- | MILiar | SHAPES / of | HOURly | OBjects,

The effect of hearing this falling rhythm emerging from the blank verse is a sort of aural interference, a technical disturbance which creates a metrical analogue for the mental disturbance the lines report. This admirable craftsmanship continues as the energy of the rocking lineation is harnessed: the cæsura in line 423 is weaker than its predecessors, enforced only by a comma; another comma end-stops the line; and in line 424, also end-stopped with a comma, the cæsura moves back one beat to split the line 4–6. This little welter of short clauses bleeds off momentum, as an eddy detracts from the force of the current: but through it all there is a steady backward movement of the cæsura, successive lines from l. 420 splitting 7–3 / 5–5 / 5–5 / 5–5 / 4–6 (or, more accurately, 7.3 / 5—5 / 5—5 / 5,5 / 4,6: the weight of the cæsura lessening from full-stop to dash to comma as it retreats). In the last three lines, 425–7, Wordsworth reaps the profit of his labour, producing a huge clause enjambed through two line-breaks: in reading aloud the sudden length of breath required is unexpected, and one's voice wants to stop after "forms", and again after "live", and again after "men", and even then is forced on beyond "mind" to gasp out "By day" and gratefully, finally, reach a comma and draw breath. Effectively 22 beats with no pause (because the natural pauses coincide with and are negated by the enjambment), this long clause interrupts the movement of the cæsura as the "huge and mighty forms" interrupt the tenor of Wordsworth's days; but the final line (427) splits 2–8, completing the retreat (1–9 is very rare) and bringing the verse paragraph to an aurally satisfying close.

You may find analysis of this kind over-detailed, but what the technical structuring achieves can be judged by comparing the 1805 with the 1850 text (O2.194/N716), with which Wordsworth had been fiddling for 45 years:

With trembling oars I turned,
And through the silent water stole my way
Back to the covert of the willow tree;
There in her mooring place I left my bark,[2]
And through the meadows homewards went, in grave
And serious mood; but after I had seen
That spectacle, for many days, my brain
Worked with a dim and undetermined sense
Of unknown modes of being; o'er my thoughts
There hung a darkness, call it solitude
Or blank desertion. No familiar shapes
Remained, no pleasant images of trees,
Of sea or sky, no colors of green fields;
But huge and mighty forms, that do not live
Like living men, moved slowly through the mind
By day, and were a trouble to my dreams.

[2] The *Oxford Anthology* has a dash here as well as the comma.

The punctuation is heavier: commas are added, lessening ambiguities and eliminating the difficulties of reading aloud; the rocking lineation is eliminated; the phrasing is made more conventional, allowing without protest clichés which are distorted in 1805 ("a trouble to" rather than "the trouble of", for example); and syntactically the passage is clearer. But to my mind (and ears) it is infinitely poorer as poetry: Wordsworth would have done better to leave well alone, and I personally regret the choice of the 1850 text by both the *Oxford* and *Norton* editors.

The *Imagist* poets of the 1910s and 1920s, such as H.D. (Hilda Doolittle, N1202) and Ezra Pound (N1186), believed that each line of a poem should contain a single clear image, and that poetry should be written by stacking together a sequence of such lines. It is certainly possible to write fine poetry like this, but to make it a rule seems to me like arguing that a car is best driven, always, in first gear. At the other extreme is the prose poem, more popular in French than English, but recently used by Geoffrey Hill in *Mercian Hymns* (1971) (N1722; see also Nlxxx). When Hill grants permission to quote from *Mercian Hymns* he does so only on condition that the lineation (and the justification of the right margin) is exactly reproduced: so although the lines may look like prose, and far more words are hyphenated around line-breaks than is usual in poetry, Hill must believe that the lineation matters. The spacing of the words sometimes has to be greater than usual to maintain the justification, as in the second paragraph of hymn VII, when one boy loses another's toy plane through the floorboards:

> Ceolred let it spin through a hole
> in the classroom floorboards, softly, into the
> rat droppings and coins.

"rat" could easily be fitted into the line above, and there is no hyphen to tie the compound noun "rat droppings" together, as there could (and even should) be. The point, I imagine, is that the wide word-spaces visually represent the gaps between the floorboards, and the "rat droppings and coins" below the floorboards are together on a line of their own below the line (with the holes in it) about the floorboards. This explains one moment, but not Hill's general decision to use this form. He is a great admirer of Eliot, who also wrote prose poems; the form allows Hill to use unusual words, and to generate a language full of metrical effects but not regularly metred; and it does not have, in English, much of a history—which, as the *Mercian Hymns* are partly about English history, was probably important. Hill in effect found a form with only internal baggage, and used it to examine a great swathe of history, from the eighth to the twentieth centuries: any form which did have the usual historical baggage would have snagged on some bits of that history, the baggage tangling with the subject; but the baggage-free prose poem allows Hill to attend to all periods without unintentionally privileging or complicating any one.

A different sort of prose poem is Allen Ginsberg's *Howl* (1956) (N1598):

I saw the best minds of my generation destroyed by madness, starving hysterical naked,
dragging themselves through the negro streets at dawn looking for an angry fix,
angelheaded hipsters burning for the ancient heavenly connection to the starry dynamo in the machinery of night,
who poverty and tatters and hollow-eyed and high sat up smoking in the supernatural darkness of cold-water flats floating across the tops of cities contemplating jazz,
who bared their brains to Heaven under the El . . .

There are many more lines beginning "who . . .", some short, some long, and all itemizing one or another way in which "the best minds of my generation" have suffered and failed. As the title *Howl* suggests, the contents and emotions of the poem are too great and chaotic to be in a regular metre or stanza; and had Ginsberg tried for a greater regularity of metre and form the power of his poem would have been lost. It's equally true, though, that if poetry as close to prose as *Howl* were common, *Howl* itself could not have been written in the same way.

Lineation is commonly taken for granted in poetry, as its absence is taken for granted in prose: but it is often a line, as line, that is memorable. This is particularly true in free verse and open form, which put a greater weight on the organization into lines; and the greatness of many distinctively modern poets (Walt Whitman [N961] is a good example) is in substantial part a mastery of lineation and the line-break.

'Nearing Forty'

Some of the effects involving lineation have already been mentioned, the pairing of catalectic and hypermetric lines under 'Metre' (pp. 16–19 above); and the short final line under 'Form' (p. 44) and 'Punctuation' (p. 72). The poem begins by alternating end-stopped and enjambed lines; the alternation gives way to repeated enjambment; and an approximate alternation, but with more enjambment than end-stopping, returns at the end. This pattern roughly matches, and interlocks with, the quatrains-into-couplets-into-quatrains form, and the relatively lighter punctuation of the last *semi-colon*.

A rather greater problem is posed by lines 12, "in simple, shining lines, in pages stretched", and 25, "or you will rise and set your lines to work". Stretched through the poem is a sequence of words which have technical poetic meanings (metred, metaphor, etc.), of which these two uses of "lines" are a part; and together these words map one of the poem's main concerns, the writing of poetry, onto another, the water-cycle. The "lines" are in both cases principally lines of poetry, but they also become the lines of falling rain, the wrinkled lines of age, and even (perhaps) the arrowed lines that geographers draw on diagrams to show the passage of water through its cycle. It is interesting that "lines" should be repeated, pushing it, as a word, towards the status of "rain" and "work", used three times each; and both times the "lines" are described positively with qualification, as "simple, shining", or as being "set . . . to work / with sadder joy". Clearly, in Walcott's idea of what it is to write poetry, to be a poet, the crafting of good lines is of prime importance, and must be got right if a poem is to work, and to do its work.

It is not surprising therefore that Walcott's own sense of lineation, and of the interplay between clause and line (the 32 *commata* and 32 lines), is very fine: and that is one reason 'Nearing Forty' is such a pleasure to read aloud. Lines such as 7, "by the bleak modesty of middle age", and 16, "ambition as a searing meteor", are not grammatical units, for they are enjambed both into and out of: but their visual existence as discrete lines, a basic unit of which the poem is composed, their aural existence as pentameters of integrity and rhythmic strength, and their syntactical existence as complete images which the grammar and the sense must digest enable them to contribute far more to the poem than the same words, in the same order, could contribute to a paragraph of prose.

Chapter Glossary

Cæsura, cæsurae: the medial pause(s) in a line; if there is no punctuation it will tend not to occur in lines shorter than a tetrameter, and to occur approximately centrally in tetrametric or longer lines; it may be forced towards the beginning or the end of a line by punctuation.

End-stopped: of a line or stanza, having a terminal mark of punctuation.

Enjamb(+ed/ment): of lines, couplets, or stanzas, not end-stopped, with the sense (and/or syntax) continuing into the next line, couplet, or stanza.

Imagists: a school of poetry in the 1910s and 1920s, advocating a poetry written in short lines each containing a clear image; Ezra Pound and H.D. were leading members.

Justified: of margins and texts, aligned straight up and down.

Lineation: the organization of a poem into lines.

Line-break: the turn of one line into the next, notated as '/ '.

Prose poem: one written and printed as prose, without the use of metrical lineation and often with a justified right margin; commoner in French literature, it was attempted by T. S. Eliot, and used by Geoffrey Hill for *Mercian Hymns* (1971); also used in modern American poetry.

Ragged: of texts and margins, not justified.

Rocking lineation: the effect of counterpointed (cæsura-to-cæsura) lines created by placing a cæsura in the same position in two or more successive lines.

Stanza break: the physical (and syntactical) space (and pause) between stanzas, marked in transcription with a double slash, '// '.

Rhyme

Poetry was spoken before it was written, and rhyme, the coincidence of sounds, has prehistoric origins, probably related to religious ritual, celebration, and memory training. Almost everyone in the West, even if they never read poetry, learns nursery rhymes and children's chants, and knows a fair number of simple rhymes, often giving information (Red sky at night, shepherd's delight) or advice (If you can't beat 'em, join 'em). Popular and comic forms of poetry are often heavily rhymed, as the limerick is, and the rhyming makes them memorable. Even in journalism, politics, and advertising, rhyming headlines and slogans remain ear-catchingly useful.

In poetry rhyme is closely bound up with lineation and layout; and can be regarded as another form of punctuation, helping to organize and display the relations of words. This can easily be seen if the lineation and layout are subtracted—as in rhymed prose. This is from Thomas Nashe's[1] *Pierce Penilesse his Supplication to the Divell*, published in 1592. (The old spelling looks unfamiliar but isn't difficult once you get used to it: if you find a word obscure, try saying it aloud.)

> Having spent many yeeres in studying how to live, and liv'de a long time without mony : having tired my youth with follie, and surfetted my minde with vanitie, I began at length to looke backe to repentaunce, & addresse my endevors to prosperitie : But all in vaine, I sate up late, and rose earely, contended with the colde, and conversed with scarcitie : for all my labours turned to losse, my vulgar Muse was despised & neglected, my paines not regarded or slightly rewarded, and I my selfe (in prime of my best wit) laid open to povertie.[2]

Despite the capitalized "But" in line 4 this is a single Ciceronian *period*,[3] with three colons and four *cola*; and the last words of the *cola* are "mony" (line 2), "prosperitie" (4), "scarcitie" (6), and "povertie" (8). All the *cola* rhyme, and the first and second pair in sense, money-prosperity, while

---

[1] For some of Nashe's poetry see O1.614.

[2] I have corrected one misprint, "erαely" for "earely", in line 5.

[3] For the distinction between a *period* and a *sentence* see pp. 122–5 below.

the third and fourth pair in the opposite sense, scarcity-poverty: which reflects the central division of the sentence marked by the capitalized "But". In the second *colon* the last words of the first and second *commata* join in the rhyme ("follie . . . vanitie"), and in the third *colon* so does the last word of the third *comma* ("earely"). If you are used to a system like this, in reading the rhyme-sound leads you to expect a mark of punctuation, and rhyme and punctuation together signal the completion of a *colon* (or of an important *comma*). The same is true in verse when rhyme and lineation coincide, and even more true if both coincide with punctuation, as in the closed couplet: the rhyme signals closure to your ears as clearly as any mark or space can to your eyes. In more open forms, with frequent enjambment, the links forged between words by rhyme are a principal means of elaborating or ironising the sense, and of controlling pace.

Vision is now very strongly our primary sense, and for most people to hear clearly how rhyme is working in any particular poem it is necessary to work out a *rhyme scheme* you can see. The conventional method indicates with letters which lines rhyme with which: the rhyme-word at the end of the first line is always *a*, and all lines that rhyme with the first will also be *a*; the second rhyme-word, and all lines that rhyme with it are *b*; and so on. Thus limericks have the rhyme scheme *aabba*, showing that lines 1, 2, and 5 rhyme together, and so do lines 3 and 4; a cross-rhymed quatrain would be *abab*, a monorhymed one *aaaa*, and an unrhymed one *abcd*; couplets would be *aabbccddee*, and so on.

In the rhyme schemes I used to indicate stanza forms and the rhymes of 'Nearing Forty' I assumed that rhyme is binary, that any two given words either do, or do not, rhyme; and I also attended only to *end-rhyme*, rhyme-words placed at the ends of their respective lines. But rhyme comes in many varieties and positions, and its effects are unpredictable. It is, however, worth being steadfastly reductive, and assuming binary end-rhyme, when you first work out the rhyme scheme of a poem, in case (as in 'Nearing Forty') the sophisticated and decorative variations of rhyme conceal a simpler underlying structure. There is also a time-consuming problem in notating rhyme schemes to show variant forms of rhyme: it is possible to use vowels against consonants, as Nabokov did (see p. 38 above); or to use upper- against lower-case letters, so that *aa* would be one kind of rhyme, and *aA* another; or to use different faces (a*a*): but there is no standard system. If you are working intensively and at leisure on a poem which uses variant rhymes it may be worth devising a notation, so that you can look at the rhyme scheme in abstract: and the only requirement then is that the notation be clear for you and your readers; but in exams you are unlikely to have the time.

In English *full-rhyme* (or *perfect* rhyme) occurs when two or more words or phrases share the same last stressed vowel and all sounds following that vowel. If the last stressed vowel is in the last syllable, so that both halves of the rhyme are stressed (CAT/BAT, aBOARD/ igNORED, in my beLIEF/that's TeneRIFE), the rhyme is *stressed* (or *masculine*); but if the stressed vowel is followed by one or more unstressed syllables (WILlow/BILlow, RAPidly/VAPidly) the rhyme is *unstressed* (or *feminine*). There is no limit to how many unstressed syllables may follow the stressed vowel, but if there are two or more the rhyme will tend to sound comic, and the tendency increases with the number of unstressed syllables. Eventually the comedy becomes silliness, which may remain funny, especially if half the rhyme is made up from monosyllables whose stress pattern is slightly wrenched, as W. S. Gilbert's 'lot o' news/hypoteneuse' (N1041) or Byron's 'merry in/heroine' (O2.330/N788): such silly rhyming is called *hudibrastic* rhyme, from its prevalence in Samuel Butler's *Hudibras* (written in 1663–80; see O1.1561).[4]

The strictest form of rhyme is *rime riche* (meaning 'rich rhyme'[5]), in which the sounds <u>before</u> the last stressed vowel must be identical, as well as those after it. Clear examples are *homographs*, words spelt identically, as 'well' (not ill) / 'well' (of water), and *homophones*, words spelt differently but pronounced identically, as 'there/their' or 'Underground/under ground'; long polysyllables differing only in their first letter (evolutionary/devolutionary) are also *rimes riches*.

Moving in the other direction, the participle endings of English, especially '-ing', allow an odd variation on full-rhyme. If the endings were stressed they would be full-rhymes; but they are usually unstressed: and it is possible to stack up rhyme-words whose stressed stems do not rhyme at all, but whose unstressed endings are identical. Shakespeare's sonnet 87 (O1.933) does this; another example is Whitman's unorthodox sonnet 'Patroling Barnegat':

---

[4] If it is a rhyme of several different words (rather than one polysyllabic word with another), it may also be called *mosaic* rhyme.

[5] It is sometimes called *identical* rhyme.

Wild, wild the storm, and the sea high running,
Steady the roar of the gale, with incessant undertone muttering,
Shouts of demoniac laughter fitfully piercing and pealing,
Waves, air, midnight, their savagest trinity lashing,
Out in the shadows there milk-white combs careering,
On beachy slush and sand spirts of snow fierce slanting,
Where through the murk the easterly death-wind breasting,
Through cutting swirl and spray watchful and firm advancing,
(That in the distance! is that a wreck? is the red signal flaring?)
Slush and sand of the beach tireless till daylight wending,
Steadily, slowly, through hoarse roar never remitting,
Along the midnight edge by those milk-white combs careering,
A group of dim, weird forms, struggling, the night confronting,
That savage trinity warily watching.

Arguably none of these end words, except the repeated "careering", are full-rhymes at all, to give an end-rhyme scheme *abcdefghijkelm*; but equally arguably the rhyme scheme is *aaaaaaaaaaaaaa*, with further *internal a*-rhymes in lines 3 ("piercing"), 8 ("cutting"), and 13 ("struggling"). Up to a point, which notation you prefer doesn't matter, because any account of the poem must notice the tolling participles, patently a principle on which the poem is constructed. Their chime amid the otherwise very varied words and images becomes like the threnody of wind in wires and rigging. I also suspect that the wave pattern made by the ragged right margin is intentional, its back-and-forth movement contrasting with the identical final letters of each line. An even odder example is the octave of Gerard Manley Hopkins's Petrarchan sonnet 'The Windhover' (O2.1469/N1062), an intense study of a wild falcon. The *a*-rhymes are stressed and the *b*-rhymes unstressed—but set stress aside, and the *a*- and *b*-rhymes rhyme:

I caught this morning morning's minion, king-
  dom of daylight's dauphin, dapple-dawn-drawn Falcon, in his riding
  Of the rolling level underneath him steady air, and striding
High there, how he hung upon the rein of a wimpling wing
In his ecstasy! then off, off forth on swing
  As a skate's heel sweeps smooth on a bow-bend: the hurl and gliding
  Rebuffed the big wind. My heart in hiding
Stirred for a bird,—the achieve of, the mastery of the thing!

Hopkins's prosody is notoriously idiosyncratic, and end-rhyming is almost the least of the sound effects he uses in these lines; but it is there amid the symphony and helps to keep the music from overwhelming the sense. The *a*-rhymes pair in meaning, 'king-/wing', because it is the bird's mastery of the air with its wings which makes it a king; 'wing/swing' because the bird banks on its wings; and 'swing/thing' because "thing" is ambiguous, referring both to the falcon itself, its anatomy and colouring, and to the intense but common beauty of its circling movement. The *b*-rhymes pair similarly, 'riding/striding' catching at the falcon's activity in flight, while 'gliding/hiding' catches at its ease and patience. The structure of the octave which these pairings reflect and help to enforce allows the complex of sounds to be deployed effectively. It is intriguing that both Whitman and Hopkins should have been moved to use such *wrenched monorhyme* (for want of a better term) in trying to describe natural phenomena (storms, falcons), and there is perhaps an analogy with the reiterative mathematics used to describe such natural fractals as coastlines and river-courses. One might think a really complicated equation would be needed to generate a curve like a coastline, but it turns out that a simple process endlessly repeated is what does the business, mathematically, poetically, and in nature.

In iambic metres an unstressed end-rhyme will almost always be an unstressed hyperbeat;[6] but a stressed rhyme can be carried by the normal terminal stress, without hyperbeats; the reverse is true in trochaic metres. A stressed hyperbeat, however, will (if rhymed) be a stressed rhyme; and an unstressed hyperbeat, an unstressed rhyme. In the version of *terza rima* devised for the heroic 'Dante' passage in part II of *Little Gidding* (ll. 80–151, O2.2006–8; and see Nlxxii) Eliot used alternating regular lines (with the normal terminal stress of any iambic line) and lines with unstressed hyperbeats, as a substitute for rhyme:

And last, the rending pain of re-enactment
    Of all that you have done, and been; the shame
    Of motives late revealed, and the awareness
Of things ill done and done to others' harm
    Which once you took for exercise of virtue.
    Then fools' approval stings and honour stains.
From wrong to wrong the exasperated spirit
    Proceeds, unless restored by that refining fire
    Where you must move in measure like a dancer.

[6] The only other possibility is for it to be catalectic, omitting the last beat.

Eliot is sombrely listing the "gifts reserved for age", and so chose the heroic line. He needed (for very complex reasons) to allude to Dante, and so wanted to use *terza rima*, but he did not want the heavy rhyme of *terza rima* to sweeten the pain he needed to express. For the same reason he could not risk unstressed rhymes becoming hudibrastic, but wanted the sad cadence of trochaic and amphibrachic words creating unstressed endings. His unorthodox answer, to use endings instead of rhyme, proved brilliantly successful, and the passage has become famous for painful honesty and gravely beautiful sound. It showed that similar patterns of stress can be heard as equivalents of rhyme; and poets learned the lesson. Leonard Cohen's 'Suzanne Takes You Down' better known as the song 'Suzanne') relies to considerable effect on a single stressed rhyme in each stanza ('blind/mind') amid lines with persistently unstressed endings.

Jesus was a sailor
when he walked upon the water
and he spent a long time watching
from a lonely wooden tower
and when he knew for certain
only drowning men could see him
he said All men will be sailors then
until the sea shall free them,

In performance Cohen exaggerates the persistently unstressed endings, emphasizing it with a falling *pitch contour* (the curve of the voice from one note to a lower or higher note) equally in the trochees (SAIlor, WAter) and the monosyllables (SEE him, FREE them)—which brings out the half-rhymes but subordinates them to cadence. Such endings are characteristic of Cohen's songs, and their cadence is partly responsible for his reputation as a melancholic singer. Conversely, upbeat songs and anthems—consider 'The Red Flag'—tend to use stressed full-rhyme.

Much modern free verse has been unrhymed, but rhyme has never been unpopular or uncommon, and it is much more usual to abandon full-rhyme than to abandon rhyme altogether. There are various kinds of *imperfect rhyme*, beginning with *half-rhyme* (or *near* or *slant* rhyme), where either the stressed vowel or the following sounds differ. While full-rhymes may chime, or confirm the sense, half-rhymes will tend to be dissonant, or question the sense. If the consonants differ, the half-rhyme will be *vowel-rhyme* ('bite/fire', 'courage/bunker'); and if the vowels differ, *pararhyme* ('lust/lost', 'honour/winter'), much used by

Wilfred Owen (O2.2050/N1276). There is also a more radical form, *eye-rhyme* (or *printers'* rhyme), where words look as if they rhyme, but are pronounced as non-rhymes: among the commonest are *-ough* endings ('cough/bough/dough/enough'), and there are also such combinations as 'picturesque/queue'.

Be careful, for pronunciation varies historically and regionally: the traditional rhyme 'move/love' could be called an eye-pararhyme, but probably used to be a full-rhyme; and for Wordsworth, born in Cumberland, 'water/matter' was a full-rhyme, though to a modern reader born in the south of England it is a pararhyme. These considerations can carry a strong ideological charge: I take the 'water/matter' example from Tony Harrison's poem 'Them and [Uz]'[7] (N1766[8]), which he wrote because at the age of 12 his English teacher stopped him from reading aloud in class a poem by Keats, on the grounds that he had a strong Leeds accent, and did not speak the *King's English*[9] in which the poem 'was written'. Keats himself was a Cockney: his living speech almost certainly bore no resemblance to 'King's English'; the language of his poetry is no more similar, and even if it were, to prevent a child from reading Keats aloud is to suppress regional variation and impose an élite language. Similar issues are raised by ethnic variations in accent, and attend 'Nearing Forty'.

Perhaps the most interesting rhyme is represented by Whitman's "careering" (p. 88 above), *autorhyme,*[10] the rhyming of a word with itself. In one sense repetition is not rhyme at all, in another the most perfect rhyme possible: either way it can have remarkable effects, and forces the voice reading aloud to do something unusual to accommodate it. Shakespeare was a master of autorhyme (see *Titus Andronicus* 3.2.1–33; *King John* 2.2.4–15; *Othello* 4.2.72–82), and its value is demonstrated in *Macbeth* 2.2.24–31, when Macbeth tells his wife that he has "done the deed" ("they" refers to the grooms, drugged by Lady Macbeth, whom Macbeth had to pass entering and leaving the room where he murdered Duncan):

---

[7] "[Uz]" represents the pronunciation of 'us' as 'uhz', common in the north of England, as opposed to 'uss', common in the south.

[8] See also p. 107, n. 5 below.

[9] Or, of course, *Queen's English*, or *BBC English*: in either case, a combination of supposed grammatical correctness and elegance with a Home Counties accent, such as BBC radio newsreaders used always to have.

[10] This term, so far as I am aware, I invented, so you may need to gloss it the first time you use it in an exam or for a new teacher; on the other hand the meaning is evident, and the only practicable alternative is the equivalent 'self-rhyme'.

MACBETH One cry'd God blesse us, and Amen the other,
  As they had seene me with these Hangmans hands:
  Listning their feare, I could not say Amen,
  When they did say God blesse us.
LADY MACBETH Consider it not so deepely.
MACBETH But wherefore could not I pronounce Amen?
  I had most need of blessing, and Amen
  Stuck in my throat.

The pause forced by the line-break in "and Amen / Stuck in my throat" is doing solid work—but it could not be so effective, and "Amen" could not stick in the reader's throat as it did in Macbeth's, if the word did not end lines 29 and 26 as well; there is also the medial use in line 24. Macbeth's insistent repetition of 'Amen' now strongly contrasts with his previous inability to say it at all; and as a single 'Amen' traditionally marks the end of a prayer its repeated use in murderous dialogue, its use followed by a question-mark (which usually implies a rising pitch), and especially the final, immediately rhyming, enjambed use (trying and failing to answer the "Amen?"), become profoundly disturbing. This murder without an Amen was an unhallowed end, and these uselessly late, volleyed Amens mark a terrible beginning. Eliot was also a fine autorhymer (see *The Waste Land* 25–9, 62–3, 162–3, 347–56, 414–21), and (like falling rhythm) autorhyme is always something to ponder. It is a formal requirement in the sestina and villanelle, having much to do with the qualities of those forms; and even in Edward Lear's limericks, where the first and last lines often form an autorhyme (see p. 8 above), the device has provoked frequent attention.

The other way in which rhyme can vary is according to its position. With end-rhyme the first variable is whether the rhyme produces couplets, each rhyme-word paired as quickly as possible; or whether the rhyme-words are separated by one or more lines (as in cross- and arch-rhyme). A line whose end-word rhymes with an earlier end-word both extends the poem (which may speed it along) and looks backward (which may slow the poem down): the tension between these two pulls of the rhyme can be used to control pace. Sylvia Plath's frightening poem 'Daddy' (N1732) returns again and again to the same rhyme-sound ('do/shoe/Achoo'), but never in a settled pattern: and one reason the poem is disturbing is because the rhyme never allows a steady pace, but forces the reading voice to spurt and tumble onwards. This technique has become much commoner in the twentieth century, perhaps because the modern world is felt to be so rapidly changing, so unsettled and adrift, that to use a more regular rhyme-scheme about anything modern is necessarily to counterpoint form and content.[11] But it may simply be yet another legacy of Eliot's, for he used rhyme brilliantly in this way: in 'The Love Song of J. Alfred Prufrock' (O2.1973/N1231), for example, there is this verse paragraph:[12]

> And indeed there will be time
> To wonder, "Do I dare?" and, "Do I dare?"
> Time to turn back and descend the stair,
> With a bald spot in the middle of my hair—
> (They will say: "How his hair is growing thin!")
> My morning coat, my collar mounting firmly to the chin,
> My necktie rich and modest, but asserted by a simple pin—
> (They will say: "But how his arms and legs are thin!")
> Do I dare
> Disturb the universe?
> In a minute there is time
> For decisions and revisions which a minute will reverse.

The rhyme in these lines (schematically *abbbccccbdad*) is working very hard: after the (apparently) unrhymed "time" there is first a sequence of three successive rhymes ('dare/stair/hair') and then one of four ('thin/chin/pin/thin'), which force the pace, and edge the pitch of the reading voice upwards as it tries to control the hysteria incipient in Prufrock's hammering neurosis; but the last of the sequence of four, "(. . . thin!")" (44), is also the first, "(. . . thin!")" (41), and begins a process of recursive autorhymes as "dare" (45) answers back to "dare?" (38), and "time" (47) to "time" (37): the neurosis subsiding into contemplative indecision. The rhyming of lines 45/38 and 47/37 sends the poem arching back over its own tracks, and within lines 46–8 there is

[11] Since at least the 1970s, however, in both the UK and USA, there has been a revival of regular formal rhyme. American exponents, include the late James Merrill (N1605) and Dana Gioia (N1845); British exponents, James Fenton (N1837), Blake Morrison, and Tony Harrison (N1764). Harrison in particular is interesting: he has written very little (if any) verse that is not formally rhymed (and metred), but is the last poet one could accuse of being stilted or artificial, and his consistent combination of strictly observed rhyming forms with topical subjects and colloquial language is a challenge to anyone who thinks regular full-rhyme inapposite to the poetic treatment of the modern world.

[12] The *Norton Anthology*, following the American edition of the *Collected Poems*, uses crotchets around ll. 41 and 44 (and elsewhere); I have restored the lunulae used in every other edition.

a more compact but complementary pattern of arched rhyme and autorhyme, as "revisions" (48) looks back to "decisions" (48), "minute" (48) further back to "minute" (47), and (the perfect last word for Prufrock) "reverse" (48) back further still to "universe" (46). Prufrock spins his wheels wildly while going nowhere; but the rhyme shows Eliot in absolute control of the skidding acceleration and braking he uses to show the tenacity of Prufrock's neurosis.

To do this Eliot had to go beyond end-rhyme and use *internal* rhyme. The strictest form of internal rhyme is *leonine* rhyme, where the word immediately preceding the cæsura rhymes with the end-word: it is popular in the third line of common metre, making the standard *abcb* into *ab(cc)b*, as in Charles Causley's (N1483) fine modern ballad 'Christ at the Cheesewring',[13] beginning:

As I walked on the wicked moor
Where seven smashed stones lie
I met a man with a skin of tan
And an emerald in his eye.

Here the stressed leonine rhyme of 'MAN/TAN' makes an audible chime, and (like a syncopated beat in music) hurries the narrative along, countering any tendency to slow down which the otherwise unrhymed *c*-line might impart,[14] and providing impetus which Causley puts to good use in a story as strange as an emerald eye. An occasional or imperfect leonine rhyme can go unnoticed, but have a claustrophobic effect—as in Betjeman's 'Death in Leamington' (N1356). Leonine rhyme is also found in the refrains of Elizabethan *roundelays* (simple songs with a chorus), such as Shakespeare's 'Under the Greenwood Tree' (O1.942/N244).

The many looser forms of internal rhyme must be judged instance by instance: they will generally have a binding or tightening effect; but will eventually fray out into *alliteration*, the repeated use of words containing the same consonant(s), and *assonance*, the repeated use of words containing the same vowel(s). Anglo-Saxon poetry, which did not use rhyme, prescribed alliteration in every line, and both it and assonance have always been basic literary resources. The best statement about them I know is Robert Louis Stevenson's in one of his *Essays in the Art of Writing*:

[13] Charles Causley, *Collected Poems* (London: Macmillan, 1992), 112.

[14] It is helped by the anapæsts substituted for iambs in the third ('with a SKIN') and fourth ('And an EM-') lines.

> Each phrase in literature is built of sounds, as each phrase in music consists of notes. One sound suggests, echoes, demands, and harmonises with another; and the art of rightly using these concordances is the final art in literature. It used to be a piece of good advice to all young writers to avoid alliteration; and the advice was sound, in as much as it prevented daubing. None the less for that was it abominable nonsense, and the mere raving of those blindest of the blind who will not see. The beauty of the contents of a phrase, or of a sentence, depends implicitly upon alliteration and upon assonance. The vowel demands to be repeated; the consonant demands to be repeated; and both cry aloud to be perpetually varied. You may follow the adventures of a letter through any passage that has particularly pleased you; find it, perhaps, denied a while to tantalise the ear; find it fired again at you in a whole broadside; or find it pass into congenerous sounds, one liquid or labial melting away into another. And you will find another, much stranger circumstance. Literature is written by and for two senses: a sort of internal ear, quick to perceive 'unheard melodies'; and the eye, which directs the pen and deciphers the printed phrase.[15]

If the artful aid of alliteration (or even assonance) is abused the fault lies with the author, not the device.

Like lineation, rhyme is often so much taken for granted that readers assume they will notice it; but that is not always so. Read Book IX of *Paradise Lost* straight through and you will probably agree that it is, as blank verse is supposed to be, unrhymed; but read aloud just the end-words of each line, and complex rhyming sequences will appear like rabbits out of a hat; or take any ten lines and ask which of the eighty-odd words rhyme with any others. Here is Eve's last unfallen parting from Adam (O1.1331/N390):

> Thus saying, from her husband's hand her hand
> Soft she withdrew, and like a wood nymph light,
> Oread or dryad, or of Delia's train,
> Betook her to the groves, but Delia's self
> In gait surpassed and goddesslike deport,

[15] Robert Louis Stevenson, 'On Some Technical Elements of Style in Literature', in *Essays in the Art of Writing* (London: Chatto & Windus, 1905), 30–2.

Though not as she with bow and quiver armed,
But with such gardening tools as art yet rude,
Guiltless of fire had formed, or angels brought.[16]

Some of the rhymes are these: husband/hand, hand/hand, hand/and, Oread/dryad, like/Betook, Delia's/Delia's, groves/bow, withdrew/bow, goddess-/guiltless; and the last four end-words ('deport/armed/rude/brought') roughly form an arch-rhymed quatrain which helps to end the sentence. Sound- and rhyme-patterning of this density is the norm in *Paradise Lost*, and the vast wreath of sound which the twelve books make together is integral to what and how the poem is and means.

[16] I quote from the *Norton Anthology*; the *Oxford* differs in capitalization and punctuation in several places.

'Nearing Forty'

Walcott was born in St Lucia (in the Windward Islands), and like many Caribbean writers seems endlessly capable of producing work in which sound is beautifully and effectively patterned. This capacity may reflect an early and sustained exposure to a culture with far more oral artistry than is now usual in the United Kingdom (cf. British dub poets, singers, and MCs); but it will also have been honed by Walcott's poetic labour, and his work as a playwright. Whatever the reason, sound and rhyme are principal facts in 'Nearing Forty'.

What, though, is the correlation of Walcott's own accent, founded on his native St Lucian[17] but affected by his long residences elsewhere,[18] with the accents which you or I as readers may bring to the poem? Clearly, the poem can be spoken aloud in any accent, and readers need not imitate a St Lucian in order to understand it; equally clearly, to hear Walcott, and perhaps any St Lucian, speak it, is to be offered access to phonetic values and rhythmic patternings which may emphasize or reveal meanings that any other accent might elide or suppress. Words containing 'th', or ending '-ing', '-sion', or '-tion', may be particularly affected, as may the pitch and cadence of polysyllables, all features commonly audible in the speech of people of Caribbean origin.[19] Line 16 ("ambition") and line 26 ("elation") in particular sound rather different to my ears if I imagine them with the medial syllables ("-bi-" and "-la-") at a higher pitch, and the "-tion's" more emphatically stressed, than would be normal in my own speech; and the most important of the sequence is line 28, where the same features bring out the "-nation" in "imagination". In 'The Schooner *Flight*' (N1714),[20] Walcott wrote "I had no nation now but the imagination.", and the same pun is *thematic* (see p. 110 below) in 'Nearing Forty'.

Just how thematic is revealed by the single greatest problem posed by pronunciation: the word "clerk" in line 29. In most southern English accents "clerk" is pronounced 'clark': and if it is so pronounced

[17] The accents of the different islands are not identical, though a St Lucian accent is certainly closer to a Jamaican or Trinidadian accent than to any non-Caribbean accent.

[18] Particularly Boston, Mass., where he teaches.

[19] It should be remembered, though, that in reggae, rap, and dub songs these phonetic features are often, for complex reasons, much exaggerated.

[20] In full in *The Star-Apple Kingdom* (1979) and the *Collected Poems*, 345–61; the line I quote begins section 3, 'Shabine Leaves the Republic', 350.

in line 29 it is a pararhyme with "work" (31). But in Caribbean (and other) accents "clerk" can move away from 'clark' towards 'clurk', and here that would make a full-rhyme with "work", an important word in the poem, with an affinity to "clerk" in meaning. Walcott's own pronunciation, on the recent autorecording,[21] is closer to 'clark' than 'clurk', but the whole recording is rather formal and precise and even an authorial instance cannot settle the matter, for voices vary with time and circumstances, and will always vary between readers. The sudden decision (or deliberate fudge) between 'clark' and 'clurk' which the speaking voice must make when it reaches "clerk" is a choice between identities, one assimilated to Englishness and another shrugging off a colonially imposed Englishness in favour of a West Indian independence (assimilated to work, and to the nation derived from imagination). These issues will recur in the chapters on diction, history, and biography, but nowhere more sharply posed than by the unstable rhyming of "clerk".

More generally, the patterns of internal rhyme, alliteration, and assonance, elaborate the structure of overlapping single-rhymed quatrains and couplets. To provide a complete schematic of the rhyme would be difficult to make helpfully clear; but the sort of thing that Walcott is about may be seen from the first seven lines (down to the first line of the first couplet): rhyme-words are underlined:

> Insomniac since four, hearing this narrow,
> rigidly metred, early-rising rain
> recounting, as its coolness numbs the marrow,
> that I am nearing forty, nearer the weak
> vision thickening to a frosted pane,
> nearer the day when I may judge my work
> by the bleak modesty of middle age

Using slashes to indicate lineation, and upper- and lower-case letters to give some indication of half-rhymes (so that *AA* and *aa* are full-rhymes, but *Aa* or *aA* half-rhymes) one could begin to notate this as: *ab/c/db/dAe/Cdc/ffE/eg* (or, sticking to end-rhymes, not the earlier *abacbcd*, but *abacbCd*: the first quatrain with a full-rhyme, *abac*, but the second and third, *acbC* and *cbCd*, already weakening, with only half-rhymes). This fuller notation shows the patterning of sound around the end-rhymes, which is neither mere ornament nor fully weight-

[21] *Derek Walcott reads a selection of his work* [from] Collected Poems 1948–84 *and* Omeros (Argo/Polygram, 1994; catalogue no. 522–222–4).

bearing; and draws attention to the thematically important pararhyme of "rain" (2) with "vision" (5), and to the sequence 'weak/work/bleak' (*eEe*), where the expected end-rhyme is an unexpected pararhyme, but the full-rhyme is supplied three words later, and the meaning of the words is made as closely related as their sounds. But even this tithe of the rhyme-words is overstretching the notation; and it has nothing to say about either 'day/may' (6), or, more seriously, about 'four/forty/day'—a sequence alluding to the biblical flood, when it rained for forty days and nights, which helps explain the connections between nearing the age of forty, listening to rain, and wondering what of one's work, if anything, is worth preserving (and capable of being preserved).

As well as this general aural method of the poem, there are a number of more specific effects involving rhyme. The first involves the central sequence of couplets: 'middle age/average', 'bled for/metaphor', 'wretched/stretched', 'gutter-/sputter', 'foresaw/meteor', 'settle/kettle', 'gap/deep'. Except for the last, a pararhyme, they look like full-rhymes: but in each case there is something wrong, usually stress.[22] "average" is not 'AVER-AGE', a spondee, but 'AV-er-age' ('AV-er-idge'), a dactyl: so 'middle age/average', an eye full-rhyme, is pronounced as a half-rhyme. Stress and enjambment similarly affect 'BLED for/METaphor', because one needs to speak it not as "bled for [pause] / the household truth" (which would emphasize the rhyme with "metaphor"), but as "bled [pause] for / the household truth" (which tends to blur or hide the rhyme). 'wretched/stretched' mixes stressed and unstressed rhyme; 'gutter-/sputter' <u>is</u> perfect, but "gutter-" is incomplete and can hardly be lingered over long enough for the rhyme to be heard clearly; and 'foresaw/meteor' behaves like 'middle age/average', because "foresaw" is a spondee and "meteor" is not the spondaic 'MEATY-OAR', but the dactylic 'MEET-i-er'. Like the enjambment, these skewed rhymes diminish the itemizing certainty which so attracted eighteenth-century poets (including Dr Johnson) to the heroic couplet; and they make the extended sequence of couplets compatible with the searching progression of the overlapping single-rhymed quatrains on either side of the sequence. Only with the closed full-rhyme 'settle/kettle' does an unperturbed couplet emerge—a moment's rest, settling for a hot drink—and it is immediately succeeded by an open half-rhyme, 'gap-deep'.

The second effect concerns "call conventional for convectional"

[22] My scansion of these examples is not intended to reflect any supposed St Lucian pronunciation, but would not (I believe) be significantly affected by such pronunciation.

(24). The polysyllabic internal rhyme is strong, ruefully matching greenhorn with more seasoned perceptions; and "convectional" is arguably the only unrhymed end-word, giving it an emotional weight which a technical polysyllable would not normally have. If there is a rhyme, it is a half-rhyme with 'settle/kettle': and as what the poem settles for is exactly an understanding of imaginative convection as neither more nor less useful than steam from a battered kettle-spout, that would be a helpful echo.

The third effect involves the autorhymes of "rain" (2, 22, 30) and "work" (6, 25, 31): pair them up (2–6, 22–25, 30–31), and it is clear that the number of lines between these key words successively reduces, until they lie snugly alongside one another, in harmony and no longer at insomniac odds. In this final pairing they are also part of a larger structure, the last quatrain, 'clerk/rain/work/weep' (*cbcj* or *Cbcj*), which links "clerk"(if it is 'clurk') and "work" (as it were, lines 1 and 3): while "work" and "weep" (3 and 4) alliterate; rain weeps (2 and 4) just as clerks work (1 and 3); and the central pairing of the autorhymes "rain" and "work" (2 and 3) isolates an outer pair, "clerk" and "weep" (1 and 4): a weeping clerk, like a resigned poet, to record the working rain. Everything becomes multiply cross-matched, like the sudden emergence, after a series of complex hand-movements, of a completed cat's cradle whose angled strings find in one another the perfect length and tension which allows the whole creation to be passed to other hands.

Finally, apart from the autorhymes the most distant full-rhymes are those in the *j*-sequence, "deep" (20), "sleep" (27), and "weep" (32). The interval again reduces, but is not eliminated: the reaching back of the last line for its full-rhyme ties what could be a loose end back into the weave of the poem; and the slow chime of "weep" (for which one's ears know there are full-rhymes even if one's eyes take a moment to find them) both sustains the ending, confirming the peaceful resolution, and (because it is a slow, distant chime and not an alarm-clock couplet) allows the deep sleep to continue beneath the working, weeping, and now "lightly falling rain".

Chapter Glossary

Alliteration: the repeated use of the same consonant(s) in two or more proximate words.

Amphibrach: a foot of three beats, the first and last unstressed, the middle stressed (uxu).

Arch-rhyme: a rhyme scheme with mirror symmetry, as *abba*.

Assonance: the repeated use of the same vowel(s) in two or more proximate words.

Autorhyme: occurs when a word is rhymed with itself (my coinage).

Colon, cola: the part(s) into which a period is divided by colons.

Comma(ta): the part(s) into which a period (or smaller unit of syntax) is divided by commas.

Common metre: also *ballad metre* or *ballad stanza*; an iambic quatrain of the form *a8b6c8b6*.

Cross-rhyme: a rhyme scheme with alternating rhymes, as *abab*.

End-rhyme: occurs between words ending lines.

Eye-rhyme: (or *printers' rhyme*) occurs between words which, having endings spelt identically, look as if they rhyme, but are not pronounced as a rhyme.

Full-rhyme: (or *perfect rhyme*) occurs when the last stressed vowel and all following sounds of two or more words or phrases are identical.

Half-rhyme: (or *near* or *slant rhyme*) occurs when either the last stressed vowel or all following sounds of two or more words or phrases are identical, but not both; includes vowel- and pararhyme.

Homographs: words with different meanings spelt identically.

Homophones: words with different meanings pronounced identically.

Internal rhyme: occurs within a line between a medial and the end-word, or between medial words in different lines; includes leonine rhyme.

Leonine rhyme: occurs between the word preceding the cæsura and the end-word of the same line.

Monorhyme: a rhyme scheme in which all lines rhyme, as *aaaa*.

Pararhyme: occurs when the last stressed vowel of two or more words or phrases differ, but the sounds following the vowel are identical.

Rhyme: the coincidence of sounds.

Rhyme scheme: a method of notating the pattern of rhymes in a stanza or poem using the alphabet. The first line, and all subsequent lines that rhyme with it, are *a*; the next line that does not rhyme, and all subsequent lines that rhyme with it, are *b*; and so on. Line-lengths may also be indicated, by placing the number of beats after the letter denoting the line.

Rime riche: (or *identical rhyme*) occurs when the sounds both before and after the last stressed vowel of two or more words or phrases are identical; principally the rhyming of homographs and homophones.

Single-rhyme: a rhyme scheme with only one set of rhyming lines, as *abcb* or *abac*.

Stressed: of an ending, with one or more stressed hypermetical beats; of a rhyme, with the stressed vowel in the last beat.

Unstressed: of an ending, with one or more unstressed hypermetrical beats; of a rhyme, with one or more unstressed beats following the last stressed vowel.

Vowel-rhyme: occurs when the last stressed vowel of two or more words or phrases is identical, but the sounds following the shared vowel differ.

Wrenched monorhyme: my coinage to describe the rhyming of unstressed participle endings.

Diction

Diction (from Latin *dicere*, to say) began by meaning 'a word', and evolved to mean the "manner in which anything is expressed in words" (*OED*); here (and in practical criticism generally) it may be most simply and usefully defined as 'the choice of words (including the reason for and consequences of that choice)'.

There are very many words to choose from, for English has the largest recorded vocabulary of any language: the second edition of the *Oxford English Dictionary* (in twenty volumes) has some 616,000 entries. It records relatively few words coined later than 1976, and is far from complete, but does record many archaic words and senses, as well as a word's *etymology* (or derivation), so it is well worth checking words in *OED2* rather than a lesser dictionary, for poets often use older senses. But no-one knows all the words, and no-one's *active* vocabulary (the words they use) is as large as their *passive* vocabulary (the words they know). That is the first constraint on poetic diction—you can't say what you don't know how to say—but a writer's active vocabulary is likely to be larger than most people's: Shakespeare's was just under 30,000 words, and Winston Churchill's is said to have been about 65,000—only about 10% of *OED2*, but quite enough to mean that in reading either author everyone will have to look up something.

Poetry tends to use words very intensively, rather than simply extensively; and poetic diction, for all its richnesses, is in some ways more constrained than other dictions. Before a poem begins there is in theory complete freedom of choice: but some kinds of words (notably scientific polysyllables) are very rare in verse; and any chosen metre, form, and rhyme will sharply limit the choices available. The particular *discourse* of a poem[1]—the sum of its actual choices of words, the

[1] *Discourse* (cf. 'discursive') is a complicated word with a range of meanings: in its strictest sense it is a quasi-technical term for a form of prose argument, and this book might well have been called (in antiquity and the Renaissance) *A Discourse on Poetic Craft*; but it now usually means something very much wider, involving the social circulation of words. The analogy between discourse/diction and scansion/prosody is my own, and of more use in practical criticism than elsewhere: but the meaning of

particular diction it achieves (and discourse is to diction, as scansion is to prosody[2])—may rule out (or rule in) slang, archaisms, or any other specifiable subset of words (or *lexical set*). In a dramatic monologue, for example, the poet must use words which the supposed speaker would use, and the speaker's age, gender, class, and occupation will narrow the poet's choices. The perception of what kinds of language are (supposedly) poetic or unpoetic is also likely to influence choice; and the requirements of truthfulness, emotional honesty, or moral probity may mean that of the whole 616,000+ there is only one that will do—or even none, in which case a new word, a *neologism* or *coinage*, may be needed. A voice under great strain may also need a non-word, a grunt or howl—Shakespeare's dramatic poetry is full of such noises—or even silence.

One reason English has such a large vocabulary is that (alone among modern European languages) it combines two major etymological groups, the word-stock of the *Germanic* (or *Teutonic*) tongues, such as German and Dutch (which have many concrete monosyllables), and the vocabulary of the *Romance* languages, those derived from Latin, such as Spanish and French (which have many abstract polysyllables). There is thus often a choice between words derived from different languages, which share a meaning but are not exact *synonyms*, words with the same meaning: consider, for example, 'canine' and 'dog-like', 'uterus' and 'womb', 'armament' and 'weapon'. Since the Renaissance, when there were great additions to the vocabulary, the choice between Germanic and Romance words has been a real one, and not only for poets: many 'four-letter words' are of Germanic origin (although some people say 'Pardon my French' if they swear), while their polite or medical equivalents are Romance: 'copulate' and 'fuck' are a good example, and using the wrong one in the wrong company (whichever way round) is likely to be embarrassing.

Sometimes parallel to, and sometimes criss-crossing with, the patterning of Romance against Germanic vocabulary is the patterning of shorter words against longer. The possible varieties and interactions of these patternings are infinite, and take place in everyday conversation as well as poetry: but it is a matter to which poets pay attention, and in poetry is likely to be more considered, and weightier. Here is the first stanza of Henry Vaughan's 'The Waterfall' (N452):

the word is not very clear at present, and some element of personal choice is involved in most uses.

[2] See pp. 1 and 10 above.

With what deep murmurs through time's silent stealth
Doth thy transparent, cool, and watery wealth
  Here flowing fall,
  And chide, and call,
As if his liquid, loose retinue stayed
Lingering, and were of this steep place afraid,
  The common pass
  Where, clear as glass,
  All must descend—
  Not to an end,
But quickened by this deep and rocky grave,
Rise to a longer course more bright and brave.

Vaughan was deeply religious (see O1.1189), and 'The Waterfall' uses its nominal image to explore the soul's approach to and passage through death. In the last four lines of this stanza Vaughan's hopes of eternal life are physically embodied in the verse lines, as the sequence of dimeters (7–10) about descending and ending give way to the last pentameters (11–12) about being "quickened" ('quick' meaning alive, as in 'the quick and the dead') by the grave. The reader should be alerted by these longer lines about "a longer course", and looking back might notice that the use of short against long lines is anticipated in the diction: "deep" (Germanic) against "murmur" (Romance), "silent" (R) against "stealth" (G), "transparent" (R) against "cool" (G), "liquid, loose" (RG) against "retinue" (R), "lingering" (G) against "steep place afraid" (GRG). The point is not any rigid patterning—the last word was Romance so the next must be Germanic—which would hobble the verse, but the play-off between the sounds and associations of words, and the different effects on scansion and vocal pitch which a polysyllable and a sequence of monosyllables have. Disturb the sequence of trisyllable, six monosyllables, bisyllable in "Lingering, and were of this steep place afraid", and that line will be less able to hold its place in the stanza; transpose "watery" (2) and "liquid" (5), and more than alliteration is lost; replace "clear as glass" (8) with 'vitreous', and though metre, meaning, and rhyme would all be preserved, the line and the stanza would be lessened, for neither at that point wants or needs a learned Latinate polysyllable. The movement of the stanza begins with the play-off of words, and Vaughan then uses the momentum those words have between them generated to reach into motion the larger play-off of lines.

Diction need not, however, be a solemn matter (it need not be anything at all). Robert Herrick's little poem 'Upon Julia's Breasts' (N321):[3]

> Display thy breasts, my Julia, there let me
> Behold that circummortal purity;
> Between whose glories, there my lips I'll lay,
> Ravished in that fair *Via Lactea*.

could easily be paraphrased in a way that would make it an offensive wolf-whistle; but Herrick's coinage of the slightly absurd "circummortal", and the horrible pun on "*Via Lactea*" (the Milky Way), make the poem jest rather than insult. Eliot did something similar when he began the solemn-sounding 'Mr. Eliot's Sunday Morning Service' with the line "Polyphiloprogenitive", a word he invented to mean 'liking to have lots of children': it's a learned joke, but it is a joke, for among the things poets are not supposed to do is to fill an entire iambic tetrameter with a single word, especially one that doesn't exist. Go one step further, and there is Mary Poppins singing "Supercalifragilisticexpialidocious".

Invented words are a particularly odd lexical set: if they don't catch on or (like *supercali . . .*) remain tied to their source, they are called *nonce words* (those invented for a specific occasion), and are often comic; but if they do catch on (become more widely applied), they become *neologisms*, and cease to be recognized, in their original sources, as new. Since the nineteenth century there has developed an attitude that poets should make do with words that exist; or that coinages are appropriate only in comic verse, as Lewis Carroll's wonderful *portmanteau* words (made by combining existing words) in 'Jabberwocky' (O2.1488/N1032); but among the reasons that English now has such a large vocabulary is that earlier poets happily invented words if they couldn't find an existing one that meant what they wanted. In Renaissance poetry especially there are many neologisms—lifelong (Browne), discourteously (Greensleeves), sunburnt (Sidney), attune, display, scorched, graceful (Spenser), waggles (Nashe), chirrup (Marlowe)—which one would not be without. But new words now are often either restrictedly scientific, or restricted to colloquial use, though some, particularly acronyms (NIMBY, from Not In My Back Yard, and DINKY, from Dual Income No Kids Yet) and coinages by dub poets and rappers (such as the portmanteau 'contagerous', from 'con-

[3] A companion poem with equally playful diction, 'Upon Julia's Clothes', may be found at O1.1117/N323.

tagious' and 'dangerous', to describe AIDS), are finding their way into wider usage.

A concentrated test of neologisms is provided by John Hollander's 'Adam's Task' (N1664), which takes as its epigraph Genesis 2: 20, "And Adam gave names to all cattle, and to the fowl of the air, and to every beast of the field". Hollander coins nineteen names of imaginary animals, in order: paw-paw-paw, glurd, spotted glurd, whitestap, implex, awagabu, verdle, McFleery's pomma, grawl, flisket, kabasch, comma-eared mashawk, pambler, rivarn, greater wherret, lesser wherret, sproal, zant, lily-eater. Before you read further, look at each of the names and decide what sort of animal you think it is. Your imagination is as good as mine: but in the poem 'paw-paw-paw' to 'awagabu' are in the first stanza, and (I think) are meant to be cattle; 'verdle' to 'comma-eared mashawk' are in the third stanza, and are fowls of the air; and 'pambler' to 'lily-eater' are in the fifth stanza, and are beasts of the field. If I am right about this grouping of the names against the terms of the epigraph, it is an interesting exercise to ponder what led Hollander to these particular coinages, and why you do like the ones you do, and don't like the ones you don't. With all the sounds there are to choose from, Hollander could easily have produced not a *jeu d'esprit* but an irritating mess.

Very different problems are posed by obscenities and racial abuse. It is easy to conflate these, and think that the problems associated with using, say, 'cunt', are the same as those with using, say, 'nigger': but this is not always so. The problem with obscenities may be misogyny, if, for example, 'cunt' is used to mean 'woman'—and that is a political and ideological matter, a sexism similar to racism; but the aversion to swear words may also be a matter of taste, and of middle-class nicety. These words are grotesquely over-used in much conversation, but have their own value and worth. When, in 'This Be The Verse' (in his *Collected Poems*[4]) Larkin wrote "They fuck you up, your mum and dad" he meant both the rueful expletive and the bitter pun on conception; equally, the litany of swearing in Tony Harrison's *v.* (in his *Selected Poems*[5]) is integral to the distress and anger which fuel the poem, and to the speech of the

---

[4] London: Faber and Faber, 1988.

[5] 2nd edition, Harmondsworth: Penguin, 1987. There is also an excellent Bloodaxe edition (Newcastle-upon-Tyne: Bloodaxe, 1989), of *v.*, which includes material relating to its broadcast by Channel 4 Television: the newspaper comments, and the ignorance of the conservative politicians who attacked the poem for its supposed 'obscenity', have to be seen to be believed. Interestingly, the Channel 4 log of telephone calls shows that the majority of hostile calls came before or during the broadcast, but that a very substantial majority of all calls, including most calls received after the broadcast, were strongly supportive.

graffitoing vandal with whom the narrator talks. Similar decisions can be appropriate in criticism: the activity of the typist and the young man in *The Waste Land*, for example (see p. 32 above), might fairly be called (even in an exam) "a lonely fuck" rather than "lonely copulation", for what they are doing has no love in it, a deal of aggression, and no true joining, which is what 'copulation' literally means (from Latin *copulare*, to fasten together). The use of these words must be judged case by case: some uses will be misogynistic or genuinely obscene; others will not: but that distinction is not always made. Lines 19 and 33 of cummings's 'i sing of Olaf glad and big' (N1284) were printed in the third edition of the *Norton Anthology* (1983) as "I will not kiss your f.ing flag" and "there is some s. I will not eat'; but in the *Complete Poems 1913–1962* (and in the fourth edition of the *Norton*) "fucking" and "shit" are printed in full, and the swearing matters. I doubt that many users of the *Norton* needed protection from those words, or hesitated in inferring them from "f.ing" and "s.": so on whose behalf did the editors *bowdlerize*[6] them?

Racial abuse, however, like misogynistic obscenity, is not a matter of taste but of ideology. Feminist writers stress the connections between obscene misogyny and violence against women; and particularly since the revelation of the *Sho'ah*[7] in 1945 the appalling ends to which the

[6] Thomas Bowdler (1754–1825) produced the *Family Shakespeare* (10 volumes, 1818), in which all rude, lewd, suggestive, or otherwise dubious words were replaced or cut. "God", for example, always becomes "Heaven", Lear's "Aye, every inch a king . . ." is cut from 22 lines to 7, and Doll Tearsheet vanishes altogether.

[7] The first word used to describe the events in Germany from 1933, by Jews from about 1936, was the Hebrew word *churban* (Yiddish *churbm*) often in the form *der driter churbm*, 'the third *churbm*': the earlier *churbms* were the destructions of the First and Second Temples. By 1940 a group of Jewish scholars in Palestine felt that what was happening was already clearly unique, and should not be described by a term which implied comparability with the past, and imposed a Deuteronomic interpretation, that the Nazis were somehow agents of God's judgement: they chose the Hebrew word *Sho'ah*, meaning 'destruction' or 'catastrophe', and still with strong biblical roots, but less specific, and in broader secular use. In English the term 'Holocaust' came into use in 1956–8, and became increasingly standard, and restricted in meaning (other and earlier holocausts were denied the word), until the unfamiliar title of Claude Lanzmann's film *Shoah* (1986) opened a debate. And debate there might well be: a 'holocaust' is "A sacrifice wholly consumed by fire; a whole burnt offering." (*Shorter OED*), and the word is used in that sense in the Septuagint. The gentile etymology and Christian associations pose a problem, particularly the idea of 'sacrifice': clearly, the Jews (and other groups) were the 'sacrifice', and the Nazis wielded knife and fire; but 'sacrificed' to whom? and in atonement for or in the hope of what? In any case, the long-standing complicity of many Christian churches with anti-Semitic violence makes any Christianized term at best dubious. For a more detailed discussion, see James E. Young, *Writing and Rewriting the Holocaust: Narrative and the Consequences of Interpretation* (Bloomington and Indianapolis: Indiana University Press, 1990), 85–9.

beliefs and assumptions embodied in racial abuse can lead has been hideously plain. This does not mean that the terms of abuse can never find a place in poetry, but does mean that their unguarded use will be contemptible and offensive, and, in all probability, any use, however guarded, will be unacceptable to some—even if, for example, it is clearly not the poet using the term personally, but a sexist or racist character within the poem. An obvious issue is the gender, race, or nationality of the poet: if a black poet uses the word 'nigger' (as Walcott has done in several poems: see N1714) it is a different thing than for a brown, yellow, or white poet to use the word. The skin-colour of the reader may affect how they judge any particular instance, but however any reader feels the premises of judgement are affected by the skin-colour of the poet. The same is true of Jewish and Gentile poets and anti-Semitic terms: in some cases, notably that of Ezra Pound, the vile prejudice is incontestable; and in others, notably that of Eliot, there is evidence that points both ways, and it is horribly easy to find oneself condemning or reprieving in a way itself partial and prejudiced, or making no distinction between the use of a racially abusive term and active moral collusion with genocide. Such issues are emotive, and difficult to think about clearly: but unless such distinctions can be made one may wind up accusing a black poet writing about racism of prejudice because they have used the word 'nigger', which would almost certainly be slanderous nonsense.

As a brief example of how abusive terms may find their value consider the opening lines of Irving Layton's (N1423) 'For My Brother Jesus':

> My father had terrible words for you
> —whoreson, bastard, *meshumad*;
> and my mother loosed Yiddish curses
> on your name and the devil's spawn
> on their way to church
> that scraped the frosted horsebuns
> from the wintry Montreal street
> to fling clattering into our passageway

"*meshumad*" means an apostate, a convert from Judaism, and carries the implication of a turncoat or betrayer; and the three insults together are the reverse of the old Christian calumny against the Jews as the 'killers of Christ'. But what matters about these lines is that they appear beneath that astonishing title, 'For My Brother Jesus': the first thing Layton does is unequivocally to call the abuses in line 2 "terrible words", and makes it clear that they were spoken by another; it is also made clear that they were provoked, aimed less at Jesus or Christian belief than at those who, claiming to be Christians, are yet prepared to throw frozen "horsebuns" into someone's doorway simply because that someone is Jewish. As a result the poem's discourse as a whole can contain the destructive energies of the words in its second line—the only words in the passage to be isolated and contained by marks of punctuation. Note also Layton's subsequent choice of "frosted horse-buns" rather than, say, 'frozen horseshit': the homelier and gentler term is appropriate to remembered childhood, line 2 is enough to deal with at one time, and the poem is trying hard to avoid the bitter tone which '-shit' could easily generate. What emerges is an unexpected perspective, humbling in its restraint, and moving in its compassion: and the amplitude of these emotions would be less if the insults of line 2, offensive in themselves, were bowdlerized away.

I have so far been concerned only with the primary senses of words, but one characteristic effect of poetry is to activate the secondary and tertiary senses of words, and set them to work. Sometimes non-primary senses are allowed to accumulate, and retroactively detonated: a striking example is Margaret Atwood's 'You Fit into Me', where 'hook' and 'eye' apparently have the sense of a clothes-fastening, and then become fish-hooks and open eyes. A less nauseating, but for some no less disturbing, instance comes in Hopkins's sonnet 'Carrion Comfort' (O2.1471/N1064), when he realizes with deep shock that he has been "wrestling with (my God!) my God.", and the different readings of 'my God', as blasphemous oath, statement of fact, and devotional vocative, jostle against one another.

This use of non-primary senses can have the quality of punning, and puns, especially *thematic* puns, those connected to the subject or theme of a work, need not be comic: who would laugh at Hamlet's "A little more than kin and less than kind", despite the 'kin/kind' and 'kind=friendly/kind=type of' puns? Of course, such puns can be comic as well as argumentative, and in Renaissance poetry often erotic as well. A famous example is in John Donne's 'A Valediction: Forbidding Mourning' (O1.1038/N275),[8] when, telling his lover not to weep because he must go away for a while, he compares the two of them to what would now be called a pair of dividers, or "twin compasses":

---

[8] Both the anthologies modernize the spelling and punctuation, I believe greatly to the detriment of the poem. For that reason I quote the 1633 text.

Our two soules therefore, which are one,
   Though I must goe, endure not yet
A breach, but an expansion,
   Like gold to ayery thinnesse beat.
If they be two, they are two so
   As stiffe twin compasses are two;
Thy soule, the fixt foot, makes no show
   To move, but doth, if the'other doe.
And though it in the center sit,
   Yet when the other far doth rome,
It leanes and hearkens after it,
   And growes erect, as that comes home.

The apparent point is to insist that however far apart Donne and his lover are, they remain joined, as a pair of dividers remain joined at the hinge even when the points are widely separated; and though the fixed point does not seem to move when the dividers are rotated to move the other point, it does in fact rotate in place, in consequence of the dividers' unity. But the hidden point is the development of the image, the notion that as the dividers close they return to a vertical position—which Donne calls "erect" by way of promising that he will 'grow erect' when he comes home, that she will 'erect' her legs in the air, and that the lovers will thus resume their lovemaking. Once the bawdy has been seen "stiffe" (26) ceases to mean only a metallic rigidity; and even "comes" (32) may not look quite so innocent. Still further back in the poem, the word "layetie" (8) (modernized in both anthologies as 'laity') is also revealed as bawdy, because the 'layetie' do lie with one another, while the Catholic clergy do not. (The thematic pun is destroyed when the spelling is modernized.) The poem as a whole carries a terrific erotic charge, but it is also in part a promise by the poet to his love that he will be faithful and abstinent while he is away, and that he will return to her.

Even more extended is the punning of a mock-epic such as Pope's 'The Rape of the Lock' (O1.1867/N547), where a sustained mismatch between the grand senses of words and the trivial subject to which they are being applied is a basic method of the poem. Pope wrote the poem in response to a feud that had broken out when one Lord Petre cut off, without permission, a lock of Miss Arabella Fermor's hair; and by exaggerating all gravity, presenting the rape of the lock as an epic with a vast machinery of sylphs and stars, Pope ridiculed the pride which was all that had really been wounded. To tread the line of gentle mockery—

pointed enough to be effective, rounded enough not to cause further offence—requires some very judicious diction, and Pope's performance in this famous poem is a lexical *tour de force*; yet even so some students are worried by his apparent devaluation of the word 'rape' (the practical and legal meaning of which is presently subject to acute theoretical and juridical debate).

Clearly, to use diction in this way depends on words having more than one sense; and despite the huge vocabulary of English many words have an astonishing range of meanings. The longer a word the less likely it is to be *polysemic*, with many senses, and the words with the biggest array of senses tend to be simple monosyllables which are, in the same spelling, verbs, adjectives, or nouns: examples are 'cast' (a stone, in bronze, of a play), 'rose' (in the world/air/morning, the colour, the flower), 'hand' (give to, of cards, a sailor, at the end of your arm), and so on. One consequence of this is that the words you will need to look up are not only those that you don't know, but also familiar but polysemic words, to make sure you consider all the relevant meanings. A great master of these words was Ben Jonson, who began his sequence *The Forrest* (1616) with the line "Some act of love's bound to rehearse": look up "bound" in the *OED* and you will find some twenty-three meanings that apply, from 'leap', through 'boundary' and 'tied', to 'setting off' ('bound for somewhere'), and a number of now obsolete meanings such as "Of persons: Dressed". One could read Jonson's line as: 'Being obliged to rehearse some act of love'; or 'On the way to rehearse some act of love'; or 'To rehearse some act of physical love'; or 'To rehearse some act showing the limits of love'; or any one of about a dozen substantial possibilities. Such dense meaning is extraordinary, but so is Jonson's poetry; and only a careful scrutiny of the poem, the whole sequence, and the *OED*, will allow any particular meaning of 'bound' to be ruled out. Nor need one wish to rule things out: I would myself incline to think that Jonson meant most of these things at once, and that this virtuoso (but perhaps not so virtuous) opening is a good guide to the remarkable sequence of poems that follow.

Finally, there is a level at which diction begins cumulatively to become imagery (though this will usually also involve syntax, the relations of more than one word). This may be a matter of a single weighty word, which is an image in its own right: in Marvell's 'The Definition of Love' (O1.1149/N438), for example, the word "planisphere" (the projection of a sphere onto a plane, as in a map of the world) must be fully and imaginatively understood if the rest of the poem is to make sense: the one word is a key to the poem. Or it may be a matter of a repeated word, such as "dust" in Herbert's 'Church Monuments' (O1.1176), used six times (there's also one "dusty"), and chosen for the multiple applicability of its single meaning—dust to dust, dust in an hourglass, worthless dust, and so on. Or again it may be a sequence of different words whose primary meanings vary widely, but some or all of whose secondary meanings participate in existing lexical sets, or form a new lexical set of their own. In all these cases the general issues of diction, and the particular issues of discourse in a specified poem, will become fused with some or all of the other matters at stake in that poem; but a poem is nothing if not words, and the issues of diction can never safely be ignored.

'Nearing Forty'

As it was not possible to discuss all 322 syllables under 'Metre', so it is not possible here to discuss all 218 words, though something could be said about most of them (and many have already been considered). Most worth noticing is the patterning of diction, which takes several forms.

Throughout the poem there is a striking balance between Romance and Germanic words, each of these pairs combining the etymological groups: 'Insomniac/four', 'recounting/coolness', 'weak vision', 'bleak modesty', 'fireless/average', 'household/metaphor', 'parallel/wretched', 'pages stretched', 'occasional insight', 'foresaw ambition', 'searing meteor', 'vision narrower', 'louvre's gap', 'cynicism/seed', 'sadder joy', 'steadier elation', 'imagination ebbs', 'water clerk'. I don't suppose that Walcott was consulting a dictionary as he wrote, but he was guided by his (very fine) ear, and the sense of etymology which those who deal in words, and often consult dictionaries, can acquire: the balance in sound, concreteness or abstraction of meaning, and association of these words makes each individually more striking and effective, and contributes a great deal to the remarkable general balance of the poem. It is also in strong contrast to the predominantly Romance diction of the Johnsonian epigraph, where 'irregular', 'combination', 'fanciful', 'invention', 'delight', 'novelty', 'common', 'satiety', 'quest', 'pleasures', 'sudden', 'exhausted', 'repose', and 'stability' are all of Latin origin. Dr Johnson, having compiled his dictionary, knew what he was about, and his predilection for these words involves his neo-classicism and authority; the diction of 'Nearing Forty', like other aspects of the poem, pits against that authority a less easily abstract truth, not abandoning Johnson's truth (for in one sense the argument of the poem follows the argument of the epigraph), but adding to it the counterbalance of a more painfully realized and personal truth.

There are also several lexical sets which overlap, the most important concerning water and fire. The water set, in order, is: 'rain', 'coolness', 'fireless', 'bled' (because blood is liquid), 'bleaching', 'rainspout', 'damp', 'wheezing' (of steam), 'kettle' (containing water), 'rain', 'convectional', 'ebbs', 'water', 'rain', 'weep'; and the fire set is: 'dawn', 'fireless', 'bled' (because in the system of humours blood is hot as well as wet), 'searing', 'meteor' (the old term was 'firedrake'), 'match', 'dry', 'kettle' (heated with fire). Although fire and water begin, naturally enough, in opposition, or join only to create bleakness ("dawn, fire-less") and suffering ("bled"), they are brought together, in the central *semi-colon*, by the "damp match" and the "dry wheezing of a dented kettle": images which realize "household" truths, and after which the fire-words are subsumed into an emotional renewal ('joy', 'elation', 'sleep') which allows the rain, once "rigidly metred, early-rising", to return, weeping but working, and only "lightly falling". Also worth pondering is Walcott's retention of rain as tears, which a lesser poet might have used in the first *semi-colon*, until the last word, when its emotional impact is commingled with the upbeat resolution.

A third lexical set orients the poem in time: 'four', 'early-rising', 'day', 'dawn', 'foresaw', 'then', 'year's', 'night', 'sleep', 'moon'. Awake before even the false dawn (8), the 'poet' moves into the early morning and makes a hot drink (17–18); a second movement through time takes him from remembered schooldays (23) to a second rising followed by work (25) "until the night when you can really sleep" (27): by the end it is again night, but a night of the new moon. (This also implies that the previous night was the dark of the moon, which would go with the insomniac lack of inspiration.) From night to night is another of the poem's cycles, like those of water and emotion; and though unobtrusive, it is vital in pacing the poem to a point of rest.

A fourth set concerning the business of poetry ('metred', 'vision', 'work', 'style', 'metaphor', 'lines', 'pages', 'ambition', 'vision', 'leaves' (of paper), 'conventional', 'lines', 'work', 'imagination', 'conventional', 'clerk', 'work') was briefly discussed under 'Lineation', and the auto-rhyming of "work" under 'Rhyme'. As well as "lines" (12, 25), two other words are repeated, "vision" (5, 19) and "conventional" (24, 29); to which may be added "narrow" (1) and "narrower" (19). The emphasis which repetition gives is subtle but significant: vision (not simply sight) is essential, for without it there is nothing for a poet to say; but the narrowing of vision with age, and the realization that it was always narrower than youthful hope imagined, must be accepted: as age's slow recognition of convention, and the predominance of convention, must be grown into without resentment: for one might as well resent the conventionality of the rain, and ignore its rôle in sustaining the cycle of life. A poetry which shirks quotidian reality and rainy days may be fine poetry such as the young will always write, but is unlikely to be a poetry of moral probity or toughness, or to be steadfastly and durably true.

Yet other lexical sets might be picked out. The terms of judgement, for example, are well worth attention ('hearing', 'recounting', 'judge', 'just', 'truth', 'gauges', 'measuring', 'weighs'), and affect other images, making the louvre's slats bars across the window; and so too is the set concerning diminution and the physical incapacities of age ('numbs', 'weak', 'bled', 'bleaching', 'fumble', 'wheezing', 'thin', 'end', 'ebbs', 'weep'). There are also alliterative patterns, within lines ('rigidly/ rising/rain', 'modesty/middle', 'false/fireless'), and more widely separated ('fireless–average' and 'foresaw–ambition', 'glad–sputter' and 'gauges–seasons'), which help bind the poem: but as with any great poem almost every reading will notice something new; and exhaustive treatment is not possible.

The more complex phrases will be considered under 'Syntax', but there are five two-word combinations more reasonably considered here. The first is the simplest: "false dawn" (8), sometimes hyphenated, is a compound noun normally used to refer to the first spill of light above the horizon which precedes the true dawn, the moment at which the leading edge of the sun's disc becomes visible; but in this unhyphenated use, where the words are metrically a spondee following a pyrrhic ('as a FALSE DAWN'), the stress on "false" partially restores its usual meaning of 'cheating' or 'untrue'. Bound up with the fact that it is raining, the rising sun presumably obscured by clouds, this disturbing flicker of a dawn with no sun (following a night with no moon) deepens the early bleakness of the poem.

The second and third combinations are related. "household truth" (10) welds together the domestic and the metaphysical. Immediately following the poem's most agonized moment, the 'home truth' of "which would be just" (9), "household truth" plants a marker to which, as to the rain, the '*poet*' (the speaker/writer: see pp. 159–60 below) returns when he invokes the values of convention and work. The same thought is embodied in the "damp match" (17) which nevertheless serves to light the gas under the kettle; but considered in isolation the common domestic object is revealed as also potentially the matching of damp with damp, a potential realized when the rain at last becomes an external weeping to match the internal sadness.

The fourth combination is "prodigious cynicism" (21), the poem's oddest and in some ways most troubling phrase. A cynic is one who is "disposed to rail or find fault . . . to deny and sneer at the sincerity and goodness of human motives and actions" (*OED*); but "prodigious"—though it can mean 'ominous, abnormal, or amazing', and is here probably best caught by the *OED*'s sense 4, "Of extraordinary size, extent, power, or amount"—has, especially in this context of remembered childhood and "seed" (21), associations with 'prodigal' and the 'Prodigal Son' of Luke 15: 11–32. The implications of bountiful generosity, of lavish being and dispensation, and of forgiveness, are sharply at odds with the wizened closure, and trammelled denial of generosity, implicit in "cynicism". The paradoxicality of finding the two words side by side is not a problem to be solved, or somehow done away with, but a wonderfully economic register of the tensions which keep taut the poem's arc, and begin to find their resolution in the equally, but less troublingly, paradoxical "sadder joy but steadier elation", and the practical response to rain which those durably balanced emotions make possible.

The final combination is "water clerk" (29), a term which was not included in the first edition of the *OED*, but which is defined in the second edition (under "**Water . . . 29**. special comb[inations].") as "an employee of a ship's chandler"; two citations are offered, from an 1898 *Barbados Freight Report*, and from Paul Theroux's *Saint Jack* (1973). A chandler supplies a ship with nautical stores and provisions, and the job of the water clerk is to meet by boat incoming ships and secure their business for the chandler who employs him or her; thereafter the clerk will also liaise between the captain and the chandler while the ship is in harbour. Such water clerking is a dogsbody sort of a job (in American slang, a 'gofer'[9]), and in that sense it is an appropriate term to find at this late stage of the poem, cohering with the acceptance of quotidian work, and the controlled farewell to the ambitions of youth; but that does not explain what this particular water clerk is up to:

> or you will rise and set your lines to work
> with sadder joy but steadier elation,
> until the night when you can really sleep,
> measuring how imagination
> ebbs, conventional as any water clerk
> who weighs the force of lightly falling rain,
> which, as the new moon moves it, does its work
> even when it seems to weep.

In this rather odd context, "weighs" is most obviously taken to mean "To consider . . . in order to assess . . . value or importance; to ponder, estimate, examine, take due account of; to balance in the mind with a view to choice or preference." (*OED v.*[1], 12); the lines might then be taken to imply that water clerks (like poets) must still go on working in

[9] A 'gofer' is one who 'goes for' this or that, fetching and carrying for someone else.

the rain, and have the opportunity, as they travel out to meet ships, or wait to do so, to consider it. The "lightly falling rain", and the degree of wind such rain implies, might also affect when a ship the clerk expects will come in. Clerks are usually office workers (again, like poets), and presumably some water clerks, whose job involves both paperwork and boating, relish getting out and about whatever the weather, while others prefer to keep dry; some no doubt complain and some are stoical: this one "weighs", suggesting careful and dutiful practicality. The lines remain unusual, and most readers would have to have some recourse to the dictionary; but this sense of 'weigh' offers a reading that makes adequate sense.

There is, however, more to it, for 'weigh' is a very polysemic monosyllable. The commonest, literal meaning of 'to weigh', "To ascertain the exact heaviness of (an object or substance) by balancing it in a pair of scales" (*OED v.*[1], 7) does not seem applicable to "lightly falling rain" (though a water clerk might well have to weigh out provisions sold to a ship); but one general archaic meaning, "To bear, carry, hold up" (*OED v.*[1], I), and one specific sense, "To raise up, exalt" (*OED v.*[1], 4b), are applicable. Water clerks must bear the rain, and hold up under it—as the "I" of 'Nearing Forty' commends the "you" for doing; and the movement of the poem is from 'bearing' the "early-rising rain", unhappily, as an insomniac, to exalting (at least after a fashion) the "lightly falling rain, / which . . . does its work". These obsolete secondary senses of 'weigh' do not press upon the poem as the primary sense does, but once a reader is aware of them they insinuate themselves persistently into the poem's fabric; and so too does one more meaning, specifically nautical but still current, "To heave up (a ship's anchor) from the ground, before sailing." (*OED v.*[1], 5). Though in no way <u>required</u> to make sense of the lines, this sense of 'weigh' would join the word to the same lexical set as "measuring" (28), "ebbs" (29), "water clerk" (29), and "work" (31); the water clerk's job ends when the ship weighs anchor, often to sail with the ebb tide, reprovisioned, redirected, and bound again for a new destination; while the clerk must busy him- or herself with another ship, and begin the cycle of the chandler's work anew. Like the new moon, the implications are of renewal and rededication, and the little constellation of secondary meanings and connections, centred on the water clerk's world, ballasts the poem's end, and does a great deal to make the balance of that ending possible.

Chapter Glossary

Active: of an individual's vocabulary, that part which is actually used.

Bowdlerize: to cut from a text, or to replace with euphemisms, anything thought 'improper'; an eponym from Thomas Bowdler (1754–1825), editor of the *Family Shakespeare* (10 volumes, 1818).

Coinage: of a word, a neologism or nonce-word; often used possessively, to indicate the coiner. Implicitly, new words are 'struck', or 'minted', rather than 'made' or 'invented'.

Diction: the choice of words (including the reasons for and consequences of that choice).

Discourse: here, the diction of a particular poem, the relations between the words it actually uses. (A specialized use of an ambiguous and polysemic term.)

Etymology: the derivation and history of a particular word, or the general study of how words evolve.

Germanic: of languages, belonging to a particular group of Indo-European languages, including modern German and Dutch, and Old English (Anglo-Saxon); of modern English words, deriving from one of these languages.

Lexical set: any set of words specified by a given criterion.

Neologism: a new word.

Nonce-word: a word invented for a particular occasion or purpose.

Passive: of an individual's vocabulary, the whole range of words that is known.

Polysemic: of words, having many senses and/or distinct meanings.

Portmanteau: a word created by merging two or more existing words.

Romance: of languages, deriving from Latin; of modern English words, deriving from Latin or a Romance language.

Teutonic: of languages or words, Germanic.

Thematic puns: those connected to the subject or theme of a work.

Syntax

English syntax, and its historical development, are complicated. Linguists and grammarians have dealt at length with such matters as the positioning of auxiliary verbs, noun phrases, and the loss of inflections. A full treatment of syntax requires this careful approach, yet such treatments often claim that the syntax of poetic language is more complicated still. The result is often to discourage readers not specifically interested in linguistics; but to grasp and use the basic points is helpful, and requires little specialized knowledge.

If *grammar* is what you can do in a language, the rules for constructing sentences that guarantee their comprehensibility, then *syntax* is what you have done. There is incorrect grammar: for example, pronouns have cases (I, me, mine), and to say 'Me hit he' or 'Him hit I' is to muddle the nominative (subject) and accusative (object) cases: but although syntax may involve incorrect grammar, there is not really, in English poetry, incorrect syntax. Instead (like punctuation) syntax may be clear or unclear, useful or pointless, verbose or economic, and so on; and the particular syntax which has been used may have considerable effects on the (shades of) meaning.

This is in part because of the analytical nature of English, and the consequent importance of word order. As I mentioned before (see p. 1, n. 1 above), in Latin *Nero interfecit Agrippinam* and *Agrippinam interfecit Nero* mean the same thing, that Nero killed Agrippina, because the cases of the words ensure that Nero always does the killing and Agrippin<u>am</u> (the accusative form of the name Agrippina) the dying. But in English 'Nero killed Agrippina' and 'Agrippina killed Nero' do not mean the same thing; and to keep 'Agrippina' as the first word, but retain the meaning of the Latin sentence, requires a passive construction, 'Agrippina was killed by Nero'. The essential meaning (who kills, who dies) is then preserved, but the emotional impact of active and passive constructions is not identical: compare 'He hit me' and 'I was hit by him'. Such things can make a difference, as the hard-headed publishers Mills & Boon know: they direct authors to pay careful attention to this matter, because active constructions used about a swooning heroine, and passive constructions about an energetic hero who will rescue her, contradict and disturb the sexist stereotypes upon which their mass-market romances depend.

A different example is split infinitives, placing a word between 'to' and the verb. Pedants say one must avoid this, and 'to boldly go', from the beginning of *Star Trek*, has become famous as a solecism. Clearly, the infinitive form creates a link between 'to' and the verb which should not be broken without good reason, or without the writer-speaker realizing that it is being broken: yet what matters is not that 'only to believe' and 'to believe only' are 'correct', and 'to only believe' 'incorrect', but that they do not all mean the same thing. In 'only to believe' 'only' governs 'to believe'; in 'to believe only' it governs what is believed; and 'to only believe' is ambiguous. Thus syntax can be exploited to shade, vary, or otherwise affect meaning: and there is no point in calling cummings's magnificently split infinitive "to in any way (however slightly or insinuatingly) insult" a 'mistake'.[1]

A decision about active versus passive constructions, or splitting an infinitive, will probably affect only one *clause*, a term now used to describe units bigger than a word or phrase, but (usually) smaller than a sentence. A short sentence may have only one clause ("I sat down."), but most sentences combine clauses ("I sat down, stretching my legs, and . . ."); and a complex sentence may have many clauses and *sub-clauses*, giving additional but not syntactically essential information, which may be simply sequential *commata*, or hierarchically organized into *cola* and/or *semi-cola*: each of which may itself be subdivided. As in the last sentence this will commonly involve prepositions ('about', 'of'), relative pronouns ('which', 'that'), and conjunctions ('and', 'but', 'or'); there may also be parentheses (clauses which are syntactically independent, and are placed within another clause) indicated by commas, dashes, or lunulae. Clearly enough, syntactical architecture is very flexible, and there are billions of possible sentences, but it is also true that the syntax of particular centuries or literary ages often shows particular trends, habits, or conventions. Compare the original prose of a seventeenth-century writer[2] such as Sir Thomas Browne (O1.1473) with that of Dr Johnson (O1.2089), Jane Austen, and Joseph Conrad

---

1 See e. e. cummings, *The Enormous Room* (Harmondsworth: Penguin, 1971), 108.

2 Prose is far more commonly and thoroughly modernized than most readers are aware. Jane Austen, for example, does not always distinguish direct and indirect speech; but almost all her editors do; and prose written before about 1700 suffers particularly badly.

(O2.1613), and you can see (and hear) the sentences changing in length, construction, and rhythm; and while the traditional prosody and form of poetry may disguise its syntax, that syntax has nevertheless changed a good deal between Shakespeare's day and our own. There has in particular been one substantial conceptual change, the evolution of the modern, grammatically defined *sentence* and the decline of the classical, rhetorically defined *period*.

Broadly speaking, the basic grounds on which a modern sentence is defined are derived from linguistics and require such elements as subject, object, and main verb; only one of each is required for a satisfactory sentence, and complete sentences are typographically signalled by initial capital letters and full-stops. Many critics and translators seem to think that this has always been what a 'sentence' is, but while the word 'sentence' (in variant forms) dates to classical antiquity, its linguistic definition is much more recent, some elements only being effectively formulated this century—and in consequence one must beware of what exactly the word means in the work of earlier writers. For example, I might have referred to the first complete 'unit' of *Pierce Penilesse* as a 'sentence', but in discussing it (under 'Rhyme'; see p. 85 above) I called it a period rather than a sentence. The distinction may be seen clearly if the punctuation of the first edition of 1592:

> Having spent many yeeres in studying how to live, and liv'de a long time without mony : having tired my youth with follie, and surfetted my minde with vanitie, I began at length to looke backe to repentaunce, & addresse my endevors to prosperitie : But all in vaine, I sate up late, and rose earely, contended with the colde, and conversed with scarcitie : for all my labours turned to losse, my vulgar Muse was despised & neglected, my paines not regarded or slightly rewarded, and I my selfe (in prime of my best wit) laid open to povertie.

is compared with the punctuation of a modernized edition:

> Having spent many years in studying how to live, and lived a long time without money; having tired my youth with folly, and surfeited my mind with vanity, I began at length to look back to repentance and address my endeavours to prosperity. But all in vain. I sat up late and rose early, contended with the cold, and conversed with scarcity; for all my labours turned to loss, my vulgar muse was despised and neglected, my pains not regarded or slightly rewarded, and I myself, in prime of my best wit, laid open to poverty.[3]

[3] Thomas Nashe, *Pierce Penniless . . . and Selected Writings*, ed. Stanley Wells (London: Edward Arnold, 1964), 26. Quoted in Parkes, *Pause and Effect*, 89.

The first edition has only one full-stop, at the very end, and is thus marked as a single unit. The integrity of that unit, and the fact that it finishes when it does, has nothing to do with the linguistic completion of a minimal grammatical sense, and everything to do with the rhythmic completion of a maximal rhetorical sense: the full-stop, in other words, does not mark the end of a complete grammatical unit, but of a complete unit of argument, a period of time, thought, and speech, in many ways more like a modern paragraph than a modern sentence. Each *colon* of a period may be grammatically self-sufficient, able to stand alone as a modern sentence, or may be only a clause; but all are linked in the argument, and so are linked together by colons, rather than separated by semi-colons or full-stops. The modernizing editor, however, has divided Nashe's single period into three sentences,[4] and so made of the argument a sequence of statements rather than a single statement. If the sentences are like lengths of scaffolding, laid end to end in a row, the period angles and bolts those lengths into a single structure.

The same issues are even more sharply visible in some Shakespearean texts. In the First Folio text of *Measure, for Measure* (1623)[5] one speech of Isabella's is printed like this:

> *Isab*. Could great men thunder
> As *Ioue* himselfe do's, *Ioue* would neuer be quiet,
> For euery pelting petty Officer
> Would vse his heauen for thunder ;
> Nothing but thunder : Mercifull heauen,
> Thou rather with thy sharpe and sulpherous bolt
> Splits the vn-wedgable and gnarled Oke,
> Then the soft Mertill : But man, proud man,
> Drest in a little briefe authoritie,
> Most ignorant of what he's most assur'd,
> (His glassie Essence) like an angry Ape
> Plaies such phantastique tricks before high heauen,
> As makes the Angels weepe: who with our spleenes,
> Would all themselues laugh mortall.

---

[4] The repunctuation is, however, rather idiosyncratic; and the middle 'sentence' must be read as "But [it was] all in vain.", with the reader supplying the subject and the verb, if it is to be read as syntactically complete. The words therefore seem to apply to what has gone before ("I began . . . to prosperity.") rather than, as in the first edition, to what follows ("I sate . . . with scarcitie;").

[5] The unexpected comma in the title is in the Folio.

The text which the printers followed for this passage was almost certainly prepared for them by Ralph Crane, a professional scribe, and it is very unlikely that this punctuation is wholly Shakespeare's; but it is patently a clear and consistent way of punctuating.[6] As in the Nashe, this period has four *cola*, the third beginning with a capitalized "But"; and while the first and third *cola* are both about man's usurpation and abuse of divine authority (and so vectored from earth to heaven), the second and fourth are about the behaviour of God and his angels (vectored from heaven to earth). The 'lengths of scaffolding' are made into something like an 'M', moving from images of fallen mankind to images of divine justice, back and forth; a single period constituting a single speech and a single argument—but this period too is done away with by modernizing editors. Here is the same passage (2.2.111–24) in the Arden 2 text (1965):

Isab. Could great men thunder
As Jove himself does, Jove would ne'er be quiet,
For every pelting petty officer
Would use his heaven for thunder; nothing but thunder.
Merciful Heaven,
Thou rather with thy sharp and sulphurous bolt
Splits the unwedgeable and gnarled oak,
Than the soft myrtle. But man, proud man,
Dress'd in a little brief authority,
Most ignorant of what he's most assured—
His glassy essence—like an angry ape
Plays such fantastic tricks before high heaven
As makes the angels weep; who, with our spleens,
Would all themselves laugh mortall.[7]

The words may not have changed, but even without the distracting effects of the relineation and the substitution of dashes for lunulae,[8] a

[6] It is also a theatrical system of punctuating, intended to help actors: try reading the 1623 and 1965 versions aloud yourself, and try giving them to friends to sightread. Which generally produces better delivery?

[7] J. W. Lever (ed.), *Measure for Measure* (London: Methuen, 1965).

[8] A substitution with major consequences. Lunulae could be (and still are) used in various conventions, in some of which they function to emphasize, and not all of which require them to be read as creating a parenthesis (cf. modern italics or underlining). Consequently, in the Folio text "(His glassie Essence)" can be read as the grammatical subject of "plaies" in the following line, which makes the sense much easier to speak because it shortens the tone contour. In the Arden text, however, "—/His glassy essence—" must be read as a parenthesis, and therefore as a relative clause in apposition to "what" in the previous line; the grammatical subject of "plays" must

reader would be hard pressed to derive from this text the balanced back-and-forth movement of Isabella's argument (earth–heaven–earth–heaven), because those four vectored movements are now broken up between the three sentences. The pattern of repunctuation is very different in detail from that of the editor who modernized Nashe, but destroys the structure of the period in much the same way, and to my mind makes it harder to read—despite the apparent 'help' of the modernized spelling: for the larger syntax of the period, the relation of *colon* to *colon*, is no longer indicated, and with it goes the exact and patterned coherence of Isabella's speech and argument. If you reduce and distort syntax, you reduce and distort meaning; and in any modernized edition of a work written before, say, 1700, whether prose, poetry, or drama, any periods that there were are almost certain to have been dismantled and destroyed.

To read any syntax its elements must be related—the referents of *relative* clauses worked out,[9] the *main* clauses linked up,[10] the parallelism of *cola* observed, and so on—yet reading poetry may involve the clear understanding, but not the elimination, of deliberate ambiguity. In writing a complex sentence there are scores of choices to make, about word-order within clauses or sub-clauses, and the order of the clauses themselves; and in poetry these choices must not only make the sentence do what the poet wants in conveying meaning and shade of meaning, but also conform to the requirements of metre, lineation, rhyme, diction, and form. It is the complexity of these requirements, and the intense awareness of language which poetry generates, which allows poets to use syntax in ways that would be out-of-place in ordinary speech or writing.

It does not do, however, to forget the conventions of syntax, and to break or ignore them has consequences: the makers of *Star Trek* intended their voice-over to excite admiration for Captain Kirk and his crew, not to become famous as a solecism. Similarly with more important or general conventions, a poet must consider before breaking with

then be "man, proud man", and an actor must use tone to link subject and verb across two sub-clauses, a parenthesis, and a simile. The Riverside, New Cambridge, World's Classics, and Everyman editions of *Measure, for Measure* differ in mild ways from the Arden 2 text, but all enforce the same modernized reading.

9 A relative clause gives additional information about a subject, verb, or object. In "The man, who was tall, came in." the phrase "who was tall" is relative to "The man".

10 Using the same example as the previous note, "The man" and "came in" are main clauses, and the relative clause "who was tall" is a sub-clause.

convention whether the consequences have been foreseen and managed, whether there is a profitable return on the breakage, and whether the cost can be borne before the profit is reaped.

The biggest test-case is *Paradise Lost*, the syntax of which is famously Latinate, placing adjectives after the nouns they govern, and ignoring the supposedly ideal sequence of subject-verb-object. The beginning of Book IX (O1.1322/N382) bristles with examples:

> No more of talk where God or angel guest
> With man, as with his friend, familiar used
> To sit indulgent, and with him partake
> Rural repast, permitting him the while
> Venial discourse unblamed. I now must change
> These notes to tragic—foul distrust, and breach
> Disloyal, on the part of man, revolt
> And disobedience; on the part of Heaven,
> Now alienated, distance and distaste,
> Anger and just rebuke, and judgement given,
> That brought into this world a world of woe,
> Sin and her shadow Death, and Misery,
> Death's harbinger.

Why Milton wrote in this way is a good question: he read and wrote Latin, so it may have sounded less odd to him than to a modern reader; and as Virgil's *Æneid* was one of Milton's principal models he may have thought it appropriate for an English epic to sound Latinate. His blindness may also be relevant, in that as he wrote he could not see his text himself, but had it read to him, and therefore (as it were) thought more with his ears than his eyes. In any case he has paid a heavy price, for the difficulty of construing his syntax puts many people off *Paradise Lost*; but he also clearly got a good return on his expenditure. The clauses between the dash in line 6 and the semi-colon in line 8 would more conventionally be ordered as 'foul distrust, and disloyal breach, revolt and disobedience on the part of man'; but by ordering them as he has Milton creates additional stress on "foul distrust, and breach" (6) and "And disobedience" (8), by isolating them within their lines; produces the finely emphatic and symmetrical line "Disloyal, on the part of man, revolt" (7); obtains as successive end-words the mutually reinforcing "breach" (6) and "revolt" (7), the latter a half-rhyme with "guest" (1) and "distaste" (9); inserts between "distrust" and "disloyal", and between "disloyal" and "disobedience", line-breaks which heighten the contrast between these human qualities and Heaven's "distance and distaste" (9); and so on. Whether these effects make the difficulty of reading the poem worthwhile is a question for each reader, and different readers have come to opposite judgements: what cannot be argued is that Milton did not know what he was doing.

Paradise Lost offers a series of lessons in the ways in which unusual syntax can be profitable, but the commonest is to delay a word until the end of a sentence or clause, as "disobedience"—a crucial word in the poem, and one used in the first line of the first book—is delayed until the end of the *semi-colon*, and thereby emphasized. A similar technique can be seen in the 1859 version of Emily Dickinson's poem 216 (N1011):

> Safe in their Alabaster Chambers—
> Untouched by Morning
> And untouched by Noon—
> Sleep the meek members of the Resurrection—
> Rafters of satin,
> And Roof of stone.
>
> Light laughs the breeze
> In her Castle above them—
> Babbles the Bee in a stolid Ear,
> Pipe the Sweet Birds in ignorant cadence—
> Ah, what sagacity perished here!

If line 7 were 'the breeze laughs light', there would be no incentive to construe it as anything but a poetic description of the wind; but as it is, it also means that the breeze is created by the laughter of light. Lines 4, 9, and 10 each begin with a verb that would conventionally be placed in the middle of the line (9, 10) or at the end (4): and in each case there are reasons. Placed at the beginning of line 4 "Sleep" follows "Noon", to which it is opposed; symmetry (reinforced by capitals) pits "Sleep" against "Resurrection"; and the sequence of rhymes is preserved ('Noon/Resurrection/satin/stone'—the last two made available by milder inversions, "Rafters of satin" and "Roof of Stone" rather than 'satin rafters' and 'stone roof'). "Babbles the Bee", because it separates the alliterating words, and gives initial stress to "Babbles" rather than "the", sounds better than 'the Bee Babbles'; and it strengthens the metre, for:

> BABBles the I BEE in a I STOLid I EAR,

makes sense as two dactyls, a trochee, and a stressed hyperbeat, the triple feet creating a babble, the trochee (still a falling rhythm) and stressed hyperbeat lessening that babble to offer metrical support to "Stolid". But:

The BEE | BABBles | in a | STOLid | EAR,

an iamb, a trochee, a pyrrhic, another trochee, and a stressed hyperbeat does nothing to support the sense, and metrically cannot decide whether it rises or falls. Line 10 is odder, and was (I suspect) prompted as much by line 9 as its own requirements; but a metrical case can be made for it:

PIPE the | SWEET BIRDS | in IG- | norant CA- | dence—

is logical, in moving from a falling trochee, through a level spondee, to a rising iamb and anapæst; it isolates "Sweet Birds" as a spondee; and plays the shift from falling to rising rhythm against "ignorant", and the trochaic cadence of "Cadence" against the lengthening rising rhythm. But 'The Sweet Birds Pipe . . .' would be two iambs, or iamb and spondee, and in either case the metrical effects would be lessened.

In 216, as in all her poems, there is also the larger syntactical oddity of Dickinson's overwhelming preference for the dash. Commas, full-stops, and especially exclamation-marks are also in evidence, but she rarely used colons or semi-colons to hierarchize (groups of) clauses. In this version of 216 there is nothing unduly problematical; but in the 1861 version (N1011) the syntax of the final lines (9–10) is constantly interrupted:

Diadems—drop—and Doges—surrender—
Soundless as dots—on a disc of snow—

The word order is conventional, and clarity would not require any dashes (though the second and fourth in line 9 could conventionally be retained); but the constant isolation of words and phrases produces a needle-sharp rat-a-tatting emphasis which brings every component of the observation into clear focus, an effect which Dickinson uses to deconstruct and itemize the miseries and hypocrisies of the very masculine (and increasingly scientific) world in which she had to live.

One consequence of this technique is that the majority of her poems are fairly short, for such sequential itemization cannot be long extended without becoming self-defeating, nothing—more—important—because—everything—is—equally—stressed. A larger version of this problem can be seen in Shelley's 'Hymn to Intellectual Beauty' (O2.408/N794), the tendency of which to become gush (or even mush) is related to its twenty-one dashes and slipshod syntax. This is only one instance of the relations between form and syntax, for clearly the length of line, and the number of lines in the unit of form, will act powerfully to condition the ways in which syntax can, or cannot, be extended. In stanzaic poetry the most general condition will be the need either to end-stop the stanza, or to fashion the syntax to accommodate enjambment across the stanza-break; and as has been mentioned, some stanzas, notably the Spenserian, are difficult to enjamb.[11] In others stanza enjambment can be brilliantly effective, as between stanzas six and seven of A. D. Hope's 'Imperial Adam' (N1374), or in MacNeice's 'The Sunlight on the Garden' (N1377):

The earth compels,
We are dying, Egypt, dying

And not expecting pardon,
Hardened in heart anew,

The line before the stanza-break quotes (substituting "We" for 'I') from Shakespeare's *Antony, and Cleopatra* (4.15.41)[12] which, in the original, is end-stopped, well-known as a complete quotation in its own right, and ends with the appropriately final "dying": so that MacNeice's unexpected continuation, "dying // And not expecting pardon, / Hardened . . . anew" (which refers back to the first stanza) is made shockingly strong.

The effects of form on syntax are not limited to stanzaic verse, and in the case of couplets syntax becomes an aspect of form, making the distinction between open and closed couplets. Open couplets will be examined in relation to the central sequence of 'Nearing Forty'; as an example of closed couplets, consider the opening ten lines of Dryden's 'Absalom and Achitophel' (O1.1602/N458),[13] which form a single sentence: aimed at the notoriously promiscuous King Charles II, these lines are among the most elegant satire in the language:

In pious times, ere priestcraft did begin,
Before polygamy was made a sin;
When man on many multiplied his kind,
Ere one to one was cursedly confined;

[11] Byron did manage it, though, in Cantos 3 and 4 of *Childe Harold's Pilgrimage*; the effect is very strange, and Byron shifted to couplets and *ottava rima* (both much easier to enjamb) in his later work.

[12] Another titular comma from the First Folio, which calls the play *The Tragedie of Antony, and Cleopatra*.

[13] I quote from the *Norton Anthology*. The *Oxford* adds commas after "prompted" and "denied" (in line 5), but omits the comma after "heart" (in line 7).

When nature prompted and no law denied
Promiscuous use of concubine and bride;
Then Israel's monarch after Heaven's own heart,
His vigorous warmth did variously impart
To wives and slaves; and, wide as his command,
Scattered his Maker's image through the land.

The measured closure of the first three couplets is plain, for all are complete *semi-cola*; and throughout the poem most couplets are end-stopped with a semi-colon or heavier mark: but within the predominant rigidity Dryden could build up and discharge great power. Here line 1 sets a syntactic pattern, "In . . . ere", which the first two couplets, parallel to one another, reiterate and amplify: their lines begin 'In/Before', 'When/Ere'; and the end-stopping of every line makes each individually a satiric shaft. The third couplet seems set to follow, line 5, like line 3, beginning "When . . .": but the internal enjambment after "denied" gives swingeing emphasis to the key word "Promiscuous", and the need to read lines 5–6 together begins to generate not pace—for lines 6 and 7 are end-stopped, and Dryden is after power, not speed—but mercilessness. "Then", at the beginning of line 7, signals the start of the attack proper, and the end-stopping comma forces attention to the phrase "after Heaven's own heart", which is the point of Dryden's arrow: for when God said "Be fruitful, and multiply" (Genesis 1: 28; 8: 17) it was hardly a charter for royal lechery. The metrical arc between "vigorous" and "variously" in line 8 is the arrow in flight to its target; and the opening of the fourth couplet as the syntax overflows line 8 and penetrates line 9 is the arrow sinking into flesh, its barbs the plural "wives", and "slaves", women whose bodies were commandeered by royal lust. The truncated fifth *semi-colon* rubs salt in the wound with the implicit impiety of "Scattered",[14] and the chastening comparison of monarch and Maker. What happens in these lines involves lineation, but also syntax: the structuring of word order to make the sense conform to, or breach, the couplet boundaries, the ordering of sense structure to place words that matter where they will count, and the controlled elegance of construction makes the indictment of inelegant and uncontrolled sexuality far more damning. Yet at the same time, as any commentary on the whole poem will rapidly tell you (see O1.1602–3, and N458 n. 5), Dryden wrote the poem largely in response to a fierce political dispute, between King Charles and the

[14] One may "plough the fields and scatter" corn—but hardly heirs to the throne.

Whig faction (led by the Earl of Shaftesbury), about the inheritance of the crown;[15] and Dryden sided with the King. As the biblical allegory of the poem unfolds King David's (Charles) venial sins come to seem much less serious than the political ambitions of Achitophel (Shaftesbury); and in retrospect the reader realizes that the exquisite syntax of these opening lines, while making them locally sharper, also restrains their satire. The very elegance of the lines enforces suave good humour, and Dryden makes the reader laugh at the profligate Charles, not wince; but his later portrait of the grasping Shaftesbury was meant to do real damage: in both aspects of his control Dryden depended on his mastery of syntax, and nowhere more so than in this beautifully balanced and double-edged opening.

By way of comparison, here are the first lines of Browning's 'The Bishop Orders His Tomb at Saint Praxed's Church' (O2.1289/N915), a dramatic monologue in blank verse spoken on his death-bed by a bishop, in "*Rome*, 15—":

> Vanity, saith the preacher, vanity!
> Draw round my bed: is Anselm keeping back?
> Nephews— sons mine . . . ah God, I know not! Well—
> She, men would have to be your mother once,
> Old Gandolf envied me, so fair she was!
> What's done is done, and she is dead beside,
> Dead long ago, and I am Bishop since,
> And as she died so must we die ourselves,
> And thence ye may perceive the world's a dream.

In a manner alien to Dryden Browning was concerned with the printed mimesis of the speaking voice: and people rarely speak in proper sentences when well, let alone when dying. He was also concerned to use the mimed voice to reveal character, and whatever his spiritual failings this Bishop has a character to reveal. His first line misquotes Ecclesiastes 1: 2, "Vanity of vanities, saith the Preacher, vanity of vanities; all is vanity", ironically setting up the Bishop's main interest, the richness and decoration of the tomb he will shortly inhabit; and the second line, the worried exhortation of those attending him, establishes the other pole of the poem. Each is a complete sentence, and with them neatly and rapidly out of the way Browning could begin the depiction of character—with an euphemism ("Nephews", which a

[15] Charles had only illegitimate children; Shaftesbury and the Whigs wanted Charles to exclude from the succession his brother James, a Roman Catholic, in favour of his illegitimate son James Scott, Duke of Monmouth.

Bishop may have), a pause, a correction of the euphemism ("sons mine", which a Roman Catholic Bishop probably shouldn't have), a longer pause, and a blasphemy followed by a fudging evasion of the corrected euphemism ("I know not", which is even worse than a frank admission of a broken vow of chastity). As a sentence "Nephews . . . not !" is grammatically hopeless, but its syntax splendidly catches both dying self-exculpation and an ingrained dishonesty which not even imminent death can obviate. The next sentence, "Well— / She, men would have to be your mother once; / Old Gandolf envied me, so fair she was!", is grammatically no better, and until the middle line is construed as 'the woman on whom men once believed I had fathered you' the meaning is unclear: but make that construction, allowing its unclarity as integral to the memorial drift of a dying mind, and to the Bishop's sins may be added geriatric cupidity (as he remembers the beauty of the woman with whom he broke his vows) and unlessened pride (as he remembers the envy of Gandolf, his predecessor as Bishop, at her beauty). There are also implications about the character of Gandolf, and the quality of episcopal succession at St Praxed's: so that Browning has again enhanced the meaning of his words by their order. The next much longer sentence (ll. 6–9) is far more grammatical, as the Bishop moves from the difficulty of confession and the drift through fragmentary memory, to the comfort of first practical, then pious, platitudes: but the syntax is still hard at work. "she is dead . . . and I am Bishop", like the thought of Gandolf's envy and the recovering grammar, signal the Bishop's renewing confidence and self-aggrandizement.[16] The glissading pronouns, from "as <u>she</u> died" to "so must <u>we</u> die" to "thence <u>ye</u> may", reduce any acknowledgement of the facts that only the Bishop is now dying, obsessed with funereal vanities, and needing, far more than his healthy sons, to "perceive the world's a dream". In his later monologues, particularly "Mr Sludge, 'the Medium' ", Browning made this revelatory syntax a fine art; and the scope and skill are already evident here.

Beyond this kind of 'positive' exploitation, where there is definite indication of un- or non-grammatical syntax, the twentieth century has also seen 'negative' exploitation in the widespread use of what might be called *raw syntax*, words strung one after another without one or more of the prepositions, pronouns, conjunctions, and punctuation which usually indicate clausal hierarchy, often to accompany free verse

---

[16] It is reminiscent of Barabas in Marlowe's *The Jew of Malta* 4.1.43–4, who, admitting fornication, comments "But that was in another country,/And besides, the wench is dead."

and open form. In the wake of Joyce's *Ulysses* (the last forty pages of which represent the drifting thoughts of Molly Bloom, and contain no marks of punctuation) raw syntax has been more radically used in prose fiction; for in poetry the use of lineation creates *de facto* syntactical units even when no other indication of the syntax is provided. The effects of raw syntax can range from the eerie evocation of psychological alienation, as in Eliot's *The Hollow Men* (O2.1998), to a rather manic comedy aimed at the neat divisions of suburban domesticity, as in Gregory Corso's 'Marriage' (N1694), to a much angrier attack on the self-assumed superiority of white hegemonism, as in Amiri Baraka's 'It's Nation Time'.[17] There is also the highly original distortion of syntax (often using other parts of speech as nouns) characteristic of such poems by cummings as 'anyone lived in a pretty how town' and 'my father moved through dooms of love' (N1286–8). Such destabilized syntax is not a tool to dismiss, given the brilliance with which Eliot and cummings were able to use it, but raw syntax seems to me of limited value in poetry, because the act of close reading is by definition to (among other things) construe, and unless the writer is generating the words and word-order randomly (as in computer 'poetry') there will be syntax implicit in the act of writing. If no syntactical construction is indicated the reader will have to seek out the implicit syntax, and failing that, will create some—for without syntax the words are only words, and might as well remain in the alphabetical sequence of the dictionary.

[17] Most easily found in the 3rd edition of the *Norton Anthology*, pp. 1358–9.

'Nearing Forty'

As a single sentence, effectively a modern period of one very complex *colon* articulated as three *semi-cola*, the poem requires of its reader an extended act of syntactical construction, which only multiple readings can clarify, but richly rewards that effort. Not surprisingly there are many sub-clauses, which must be identified before the high road of the main clauses can be trodden; and one way of doing this is to pick out words crucial to the main syntax, often the prepositions and conjunctions which begin *commata*. Treated in this way the first *semi-colon* becomes: "Insomniac since four, hearing . . . that I am nearing forty . . . when I may judge . . . which would be just, because . . . ;". The pattern of compact moments of syntactical reorientation interspaced with much longer elaborative developments (the qualities of the rain, of the weakening vision, of the judgement, of the reasons for its justice) is an alternative to formal analysis as an explanation of the way in which the poem moves forward. The compact moments are stress points of the syntax, and (in true testimony to Walcott's craft) are aurally linked: four/forty, hearing/nearing, when–judge/which–just. It is also notable that as the period begins to build up, and the complexity of the syntax to grow, the natural visual stress given to the first word of each line is employed to help the reader construe, by using it to promote important small words: "that" (4), "by" (7), "as" (8), "which" (9), "that" (11), "in" (12). Taken together, these considerations partly account for the impact of "which would be just" (9): for, as well as being fraught with the pain of confessional honesty, it is syntactically self-contained in a way which sets it against the elaborative clauses about coolness, weak vision, and bleak modesty; and the simplicity of "which" is strained by the emotional freight that as a relative pronoun it gathers into itself, strain which the reading voice must register.

A similar pattern emerges from the second *semi-colon*: "glad . . . you who . . . will fumble . . . and . . . settle . . . then . . . recall . . . which . . . ;". This time the elaborations are of what is settled for and what recalled, and the syntactical complexity is again made easier to follow by the linear positioning of "will" (17), "for" (18, 19), "then" (20), and "which" (23). This central section is syntactically compressed in the frequency with which words needed for the full construction have to be inferred from single, earlier uses: in line 17, for example, one needs to read "will fumble . . . and . . . [will] settle"; in line 20 "[and] then . . . [you will] recall"; and in line 22 "[recall how . . . prodigious cynicism] gauges our seasons". These syntactical eddies are appropriate to meditative and rueful memory, as the more sequential syntax of the first *semi-colon* was needed for the painful and bleak business of enumerative judgement.

The last and shortest *semi-colon* returns to the sequentiality of the first, "who" (30) referring only to the "water clerk" (29). The greater simplicity of construction, aided by the easier flow of the lines (only 29 and 31 have medial punctuation) and the momentum of the more strongly rising metre, underpins the emotional resolution and sense of restored balance which enable the poem to close.

Although many of the mathematically possible relations between the 218 words are precluded by grammar, lineation, and punctuation, the syntax of such a period is nevertheless multiply complex, and the approach I have taken above only one of many possible approaches. The largest syntactical divisions, into three *semi-cola*, were considered under 'Punctuation' (see pp. 71–2 above); and one could, for example, take an extremely robust view, and pick out only the first and last words of each, producing: "Insomniac . . . rainspout; glad . . . conventional; or . . . weep": which (in further testimony to Walcott's craft) is about as terse a summary of the poem's thought as can be imagined. How exactly you respond to the syntax is up to you: the only things ruled out absolutely are to ignore it, or to think that it simply happens of its own accord.

Two further points are worth noticing here: the manipulation of syntax and enjambment in the open couplets, and the complex phrases of lines 10–14 (elaborating on "the household truth") and 28–32 (imagination, the water clerk, and the moon).

The first couplet (ll. 7–8) is end-stopped by the comma after "average"; the penultimate couplet (17–18) is end-stopped by the comma after "kettle"; and the last (19–20) is different, a half-rhyme ('gap/deep') with the first line end-stopped and the second out-rhyming, with 'sleep' (27) and 'weep' (32), matters which have previously been noticed: but the second to fifth couplets (9–16) are open, and all are internally as well as externally enjambed (including the extraordinary "gutter-/ing"). The momentum this imparts helps to prevent the poem becoming mired in self-judgement, but it is worth looking more closely:

fireless and average,
which would be just, because your life bled for
the household truth, the style past metaphor
that finds its parallel however wretched
in simple, shining lines, in pages stretched
plain as a bleaching bedsheet under a gutter-
ing rainspout; glad for the sputter
of occasional insight, you who foresaw
ambition as a searing meteor
will fumble a damp match and, smiling, settle
for the dry wheezing of a dented kettle,
for vision . . .

This is no rocking lineation, but rather a spurt of syntax (like rainwater from the gutter's spout) which begins after the phrase I find myself obliged to read most slowly and with the greatest pain: "which would be just". Having forced itself to that admission, the poem urgently needs to explain it and achieves an explanation with the idea of "household truth": but that idea itself then requires explanation in terms of writing. "however wretched" qualifies "parallel", and in prose would probably be indicated by commas: 'finds its parallel, however wretched, in simple': by omitting these commas Walcott preserves the openness of the couplet, and keeps up the pace because the voice must take the words as if they were a hyphenated compound noun ('parallel-however-wretched'), which makes them a stronger parallel to the "household truth". Conversely, ", shining lines," <u>is</u> isolated by commas, which slow the voice to allow time for admiration; but the internal syntactical parallelism of line 12 ("in . . . in . . .") keeps things moving, for too long a pause after "lines," would endanger the necessary construction of "finds its parallel . . . in pages stretched". The extraordinary final clause of the *semi-colon*, "in pages . . . rainspout", again batters through two line-breaks, but is marked also by a pulsing rhythm and *plosive* diction[18] (all Ps and Bs) which disturb the momentum: yet because the syntax is actually straightforward (in what other order would you place these words?) it is not difficult to make it through to the semi-colon. That mark is a strong pause, but used in the middle of a line cannot be too long a pause: so the reader, like the

[18] *Plosive* is one of the ways of characterizing the manner in which a letter is articulated, and means that in the articulation the vocal tract is completely closed, and then opened, producing a small explosion of breath/sound—as happens in English with Ps and Bs. For more detail, see David Crystal, *The Cambridge Encyclopedia of Language* (Cambridge: Cambridge University Press, 1987), 152–68.

poem, cannot afford to puddle under the rainspout, but must go on. The “searing meteor” is no more than a shooting star, for line 16 is enjambed both in to and out of: but its blaze, burning out as a candle gutters, marks the last of the open couplets; and again there are absent commas. In prose one would read: “you, who foresaw ambition as a searing meteor, will fumble”: and as before the absence of commas, as well as keeping the couplet open, acts to compound, making the subject not simply “you” but ‘you-who-foresaw-ambition-as-a-searing-meteor’. If it had been isolated by commas the qualification of “you” could be left behind, but thus compounded it must be carried on to create a potent contrast between the subject and the verbs “fumble” and “settle”. And again an absence of commas is later matched by a presence, this time around “, smiling,”, braking the momentum as the sequence of open couplets ends, allowing the time for a smile, but making it, in its isolation, inward and sad. The subtle but highly effective control which Walcott effects in these lines by playing lineation, enjambment, and syntax off against one another is very close to the poem’s heart.

In lines 10–14, it may seem that "the style past metaphor" is contradictorily illustrated by a metaphor, the "bleaching bedsheet". A metaphor is literally “The figure of speech in which a name or descriptive term is transferred to some object to which it is not properly applicable” (*OED*): but the “in . . . in” syntax of line 12 suggests a “parallel”, not a metaphor, and there is a question about how to read these lines. Is “the style past metaphor” an explanation of “the household truth”? or a second thing which “your life bled for”? “the style . . . that finds its parallel . . . in simple . . . lines” can be understood as a way of being which finds expression in more direct writing, as the poem itself eventually finds in the simpler syntax of the third *semi-colon*; but is the bedsheet outside, actually being bleached by the rain? or is it, like the poet, bleaching and wearing thin with age, and “under a gutter-/ing rainspout” because, like the spouting poet lying under it, it is in a room past the window of which rainwater from the gutter is falling? For me, the second reading makes more satisfying sense, but the syntax allows either, and the ambiguity is arguably one of the poem’s few weaknesses.

Finally, there are the last and very moving lines:

> or you will rise and set your lines to work
> with sadder joy but steadier elation,
> until the night when you can really sleep,
> measuring how imagination

ebbs, conventional as any water clerk
who weighs the force of lightly falling rain,
which, as the new moon moves it, does its work
even when it seems to weep.

More missing commas (after "clerk" and "work") declare their absence, so that at this very last moment the working is not confidently final—'does its work, even when . . .'—but soundlessly and efficiently compounded with the weeping. But there is also a slight problem, for if "conventional . . . rain" (29–30) is taken as a sub-clause (which the commas that *are* present indicate), the main clause must run from "ebbs" (29) to "which" (31); and "which", "it", and "its" (31) must then refer to "imagination" (28). In one way that reading makes good sense, for if "imagination / ebbs" it is being imagined as a tide, and the moon does move the tides; moreover, at the new (as at the full) moon, the tide will be a spring tide, flooding higher than the neap tides which occur near the first and last quarters. Yet tides do not (to me at least) readily "seem to weep", so "it" (32) would more satisfactorily be taken to refer to the "lightly falling rain"; and "its" (31) and "it" (32), despite being in the same clause, would then have different referents—at which point a grammarian or anyone guided by the MLA handbook would reach for their red pencils: Lost referent! a pronoun dangerously adrift. As with the bedsheet there is a genuine ambiguity here, a degree of torque within the syntactical structure which brings together the falling rain and the ebbing tide; and like the poet the reader must surrender to the movement and pass beyond the restrictive logic of rules to faith in the boundless cycle, believing that what goes out with the tide will come in with the rain.

Chapter Glossary

Clause: a word with no fully agreed definition, but used to mean units of syntax larger than a word or phrase, but smaller than a sentence. It is possible however for a sentence to have only one clause. Sub-, relative, and main clauses are (among others) distinguished.

Grammar: the rules governing the cases of words and the 'permissible' syntax of any given language.

Main clause(s): those clauses which deal directly with or continue the principal action of a sentence; distinguished from sub-clauses.

Period: a classical rhetorically defined unit of syntax and argument, composed of *cola* and *commata*; closer to the modern paragraph than the modern sentence; also, latterly and in the USA, a full-stop.

Raw syntax: my coinage to describe sequences of words which lack one or more of the elements (such as prepositions, pronouns, conjunctions, and punctuation) which conventionally indicate clausal hierarchy and other aspects of syntactical construction.

Relative clause: one which gives additional but syntactically inessential information about a subject, verb, or object; commonly signalled by 'who', 'which', or 'that'.

Sentence: in modern use, the largest unit of syntax, composed of one or more clauses, and normally containing at least one grammatical subject, one transitive or intransitive verb, and if appropriate an object; typographically, sentences begin with a capital letter and end with a full-stop.

Sub-clause: any clause that is not a main clause, including all relative clauses, parenthetical clauses, etc.

Syntax: the relations between words and clauses (of whatever kind) within a period or sentence.

History

The rôle of historical knowledge in practical criticism has always been uncertain. The book that first theorized the discipline, I. A. Richards's *Practical Criticism* (1929), reports an experiment Richards conducted, giving his students passages of poetry for comment without identifying author, date, or title. Richards wanted them to respond to what they actually read on the page, rather than to a name or date about which they had assumptions; and so far as it goes this is a sensible procedure. For example, Eliot has a reputation as a 'difficult' poet, and if you give a class a passage ascribed to Eliot, many students seem unable to respond because 'Eliot's too difficult for me'; but give them the same passage unascribed, and they respond to what they do understand and ask good questions about what they don't. 'Shakespeare' has a similar effect, because 'If it's by Shakespeare it must be perfect'—as if Shakespeare wrote from his earliest youth with the greatness of his adult vision, and never had a bad day or made a wrong decision. This is nonsense, but the position Shakespeare occupies in the canon of English literature, and the unthinking praise of him known as *Bardolatry*, have made his name deeply inhibiting to criticism.

More recently, the thinking which prompted Richards to attempt to exclude half-baked historical assumptions has been greatly extended in the theoretical literary criticism derived from the works of Marx, Freud, Barthes, Derrida, and from some feminist thinking. Each theoretical model (Marxism, psychoanalysis, structuralism, deconstruction) seeks in one way or another for general theories of poetry and poetics,[1] ways of reading and understanding as applicable to *Beowulf* as to *The Waste Land*, as helpful about Chaucer as about Dryden or Pope: but anything that general must reduce the importance of the immediate historical context in which those authors lived, those works were written. There

[1] Marxism does not, of course, dismiss history, but Marxist critics often seem more interested in the Marxist theory of history than in anything else, and so tend to flatten historical particularities in much the same way as thoroughly ahistorical psychoanalysts and structuralists.

are things which apply as much to the unknown author of *Beowulf* in the first millenium CE as to Eliot in the twentieth century—both were white, male, formally innovative Christian poets, for starters—but equally, there are clearly things which differentiate the two writers, many of which have to do with the differences between the times in which they lived: and it is not in the least obvious that a better understanding of either can be achieved by the principled dismissal of historical facts and contrasts.

Neither is it obviously possible to dismiss history in this way, and in the last twenty years there has been a double debate: among literary critics the issue has tended to be the 'relevance' of history to texts, and the possibility of reading ahistorically; and among historians, the 'relevance' of textual studies to history, and the possibility of atextual history. Older history books tend to claim, at least implicitly, an 'objective' status, and are written as if their authors were simply revealing the natural relations of facts; so the problem for historians has been a new understanding that history books, like fictional texts, inevitably make assumptions, construct selective interpretations, and deploy rhetoric, and that *value-free* history is not possible.[2] And in history, proverbially 'written by the winners', the stakes are usually higher than in fiction: in Germany, central issues in the recent *Historikerstreit*, or 'battle of the historians', have been how German historians can write of Germany's defeat, and how they may write of Nazi history. Which ways of writing German history help to defeat neo-Nazism? and which ways intentionally or unintentionally collude with it? The issue is vital because many neo-Nazis are apologists for Auschwitz, attempting to warp history by editing the evidence and abusing historical method to deny that the *Sho'ah*[3] happened. To these perverted 'historians' the debate about the reliability of history books and the rhetoric of historians was a golden opportunity for disinformation, and what began as timely academic house-cleaning became in the mass media political dynamite.

In the study of literature the problems and moral stakes are not often so intense, but the case of Salman Rushdie is a sharp warning, and in

---

[2] The extreme version of this argument is that 'history' is texts, that whatever 'actually happened', those events are only available through, and are inevitably masked by, texts that supposedly report but also rhetorically construct them. This can seem counter to common sense, and of course things do happen, but it is patently true that the vast bulk of the 'historical facts' that any person 'knows' they have learned through the media of written or audio-visual 'texts'.

[3] See p. 108, n. 7 above.

many texts, especially modern ones, there are historical and moral issues which should not be ignored. In English literature the largest and most difficult issue is probably the complicity of canonical texts with imperialism: whether one is reading *The Faerie Queene* knowing that Spenser helped administer and enforce Elizabeth I's brutal Irish policy, or wondering why Forster's *A Passage to India* has been reprinted more than fifty times since the first paperback edition in 1936, the connections between literature and imperial or post-imperial politics are not easily or comfortably dismissed. In this light history and (in the broad sense) politics are very closely intertwined; and a reading ignorant of history is as much a political act as an informed reading: the question is only whether the ignorance results from blindness, unobservance, censorship, or averting one's eyes.

One might also ask why it should ever be thought desirable to exclude history from reading. To begin with, some literature is patently about specific historical events and one may well ask what kind of sense it can make if one somehow subtracts that history. Take Marvell's great poem 'An Horatian Ode, Upon Cromwell's Return from Ireland' (O1.1162/N444), for which the editors of the *Norton Anthology* provide seventeen notes, more than half explicit provisions of historical fact:[4] if one knows nothing about the English Civil War, the execution of King Charles I, the part played by Oliver Cromwell, the bloody campaign he fought in Ireland, and the political events catalysed by his return to the centre stage of post-regicide politics, what kind of sense is it possible to make of the poem? and if there is that in the poem which is in all poems, what and where is the interest or delight of this particular poem if its historical specificities are stripped away to leave it as a bald universal truth? Why read this poem and not any other poem that can equally be stripped to that same bald universal truth?

Nor does the history need to be so central and explicit for it to matter. Robert Browning's 'My Last Duchess' (O2.1288/N911) was probably prompted (as both the *Norton* and *Oxford* editors again note) by the lives of Alfonso II d'Este, a sixteenth-century duke of Ferrara, and his first wife, whom he is thought to have had murdered; one does not need to know these names to enjoy the poem: but if one knows nothing of arranged marriage or of the existence and function of marriage-brokers, nothing of Renaissance attitudes to art or of Italian and aristocratic pride, the extent to which the poem can be understood

[4] The annotations in the *Oxford Anthology* are differently organized, but the editors give much the same information as is in the *Norton* in a headnote.

must be limited. In Browning's duke's willingness to have his wife murdered because she smiled at somebody else, and to admit that murder to the marriage-broker with whom he is negotiating for a second wife, there is a portrait of masculine pride, selfishness, and uxoricidal violence which is not historically limited: one has only to read the daily papers to find accounts of men who kill women for much the same vile unreasons. But Browning's portrait is set in a particular historical period, and contains words and references made meaningless if the poem is abstracted from that period; he could have chosen a different setting for a different speaker, but this Italian setting and speaker, an aristocratic foreigner of a much earlier period, were what Browning did choose, and employed his craft to realize: and the possible reasons for that choice offer good ways into the poem.

Another point is that whether or not a poem explicitly deals with history, it must have been written at an historical moment; and one way of approaching a poem (or any artwork) is to locate it on the axis of history. The *Norton* and *Oxford* anthologies, like many others, are organized chronologically, proceeding from 'Old English Poetry' (O1.19) and 'Caedmon's Hymn' (N1) to 'English Literary History in Process' (O2.2168) and the work of Cynthia Zarin, born in 1959 (N1880). Riffle through the pages of either and it is clear that each of the topics already discussed, from 'Metre' to 'Syntax', has its own history, and that the intertwining of these histories makes a thirteenth-century lyric very different from the work of Silko. An ability to discern in reading the difference between the way Dryden handled the heroic couplet in the last quarter of the seventeenth century, and the way Pope handled it in the first half of the eighteenth, can only be acquired through an extensive and intensive experience of reading: but it does not take a reading superstar to notice that the spelling, diction, syntax, form etc. of Chaucer are very different from those of Auden; and the dimmest historical awareness will place Chaucer's "In Flandres whilom was a compaignye / Of yonge folk that haunteden folye" (O1.263/N41) as something written much earlier than Auden's "Watch, then, the band of rivals as they climb up and down / Their steep stone gennels in twos and threes" (O2.2108/N1370). And that is a mere beginning: most A-level English courses involve the study of poetry drawn from periods between the late-mediæval world of Chaucer and the twentieth century, and as the terms *Metaphysical, Augustan, Romantic,* and *Victorian* (to name only a few) come to be understood, and supported by known examples of those poetries, so the historical sense will be refined. Since the work of Christopher Hill on the literature of the

English Civil War, historians have acknowledged that the self-expression, commentary, and investigation embodied in literature are resources for the historian; and the reverse is equally true. To understand what Metaphysical poetry is, to relate its characteristic themes to its characteristic forms, is certainly more difficult, and probably impossible, without some knowledge of political and social history, without some understanding of subjects as diverse as patronage, printing, religious belief and sexual mores; and to pretend that there is no relation between the Enlightenment and the closed-couplet lucidity of Augustan verse, or between the confused social and poetic fluidities of the twentieth century, seems to me wilfully perverse.

There is, in any case, one body of historical knowledge to which all readers must have constant recourse in reading all older literature: the earlier senses of words which have changed their meaning between the time of writing and the time of reading. An obvious current example is 'gay', which now almost always has the primary meaning of '(male) homosexual(ity)'; but which until the second half of the twentieth century simply meant 'cheerful'. When Dickens described a character as 'gay', or as having a 'gay time', he did not mean that they were homosexual, and any reader who believes the word to mean that in Dickens is demonstrably misreading (and is likely to become very confused).[5] Another example (which still gives many readers trouble) is 'silly', which once meant—and in some places still does—'feeble; defenceless; deserving of pity'; but the modern sense ('foolish, trifling') became strong in Shakespeare's day (and works), and has now largely eclipsed the older and larger meaning. 'Officious', on the other hand, was to Shakespeare for the most part simply how any officer (including any civil office-holder) did and should behave; the pejorative modern sense of 'interfering; over-assertive of authority' was just emerging (the *OED*'s earliest citation is 1602), but does not seem to have gained much ground until later in the seventeenth century. The *OED*'s inclusion of these older senses, and its dating of all senses by earliest and latest quotations, is precisely why it must be the *OED* you consult whenever possible.

There is also the meaning given to a particular form or technique by its previous use. A poet cannot write a sonnet without knowing what a sonnet is—but to know that implies some knowledge of existing sonnets, of how and what they are, of the form's capacities and history,

[5] There may of course be among Dickens's characters some whom a reader may very reasonably believe to be homosexual; the point is that the word 'gay' does not convey that information.

which will bear upon the new act of writing. And within the sonnet (or any other form) there may be dozens of techniques, and even individual words, learned from a previous poem: all of which precedent will bear upon the meaning of this new poem. In the case of sonnets I have already mentioned Yeats's 'Leda and the Swan' as using its form ironically (see pp. 23, 35 and 37 above), the poet forcing together the association with courtship and the relation of a rape despite their antipathy; but such uses of form do not have to be a matter of intent, as they were for Yeats. A poet may have forgotten where they first encountered a phrase or a technique, and a reader may know or recognize what the poet did not: but neither ignorant writing nor ignorant reading can alter the existence of that phrase or technique in the two poems, or the relationship in time which exists between them—a relationship which can enrich a more informed reading of the older poem as much as of the newer. That web of relationships between one text and other texts is now often called *intertextuality*, and many critics seem happy to imagine that intertextuality cancels history, as if texts and books did not in reading constantly declare themselves to be fashioned by different minds formed in different ages and places. Eliot, as one might expect, saw rather more clearly, and made the point much more elegantly, in his essay 'Tradition and the Individual Talent', when he said that the past is altered by the present as much as the present by the past: and in both kinds of operation it is as well to know something of both present and past, whose interaction makes history.

A knowledge of how some words have shifted sense is a simple and necessary beginning; and the histories of forms are the next and equally important step; but there is no limit to the growth and refinement of one's sense of literary history. I still use my *OED* almost every working day, and any number of oddities in literary history continue to intrigue and puzzle me: why, for example, Marvell, in the middle of the seventeenth century could use iambic tetrameter with the utmost gravity and delicacy, while fifty years after his death it had become a predominantly comic metre? or why the triple rhymes of *ottava rima* are far from comic in the hands of Fayrfax, but thoroughly comic in the hands of Byron? or why longer triple metres should have had a vogue in the later nineteenth century? I do not know the answers: but among them will be historical facts and processes, just as among the reasons which made Dryden write 'Absalom and Achitophel' as he did (see pp. 129–30 above) were the developing Augustan passions for clarity and exactitude of language and for satire, passions satisfyingly reconciled in the heroic couplet; and among the reasons which made Browning write 'The Bishop Orders His Tomb at St Praxed's' as he did (see p. 131 above) were the Romantic legacy of interest in mental pathology, and the remarkable developments of printing and the *mise-en-page* of the voice, which began in the eighteenth century and culminated in Browning's own legacy to Eliot.

There is, though, one obvious limit to the history which can be brought to bear on a poem if that poem is set as an unseen in an exam: the knowledge which the candidate has available in their head. The acquisition of a sense of history and of literary developments and influences takes time to grow, and continues to grow throughout one's reading life. But you can cultivate that sense or ignore it; you can try to bring the knowledge you have to bear on a poem, or bash ahead not giving a hoot for history or accuracy; you can care about your reading of a poem, even under exam conditions, or treat it simply as a chore to be got out of the way. The discovery and exploration of history, whether political, social, cultural, or literary, can be pursued in many ways, and rapidly passes beyond my scope here: a knowledge of fashion history, for example, can be invaluable in reading the poetry both of the Renaissance and of the 1960s, and a visit to a museum which has old clothing (such as the Victoria and Albert Museum in London) can be a revelation.[6] It is a general pursuit, with consequences for far more than reading, but as a reader I have always found it worth cultivating a sense of history, for as much as my senses of vision and hearing it can enhance my enjoyment and understanding of the poems (and prose) that I read.

---

[6] As an example, find out what a 'farthingale' is and looked like, and then read Donne's 'Elegy XIX' (O1. 1023–4/N281–2), esp. ll. 15–16.

'Nearing Forty'

The title suggests a closer involvement with biography than history at large, and the lyric inwardness of the poem excludes the historical concerns courted by satirical and narrative poetry. That in no way lessens the importance of locating Walcott as a Caribbean poet, whose island and people have suffered a violent history, often at British hands, but it does focus that importance on Walcott as an individual, where I will come to it under 'Biography'. In two important ways, however, a less personal history is explicitly and complicatedly invoked: by the epigraph and by a particular intertextual association of "water clerk" (29).

The quotation serving as the epigraph comes from the seventh paragraph of the *Preface* to Johnson's great edition of Shakespeare, published in 1765; and the poem seeks to follow its epigraph from "irregular combination" to "stability", while testing Johnson's certainty by pitting it (and its prose cadences) against poetic justice, a harsh self-judgement and a "household truth" acknowledged as a form of diminishment.

Literary judgements and understandings of the eighteenth century are presently under reappraisal, and the older models, concentrated on the intellectual predominance of reason and the linguistic predominance of elegance, have been shown up as ideologically simplified: but the tastes for reason and elegance must be embodied in any new models, and are well exemplified by Johnson. His ability to declare without qualification that "the pleasures of sudden wonder are soon exhausted and the mind can only repose on the stability of truth" is characteristic of his thinking, and came more easily in the fairly stable and self-assured mid-eighteenth century than it would have done in the mid-seventeenth, when England was racked by civil war—or in the mid-twentieth. We do not yet have the benefits of historical hindsight on our own century, but there is no doubt that it has been deeply unsettled politically, socially, and culturally, and that this was manifest to Walcott when he wrote. My point is not that these acute twentieth-century problems are what 'Nearing Forty' is 'about', but that they are a background of failures and uncertainties against which Walcott's ability to write of "judg[ing] my work / by the bleak modesty of middle age / as a false dawn" makes deeper and fuller sense, as the successes and certainties of the eighteenth century are a background against which Johnson's willingness to make absolute pronouncements also makes deeper sense.

Although the details of eighteenth- and twentieth-century histories and perceptions of history are complex, this use of an epigraph is not in itself a complicated way of invoking a historical comparison: any epigraph might do as much. What does complicate things is the point in the *Preface* from which the epigraph is taken: Johnson is elaborating on Ben Jonson's statement (see O1.1066/N310) that Shakespeare "was not of an age, but for all time", that Shakespeare's truths were not limited and relative, but universal and ahistorical:

> Nothing can please many, and please long, but just representations of general nature. Particular manners can be known only to a few, and therefore few only can judge how nearly they are copied. The irregular combinations of fanciful invention may delight a-while, by that novelty of which the common satiety of life sends us all in quest; but the pleasures of sudden wonder are soon exhausted, and the mind can only repose on the stability of truth.
>
> *Shakespeare* is above all writers, at least above all modern writers, the poet of nature; the poet that holds up to his readers a faithful mirrour of manners and of life. His characters are not modified by the customs of particular places, unpractised by the rest of the world; by the peculiarities of studies or professions, which can operate but upon small numbers; or by the accidents of transient fashions or temporary opinions: they are the genuine progeny of common humanity, such as the world will always supply, and observation will always find. His persons act and speak by the influence of those general passions and principles by which all minds are agitated, and the whole system of life is continued in motion. In the writings of other poets a character is too often an individual; in those of Shakespeare it is commonly a species.
>
> It is from this wide extension of design that so much instruction is derived. It is this which fills the plays of *Shakespeare* with practical axioms and domestick wisdom. It was said of *Euripides*, that every verse was a precept; and it may be said of *Shakespeare*, that from his works may be collected a system of civil and œconomical prudence. Yet his real power is not shewn in the splendour of particular passages, but by the progress of his fable, and the tenour of his dialogue; and he that tries to recommend him by select quotations, will succeed like the pedant in *Hierocles*, who, when he offered his house for sale, carried a brick in his pocket as a specimen.

Only the brief extract which Walcott quotes must be taken into consideration, but the ellipsis following the epigraph points out (among other things) that there is more than is quoted, and it is clear that 'Nearing Forty' draws more than its epigraph from this passage: the model excellence which Johnson attributes to Shakespeare is very close to the praise which Walcott's poem gives to "your life" (9). Most crucial is the relation between Johnson's "domestick wisdom" and "œconomical prudence",[7] and Walcott's "household truth", but beyond this striking echo is the whole movement of Johnson's argument towards Shakespeare's practical value rather than rhetorical splendour, and the equivalent movement in Walcott's poem towards the endorsement of quotidian and water-clerkly work. It is not the "fanciful invention" or the "searing meteor" which endures, but the workaday world; and though the natures of fancy and work changed in various ways between Shakespeare's time and Johnson's, and again between Johnson's and Walcott's, the distinction between them, and the truth of that distinction, did not change. Walcott's poem squares up to his own ageing, to the passing of young fancies, the recognition of bleaker truths; and in that painful transition it is implicitly a comfort to know that what the poet discovers, and must acknowledge, is a timeless truth, discovered and acknowledged by great precursors, even Shakespeare and Johnson. But there is a doubleness in this, for the epigraphic truth that transcends history is itself taken from the literary history which has preserved Johnson and made his *Preface* available, two centuries later, to Walcott. Moreover, it is a fragment of history that reaches back to a still older history in Shakespeare, and its value to Walcott is precisely the historical endorsement, a truth verified by Johnson, and through Johnson by Shakespeare. You may think this a paradox; but it may equally be understood as a loop of opening and closing historical perspectives, a history cycle to accompany the cycles of water and emotion: just as the knowledge that one's predicament is an age-old predicament may at one moment be comforting, and at another seem a lessening of self.

The intertextual spark that connects with "water clerk" is not formally acknowledged in the same way as the epigraph, and the term is

[7] Johnson is probably using "œconomical" in the *OED*'s sense "1. Pertaining to a household or its management; resembling what prevails in a household.", and "prudence" in the *OED*'s sense "2. Wisdom; knowledge of or skill in a matter. Cf. JURISPRUDENCE.". The phrase "civil and œconomical prudence" implies that from Shakespeare may be learned all that is necessary for the wise management of state and household alike.

not a quotation as such; but in so far as Walcott's intent is held to matter, I think it highly likely that he was aware of his reference. In first attempting to understand the presence of this "water clerk / who weighs the force of lightly falling rain" (see pp. 117–18 above), I mentioned that *OED2* offered two illustrative quotations, one from 1898 and one from 1973. These, both from obscure sources, are cited because they are the earliest and latest uses known to the editors; beyond harbour life the term is not common—encountering it in the poem I had to hunt for the meaning—but in the *OED* offices there are ten further recorded usages,[8] and all are from the same high-canonical text: Joseph Conrad's *Lord Jim* (1900).

Conrad's name is a very interesting one to encounter in any investigation of Walcott, for a score of specific issues, from racial miscegenation to the sight from the beach of a schooner under sail, run persistently through the works of both writers, and Conrad's novel of lost honour, with its analyses of Jim's self-esteem, ambition, and decline, is immediately suggestive of many links with the poem. Conrad (1857–1924) was forty-three when *Lord Jim* was published, and the novel offers perspectives on life and ambition from just beyond the rubicon that Walcott's poem contemplates and fears. More specifically, the novel has three extended references to water clerking in general, or to Jim's in particular, and each serves to focus the textual links, bringing to the end of the poem a degree of darkness that greatly deepens the complexity of its balance. The connection begins with the novel's opening paragraphs:

> He was an inch, perhaps two, under six feet, powerfully built, and he advanced straight at you with a slight stoop of the shoulders, head forward, and a fixed from-under stare which made you think of a charging bull. His voice was deep, loud, and his manner displayed a kind of dogged self-assertion which had nothing aggressive in it. It seemed a necessity, and it was directed apparently as much at himself as at anybody else. He was spotlessly neat, apparelled in immaculate white from shoes to hat, and in the various Eastern ports where he got his living as ship-chandler's water-clerk he was very popular.
>
> A water-clerk need not pass an examination in anything under the sun, but he must have Ability in the abstract and demonstrate it practically. His work consisted in racing under sail, steam, or oars against other water-clerks for any ship about to anchor, greeting her captain cheerily, forcing upon him a card—the business card of the ship-

[8] I am indebted to Dr Philip Durkin of the *OED* staff for searching them out.

chandler—and on his first visit on shore piloting him firmly but without ostentation to a vast, cavern-like shop which is full of things that are eaten and drunk on board ship; where you can get everything to make her sea-worthy and beautiful, from a set of chain-hooks for her cable to a book of gold-leaf for the carvings of her stern; and where her commander is received like a brother by a ship-chandler he has never seen before. There is a cool parlour, easy chairs, bottles, cigars, writing implements, a copy of harbour regulations, and a warmth of welcome that melts the salt of a three months' passage out of a seaman's heart. The connexion thus begun is kept up, as long as the ship remains in harbour, by the daily visits of the water-clerk. To the captain he is faithful like a friend and attentive like a son, with the patience of Job, the unselfish devotion of a woman, and the jollity of a boon companion. Later on the bill is sent in. It is a beautiful and humane occupation. Therefore good water-clerks are scarce. When a water-clerk who possesses Ability in the abstract has also the advantage of having been brought up to the sea, he is worth to his employer a lot of money and some humouring. Jim had always good wages and as much humouring as would have bought the fidelity of a fiend. Nevertheless, with black ingratitude he would throw up the job suddenly and depart. To his employers the reasons he gave were obviously inadequate. They said 'Confounded fool!' as soon as his back was turned. This was their criticism of his exquisite sensibility.

To the white men in the waterside business and to the captains of ships he was just Jim—nothing more. He had, of course, another name, but he was anxious that it should not be pronounced. His incognito, which had as many holes as a sieve, was not meant to hide a personality but a fact. When the fact broke through the incognito he would leave suddenly the seaport where he happened to be at the time and go to another—generally farther east. He kept to seaports because he was a seaman in exile from the sea, and had Ability in the abstract, which is good for no other work but that of a water-clerk. He retreated in good order towards the rising sun, and the fact followed him casually but inevitably. Thus in the course of years he was known successively in Bombay, in Calcutta, in Rangoon, in Penang, in Batavia—and in each of these halting-places was just Jim the water-clerk. Afterwards, when his keen perception of the Intolerable drove him away for good from seaports and white men, even into the virgin forests, the Malays of the jungle village, where he had elected to conceal his deplorable faculty, added a word to the

> monosyllable of his incognito. They called him Tuan Jim: as one might say—Lord Jim.[9]

The *OED*'s citations, though functionally informative, left the poem's water clerk an impersonal figure; but the literary echo of Conrad suggests an identification of that water clerk with a particular water clerk, Jim, and so briefly gives the figure a gendered identity and history: a past he flees, a fate he lives, and a destiny he approaches. A principal consequence of such intertextuality is often to make readers conscious of the rhetorized, self-dramatizing aspects of a work, and here the self-dramatizing affects the poem's presentation of "you" (and implicitly of "I") as happily buckling down to clerkly work. The casting of Conrad's tale as a tragedy, his presentation of Jim as a figure of potential heroism and nobility, living a life filled with exotic names and shadows, momentarily sneaks back into the poem a high romantic world and imagined destiny ("ambition as a searing meteor") which had previously seemed to have been transcended and released. Yet Conrad was as aware of the problems of youthful ambition, of ageing, and of a "keen perception of the Intolerable", as Walcott shows himself to be; and each subsequent return in *Lord Jim* to the matter of the water-clerking is in a more sombre and more jagged vein. Both returns occur in the portion of the novel narrated by Marlow, whose voice is at odds with the third-person voice of the opening; the first is in chapter 13, by which time Conrad's readers have learned that the "fact" from which Jim flees is that he once, when chief mate of a ship called the *Patna*, behaved as a coward, abandoning ship with the other officers while the hands and passengers were still on board:

> [Jim] was then working for De Jongh, on my recommendation. Water-clerk. "My representative afloat", as De Jongh called him. You can't imagine a mode of life more barren of consolation, less capable of being invested with a spark of glamour—unless it be the business of an insurance canvasser. [. . .] I don't know how Jim's soul accommodated itself to the new conditions of his life—I was kept too busy in getting him something to do that would keep body and soul together—but I am pretty certain his adventurous fancy was suffering all the pangs of starvation. It had certainly nothing to feed upon in this new calling. It was distressing to see him at it, though he tackled it with a stubborn serenity for which I must give him full credit. I kept my eye on his shabby plodding with a sort of notion that it was a pun-

[9] Joseph Conrad, *Lord Jim* (Harmondsworth: Penguin, 1949), ch. 1 (pp. 9–10).

> ishment for the heroics of his fancy—an expiation for his craving after more glamour than he could carry. He had loved too well to imagine himself a glorious racehorse, and now he was condemned to toil without honour like a costermonger's donkey. He did it very well. He shut himself in, put his head down, said never a word. Very well; very well indeed—except for certain fantastic and violent outbreaks, on the deplorable occasions when the irrepressible *Patna* case cropped up.[10]

The complex lexical echoes which unite Conrad's text with both Johnson's and Walcott's—fanciful, fancy, imagine, imagination, sudden wonder, violent outbreaks, searing meteor, steadier elation, stubborn serenity—underpin a common theme, of learning to settle for the workaday world, without the consolation of what was perhaps always an overreaching fantasy and is in any case lost. Johnson dismisses the fantasy, Conrad has Marlow suppose Jim grieves for it, and Walcott inherits both to complicate his own attempts to find a resolution. Conrad's sense of Jim's fallen position is, however, dynamic (or unstable), and in the contrast between the first exposition of water clerking (the skill of the job) and this exposition (the menial diminishment of the job) the intertextuality truly begins to bite. Walcott's poem is seeking resolution, in the most banal terms 'to look on the bright side', to find in the image of the working water clerk a source of consolation; but Conrad's novel tends to tragedy, and Marlow's recharacterization of water clerking as "barren of consolation" is a step on that tragic road. As such it is an intertextual current running counter to the movement of 'Nearing Forty' at the moment when they connect, an undertow beneath the rhetorical crest of Walcott's ending.

The novel's third and final return to the subject of water clerking, in chapter 18, throws the intertextual relations into relief. Marlow is recounting the reactions of one Egström, a chandler who had employed Jim, to Jim's abrupt and unexplained decision to quit his job in the middle of a working day:

> ' "When I understood what he was up to, my arms fell—so! Can't get a man like that every day, you know, sir; a regular devil for sailing a boat; ready to go out miles to sea to meet ships in any sort of weather. More than once a captain would come in here full of it, and the first thing he would say would be, 'That's a reckless sort of lunatic you've got for water-clerk, Egström. I was feeling my way in at daylight under short canvas when there comes flying out of the mist

[10] *Lord Jim*, ch. 13 (pp. 116–17). A long digression is omitted.

> right under my forefront a boat half under water, sprays going over the masthead, two frightened niggers on the bottom boards, a yelling fiend at the tiller. Hey! hey! Ship ahoy! ahoy! Captain! Hey! hey! Egström & Blake's man first to speak to you! Hey! hey! Egström & Blake! Hallo! hey! whoop! Kick the niggers—out reefs—a squall on at the time—shoots ahead whooping and yelling to me to make sail and he would give me a lead in—more like a demon than a man. Never saw a boat handled like that in all my life. Couldn't have been drunk—was he? Such a quiet, soft-spoken chap, too—blush like a girl when he came on board. . . .' I tell you, Captain Marlow, nobody had a chance against us with a strange ship when Jim was out. The other ship-chandlers just keep their old customers, and . . ."
>
> 'Egström appeared overcome with emotion.
>
> ' "Why, sir—it seems as though he wouldn't mind going a hundred miles out to sea in an old shoe to nab a ship for the firm." '[11]

"conventional as <u>any</u> water clerk" . . .? On this account, there was in Jim's water clerking a degree of panache or élan sufficient to proclaim desperation. Not just any water clerk, but a regular devil, a fiend of a water clerk, careless of all weathers; hardly one "who weighs the force of lightly falling rain", however that phrase may be read. With this discovery the oddity of Walcott's words is partly explained: "water clerk" creates the intertextual invocation of Jim's decline from first mate towards an obscure death, but the preceding qualification of the clerk as "conventional" keeps apart a water clerk of Jim's recklessness and the water clerk imagined in the poem. One distinct complication, though, is the presence in Conrad's third passage of the reiterated "niggers"—which (however one may point out that it is in reported speech, that it would in 1900 have been acceptable, and all the rest of it) is now redolent with offence. Egström's story (and more largely Marlow's and Conrad's) is structured around Jim's class-conscious self-estimation by professional and racial criteria, his need to demonstrate personal courage and social standing; and though Conrad may in *Lord Jim* as a whole criticize the imperial honour-codes by which Jim lives and is hounded, the historical fact and consequences of those codes for many colonial subjects (including Walcott) remain, intransigent and unpalatable. To follow this strand of the intertextuality, however, would lead beyond history at large and towards more personal territory, and I will leave it here, but return to it under 'Biography' (see pp. 165–6 below).

---

[11] *Lord Jim*, ch. 18 (pp. 148–9).

I knew 'Nearing Forty' very well (or so I thought) before being prompted by writing this book to go beyond the *OED*'s bare definition of 'water clerk', and so to discover the connection with Conrad. More than any other detail it has unsettled my sense of the poem as a whole, and it seems to me now to stand in the same relation to the poem's end as Johnson does to its beginning, Conrad's text silently triangulating itself with Johnson's and Walcott's. The impossibility for Jim of settling to the diminished, quotidian world of water clerking, and the instability which the 'truth' repeatedly creates in his life, opens before the reader's eyes the deep pit which yawns beneath the final balance of 'Nearing Forty'.

Beyond the intertextual the most important histories in the poem are the literary histories of the component forms and images. The iambic pentameter, sonorous, flexible, strong, and deeply traditional, affords the 'poet'—the speaker/writer who is but also is not Walcott[12]—the prosodic space to be lyrical while containing and marshalling emotion, and so supports the quest for an harmonious acceptance of the truth which the epigraph proclaims. Closed heroic couplets were predominant in Johnson's day, corresponding as a form with the moral self-certainty expressed in Johnson's oracular prose, and Walcott's central sequence of couplets alludes to the history behind the epigraph; but the moral self-certainty was also a part of the age's imperialism and a reason so many eighteenth-century British merchants could in all conscience become slave-traders. Walcott's position as a post-independence West Indian and a colonial descendant of slaves gives him a very different perspective from that of the imperial slavemasters, and he qualifies his allusion to the poetry of their age—for his couplets are open, their rhymes slightly skewed, and the poem must break out of them to find its rest. Troubled and disturbed by its Johnsonian and Conradian intertextualities, the poem turns at the very last to the picture of the new moon controlling the lines of falling rain, and implicitly summoning renewed lines of poetry. Thus Walcott invokes a symbol of the poetic muse in self-benediction; both symbol and imagined benediction are utterly traditional, but historically the moon was invoked and used poetically far more in the Renaissance (before Johnson) and in Romantic poetry (after Johnson) than in Augustan poetry. It marks a moment when Walcott passes beyond Johnson and

[12] For more on this distinction see pp. 159–60 below.

Conrad, or puts them back into the old histories to which they belong; and the lunatic hope which the new moon expresses for the future is the 'poet's' final answer to both the dead certainties of his Johnsonian epigraph and the 'reckless lunacy' of Lord Jim.

Chapter Glossary

Augustan: of poetry, that of the later-seventeenth and first half of the eighteenth centuries. The boundaries are ragged and variable, but in schemata 'Augustan' follows 'Restoration' and is followed (after a gap) by 'Romantic'. The term derives from the Roman age of the Emperor Augustus, and hence is self-consciously imperialistic; the most obvious formal feature of Augustan poetry is the prevalence of closed heroic couplets.

Bardolatry: the worship of Shakespeare.

Historikerstreit: German, literally 'the battle of historians'; a sharp debate beginning in 1986–7 initially about whether it was acceptable to argue that the story of the Wehrmacht's defence of Germany's Eastern Front in 1944–5 deserved to be told as a tragedy. The principal figures involved were Ernst Nolte, Andreas Hillgruber, and Jürgen Habermas.

Intertextuality: generally, the relations between texts; more specifically, the aspects of a given text which derive meaning from relations with another text or texts.

Metaphysical: of poetry, that of the later sixteenth and first half of the seventeenth centuries; characterized by complex stanza forms and arguments, and by elaborate comparisons (or *conceits*).

Mise-en-page: the actual layout of a given poem (or prose text) on a given page.

Romantic: of poetry, that of the later eighteenth and first half of the nineteenth centuries; a part of the general Romantic movement, a reaction against the Enlightenment, such poetry is characteristically vigorous, formally innovative, and concerned with nature and subjective emotion.

'Value-free' history: history supposedly written objectively, without ideological selection or emphasis of material; presently regarded as a chimæra.

Victorian: of poetry, literally that written during the reign of Victoria (1837–1901), but used in schemata of literary history to fill the gap between 'Romantic' and 'Modernist' poetry.

Biography

Critics and theorists who dismiss history often have equally little time for that particular form of history which is an author's biography. This 'death of the author' has been often proclaimed, and its classic statement was made by the American 'New Critics' W. K. Wimsatt and M. C. Beardsley in 'The Intentional Fallacy' (1946):

> The poem is not the critic's own and not the author's (it is detached from the author at birth and goes about the world beyond his [*sic*] power to intend about it or control it). The poem belongs to the public. It is embodied in language, the peculiar possession of the public, and it is about the human being, an object of public knowledge. What is said about the poem is subject to the same scrutiny as any statement in linguistics or in the general science of psychology.[1]

The extreme version of this is the argument that the reader-critic should not be bothered in any way with the identity, experience, or intention of the author, a point-of-view most associated with Roland Barthes (who in 1968 coined the phrase 'the death of the author').[2] At the same time a different question was posed by Michel Foucault: 'What is an author?' (1969)[3] examined the cultural and commercial function of labelling texts with a name, and asked how the practice of ascribing (most) texts affects readers.

Again, a sound basic point is being made: Wimsatt, Beardsley, Barthes, and Foucault were all reacting against the ingrained habits of *expressionist* criticism,[4] which regarded a poem as expressing the inten-

[1] In W. K. Wimsatt, Jr., *The Verbal Icon* (1954) and David Lodge (ed.), *20th Century Literary Criticism: A Reader* (London and New York: Longman, 1972).

[2] In an essay of that name (1968), most readily available in various anthologies of criticism, such as David Lodge (ed.), *Modern Criticism and Theory: A Reader* (London and New York: Longman, 1988), or Dennis Walder (ed.), *Literature in the Modern World: Critical Essays and Documents* (Oxford and New York: Oxford University Press, 1990). Barthes was partly echoing Nietzsche's "*Gott ist tot*", 'God is dead'.

[3] Reprinted in Lodge, *Modern Criticism and Theory*.

[4] Beware! 'Expressionism' is not, in this context, the same thing as in art history or in drama.

tion of the author, and as somehow determined and limited by that intention. At its worst such biographically-driven criticism is completely ludicrous, and speculatively relates minute details of texts to spurious reconstructions of lives without judgement or scruple: a good example is the endless pursuit of who the 'lovely boy' and the 'dark lady' of Shakespeare's sonnets 'really' were, as if knowing that (supposing we could know that for certain) would somehow 'solve' the literary problems posed by the dense complexity of Shakespeare's sequence. Even watered-down versions of this expressionism will not do, though, for the underlying principle is fundamentally in error. Whatever one's beliefs about Salman Rushdie and *The Satanic Verses*, events have shown very clearly that what an author intends readers to understand, and what readers do understand, are not necessarily the same thing; and that it may not be good enough, when they diverge, for the author to say 'But what I meant was . . .'. What is true of intention in this extreme case is true in every case, and no work can have its meaning fixed by intention.

There is also a good question as to how one knows what the author's intentions were. If the author is alive one might ask, but without going so far as to think they might lie, it would be naïve to take an answer at face value: any number of reasons, including the sheer complexity of artistic 'intention', make even the fullest statement of intent at best partial. If the author is dead, perhaps long dead, intention becomes even more difficult to discover and to interpret. It must be accepted, therefore, that absolute knowledge of intent cannot be obtained, and that such partial knowledge as may be obtainable must be treated with great caution.

It is also plainly and obviously true that art is not necessarily autobiography. In drama, most evidently, an author presents an argument or a view in distinct voices; one character may to a much greater extent than others be a mouthpiece for the author, but character and author are never simple equivalents. Many novels are also constructed from dialogue as well as narration, and again the views of characters and narrators (especially unreliable narrators) cannot be easily attributed directly to authors. So too in poetry; and a poem does not have to be a dramatic monologue supposedly spoken by an individual for there to be an appreciable gap between the poet (as historical documents and biography might reveal them) and the *persona* who appears to write (or to speak) a particular poem. Different critics make this distinction in different ways: some refer to the persona, while I personally distinguish the *poet* (say, William Wordsworth, 1770–1850) from the '*poet*', the rhetorically constructed persona inferred from a given poem (say, the 'individual' designated by 'I' and 'me' in *The Prelude*). How exactly you signal the distinction doesn't much matter; but that you do signal it, and remember it in reading, is vital.

With all these difficulties of biographical criticism noted, however, there are equally severe problems and inconsistencies in the arguments of those who wish to ignore biography. It is not at all clear why the manifest problem with interpreting a statement of intention makes it preferable to ignore such statements altogether, or why difficulties with authorial intention justify the wholesale ditching of biographical enquiry. Just as all poems must have been written at a particular historical moment, so they must have been written by a particular person, whose nationality, age, education, experiences, and so forth, will partly determine what poems, and what kinds of poem, they can and do write. It is of course possible to abuse biographical criticism, and to use it abusively, as it is possible to abuse and be abusive with other theories; but something is not rendered of no value because it can be abused.

To turn to some examples, consider Coleridge's 'The Rime of the Ancient Mariner' (O2.238/N744). Given the supernatural story no-one would suppose the poem autobiographical, and the knowledge that in its first appearance[5] a part of Coleridge's intention was to revive balladic poetry, while interesting, is very secondary. What does interest me is the knowledge that when he wrote it Coleridge had never been to sea, and though he had lived in harbour-towns does not seem ever to have been aboard a ship: in other words, the extensive knowledge and powerful evocation of sea-life were wholly generated from his reading of sea-stories. When I first discovered this (from John Livingston Lowes's *The Road to Xanadu*) I could barely credit it, and went back to the poem with an astonished admiration for the fertile coherence of Coleridge's imagination: but as I re-read I realized that if Coleridge had had first-hand experience of a long voyage he would have written a different poem. The knowledge that he was imagining everything in the poem, rather than remembering something and adding imagination to the memory, was of material assistance in seeing, as I read, how the poem was shaped, and in understanding how Coleridge had been able to eliminate any barrier or discontinuity between the unusual (such as killing an albatross) and the supernatural (the consequences of that killing).

[5] In Wordsworth's and Coleridge's joint volume *Lyrical Ballads*, 1798; a revised version appeared in 1800.

Other examples abound, as varied in their nature and importance as the lives and works of poets. The course of Donne's poetry from the secular to the sacred has a powerful analogue in his career, culminating in his appointment as Dean of St Paul's; Milton's 'When I Consider How My Light Is Spent' (O1.1220/N378) must puzzle those unwilling to remember his blindness, and both that physical handicap and his political career as a Republican play very interestingly against *Paradise Lost*; Smart's *Jubilate Agno* (O1.2217/N625) is movingly illuminated by the knowledge of his confinement to an asylum; and Hopkins's 'No Worst, There Is None' (O2.1472/N1065) and Roethke's 'In a Dark Time' (N1393) are both deepened by knowledge of the battles with mania and despair which those poets faced.

The importance of biography, like that of history, can range from the immediate and self-evident to the broad and general influence of background, as John Clare's rural life stands behind his rural poems (O2.571/N822). But even if a poem is evidently and explicitly written in response to a particular experience, as Tennyson's 'In Memoriam A. H. H.' (O2.1226/N899) repeatedly declares itself the product of grief for Arthur Hallam, the nature of the response is not always straightforward. Tennyson's great sequence of poems was written over some seventeen years, and the poems vary in length; but all use the same stanza, arch-rhymed quatrains in iambic tetrameter, and the continuity of form is part and parcel of the poem's dominant concern with unremitting grief. Look through the selections from 'In Memoriam' in the *Norton* or *Oxford* anthologies and the importance of form is apparent: the arch-rhyme (*abba*) makes each stanza self-contained, ending in a closure that looks backward; and in many lines the symmetry of rhyme is reflected in a central cæsura splitting the line symmetrically 2–2. Both are prosodic expressions of the rocking movement of grief, back and forth; and one could say that the continuity of form expresses the persistence of Tennyson's grief; but it might be the other way around. Tennyson's grief was remarkably prolonged, and he wrote the earliest of the 'In Memoriam' poems within a few days of hearing that Hallam was dead. In them the form, and the grieving rock of the lines and quatrains, is from the first fully achieved: so the question becomes whether Tennyson instinctively divined the form that he would need for the extended grief he was just entering, or whether the form he seized upon in his first grief came to trap him within that grief, and to prolong its grip on him. Its prosody and form give to 'In Memoriam' a curtness which contains the grief, preventing it from dissipating and keeping it warm; had Tennyson written instead, say, an heroic elegy for

Hallam, rhetorically trumpeting his grief, the grief might have been cooled, or been cathartically discharged, so much the sooner. Tennyson's form and his history of grief are entwined, and if one was cause and one effect it is not in the least obvious which is which.

A final and most pointed example is offered by Geoffrey Hill's 'September Song' (N1721), one of the very few poems in English to treat responsibly and honourably the terrible subject of the *Sho'ah*. As one would expect, the poem is not an easy one: its subtitle, "BORN 19.6.32 – DEPORTED 24.9.42", and the reference to Zyklon, the lethal poison used in the gas chambers of the extermination camps, make it clear that the poem is about a child victim of the Nazis; but the exact thought of the poem is difficult to follow without a piece of biographical information (which the Norton editors supply), that Hill was himself born on the 18th June, 1932, one day before the birthdate of his imagined victim. What this knowledge clarifies is that Hill does not simply mourn the child whose murder he imagines, but ponders also the chance that placed his own birth safely in England, and the other child's birth the next day fatally in Germany or one of the countries which Germany had, by 1942, invaded. No responsibility for the murder can lie at Hill's door, but as a human being he found himself nevertheless possessed by the guilt of being a survivor (his first volume was *For the Unfallen*), and as a poet he found the need to express as best he could his commingled senses of gratitude, pity, horror, and anger—senses which were fuelled not only by his imagination of the child's death, but by his knowledge of his own life. He had therefore to incorporate himself into the poem, but needed to do so in a way that did not displace from the centre of the poem the child who died, for to displace the true victim would be to slide from an expression of pity to an impression of self-pity. One of the ways he found of doing this was to place his own use of the word 'I' in parenthesis (see p. 66 above), and another was the oblique relation of the subtitle to his own birthdate, unstated in the poem, but readily available to any reader who cares to investigate. In any poem such a procedure would challenge those who would dismiss biography, and in a poem of this stature, achieving this kind of moral probity, it is a challenge which to my mind cannot be answered.

'Nearing Forty'

As a St Lucian creole, spiritually tenter-hooked between European and African inheritances but offered by politics and history a chance of an independent St Lucian and West Indian identity painted by both continents, Walcott's whole work has been of necessity deeply autobiographical. At the largest scale this preoccupation was expressed in his verse autobiography *Another Life* (1972); but there are many lesser levels, attested by the recurrence of St Lucian place-names throughout his work (the Roseau Valley, Castries, Gros Ilet), and by protagonists like Shabine in 'The Schooner *Flight*' (from *The Star-apple Kingdom*, 1979) who share Walcott's mixed racial and cultural inheritances. The 'I' of a Walcott poem (even of *Another Life*) cannot be simplistically identified with Walcott himself, as if the poem were an interview—even here there is a 'poet' as well as Walcott the poet—but neither can it be pretended that there is no connection between poet and 'poet'.

The autobiography of 'Nearing Forty' begins with its title, for the poem was first published in *The Gulf* in 1969, the year before Walcott's fortieth birthday: so the poem does express one aspect of his response to his (as the cliché has it) mid-life crisis, the moments at which one recognizes oneself as middle-aged, with half or more than half of one's life already lived. This may be obvious, but it is not therefore unimportant: consider what it would mean to discover that Walcott had written the poem at the age of twenty, or at the age of eighty—everything would be changed. Two of the canonical poems which most vividly evoke the experience of age, Tennyson's 'Tithonus' (O2.1204/N909) and Eliot's 'The Love Song of J. Alfred Prufrock' (O2.1971/N1230), were written by poets still in their twenties,[6] and knowledge of the astonishing discrepancy between what they could then have known and what they imagined presses on the reading of those poems. It is equally important to know that no such oddity attends 'Nearing Forty', that the poet and the 'poet' were both nearing forty and that the poem could therefore draw as much on experience as on imagination.

The epigraph, and the literary histories implicit in the poem, are

[6] Strictly speaking, the young Tennyson wrote 'Tithon', and an older Tennyson revised this to become the 'Tithonus' that is now famous.

biographical testimonies of a different sort: to Walcott's education, and to his deep and wide reading. It may have been an imperial and colonial education, and in those ways politically compromised, but it was by Western standards a thorough and classically-grounded education that provided access to a rich tradition of letters which Walcott's work began by imitating, and has now joined. Most recently and astonishingly he has in *Omeros* (1990: N1716) insisted on the similarity of the Mediterranean and Caribbean archipelagoes, mapping the Homeric heroes of the *Iliad* onto St Lucian fishermen and staring down any objections from less imaginative classical scholars; in the following year he restated his point in an equally creolized Homeric drama, *The Odyssey*, premièred by the Royal Shakespeare Company at Stratford. But for a West Indian of Walcott's age the journey from St Lucia to Stratford has been no easy matter: in a *South Bank Show* devoted to him, Walcott remarked that while his own experience of colonialism was largely benign,[7] he was nevertheless aware of being of a generation of West Indian poets who hesitated on the verge of writing down the words 'mango' or 'breadfruit' because they were conscious that these tropical trees could not have the same literary dignity and importance as an oak in Shakespeare's Warwickshire. The remark reveals the way in which even a poet of the greatest talent, if they are of colonial birth, can be intimidated as well as enriched by an induction into the imperial mother tongue and literature; and how, in Walcott's generation, which faced and celebrated West Indian independence, that intimidation was confronted by a nascent nationalism which demanded to know why a mango was not as good as any oak. The work of younger West Indian artists, and of younger black writers in the UK and the US—reggae singers, dub poets, and rappers, for example—tends to show that nationalism with far more overt aggression than Walcott's work: which is poetically neither better nor worse, but is different, and reflects a generational difference of attitudes. Other poems of Walcott's deal with these matters more explicitly, but they are relevant to 'Nearing Forty', in the background they provide to Walcott's severe self-judgement, and because the poem is, unobtrusively but suggestively, West Indian.

[7] He mentioned specifically memories of a village policeman whose hat the village schoolboys would knock off when they could, but who was more-or-less polite to the boys even so, and drew a contrast with Gendarmes in Martinique and 'South American cops'. Throughout this part of the interview Walcott was at pains to make it clear that he was talking specifically of his personal experience in St Lucia, and was quite aware both of the horrors of the historical record and that many of his contemporaries had experiences quite different from his own.

To me, as a British reader, the most obvious Caribbean references are the dedication to John Figueroa (a distinguished West Indian educator and poet), the image of the "year's end rain", and the "louvre's gap". The noisiness of the rain and the domestic architecture suggested by its audibility and by the louvres, the presence of a bedsheet but not a blanket, do not suggest to me an English climate but a tropical rainy season, cooler but still warm, agriculturally essential but often emotionally oppressive. But at least one Jamaican reader[8] finds the poem insidiously British, full of talk about the weather and fears of a persistent dampness which is anything but West Indian. For this reader, who like Walcott has had to leave the Caribbean in pursuit of education and employment, the poem's distinction between happier memories of youth and a present rainy melancholia spoke of an island childhood, when it not only seemed but usually was sunny, and of time spent as an adult in Britain, almost always feeling cold and often getting wet in the endless and miserable rain—yet the longing to return to the Caribbean is qualified by the same desires that forced departure, the appreciation that though paradisal it is also constricting. These feelings I believe Walcott to share, and if the hot island of childhood is a former colony of the cold country of adulthood such feelings are not only emotional and physical, but also political and ideological. A truly hostile reading of 'Nearing Forty' could argue that in endorsing a stoical and clerkish acceptance of rainy days as maturer and wiser than sunny juvenile imaginings, Walcott reflects the old imperial argument that tropical peoples, living carelessly in their permanent sun, needed looking after by Englishmen who knew how to get things done on time and whatever the weather. So far as I am aware this particular poem has not been so criticized, but Walcott has been attacked by some West Indian critics and readers (notably the poet Kamau Brathwaite: N1690) for looking too much to his European learning and too little to his African inheritance; and to someone who did believe that his other work and career outside the Caribbean left Walcott vulnerable to a charge of slighting Africa, 'Nearing Forty' would also be vulnerable to political attack on the grounds that its engagement with Johnson and Shakespeare, like its preoccupation with rain, exclude engagements with African traditions and a tropical climate which are equally a part of Walcott's life.

Such an argument would, however, have to confront also the intertextual presence of Conrad's *Lord Jim*, and could seize upon the

[8] Dr Francis Ingledew of Fairleigh Dickinson University, to whom I am indebted.

presence in Egström's account of Jim of the "frightened niggers" whom Jim is reported to have kicked (see pp. 153–4 above). The association of Walcott's "water clerk" with Jim brings with it Jim's dependence on a brutal and racist society, and his dramatization as the white man who gets things done, which interlocks with the argument about inadequate blackness, and the charge that Walcott has somehow curried white favour and canonical admission by cleaving to his European inheritance at the expense of his African one. The name of Conrad is a double-edged sword, though; for the novelist's name at birth was not Joseph Conrad but Konrad Korzeniowski, and he was not a spuriously privileged imperial Englishman but a naturalized Pole (most of Poland then belonging to Russia) who (like all good sailors) worked his way up the nautical ranks. One might also argue that Conrad called it as he saw it, and no-one who has read *The Nigger of the* Narcissus (1897) could believe that its author would use the word 'nigger' careless of the prejudice which possesses it. Nor does Walcott do so, in his own direct uses of the word, as in 'The Schooner *Flight*'.[9] As a professional sailor exploring an acquired Britishness, and (like Walcott) in transit between the tropics and colder latitudes for much of his life, Conrad is not easy to press into service for any prosecution of Walcott.

I do not myself believe that, either in 'Nearing Forty' or anywhere else, the prosecution has so much as a leg to stand on. The poem's rain seems to me Caribbean rather than English, and Walcott to negotiate on equal terms with his epigraph and constituent forms, ruefully aware of Johnson's limitations as well as those of "greenhorns at school" (23), accommodating Conrad to his own ends, and in general manipulating and qualifying his British literary inheritance to achieve a resolution which cannot be accommodated by a polemical and personalized reading. But in considering a poem biographically it is usually necessary to do more than to consider it on its own, for although to us, as readers, it may be isolated on the page, its composition was for the poet an act of creation among other acts of creation; and it may well make more sense to consider a poetic career volume by volume than poem by poem. Some indication of how 'Nearing Forty' parallels other poems in *The Gulf* is given by Lloyd Brown in *West Indian Poetry* (2nd edn, 1984). To deal with the problem of the poetic 'I' that is and is not Walcott, he refers to that 'I' as "Walcott's poet":

---

[9] First published in *The Star-Apple Kingdom* (1979), this important poem may also be found in Walcott's *Collected poems 1948–84*. The protagonist, Shabine, explicitly refers to himself several times as a "red nigger", i.e. someone of visibly mixed racial inheritance. See also N1711.

> In [. . .] *The Gulf*, Walcott's poet is marked by an even greater sense of isolation [than in previous volumes]. And this greater isolation is paralleled by the divisions, or gulfs, which the poet himself perceives in the world around him. [. . .] The poet's personal sense of alienation and separation is [. . .] a private extension of the divisions which he sees in the world of the 1960's: the Vietnamese War ("Postcards"), racial violence in the United States ("Blues"), and the civil war in Nigeria ("Negatives"). The gulf is everywhere, compelling our awareness of the very real divisions which mock our most passionate attempts at unity or intimacy [. . .].
>
> The Caribbean landscape itself reflects the human gulf. [. . .] And the prospects for the future are not reassuring: "The Gulf, your gulf, is daily widening."

I for one would count a poem like 'Nearing Forty', ruthlessly self-judgemental but fighting hard in its content to reach a personal and philosophical accommodation with ageing, and in its form to reach a literary and political accommodation with Walcott's precursors in the imperial canon, among "our most passionate attempts at unity or intimacy": but the attempt would not be needed were it not for the gulfs, between its "I" and "you", and (more severely) between the younger "I", the greenhorn schoolchild, callow but passionately hopeful, and the older "I" whose passions have been withered by sleeplessness and knowledge. What unity can be hoped to bridge the gulfs between nations if nations themselves are internally divided? if individual citizens feel divided from their own former selves? Yet Walcott found that his life, genes, culture, nation, and times made him painfully aware of such gulfs echoing on many scales; and that is in part what 'Nearing Forty' reports.

This barely begins the investigations that biographical knowledge might prompt or assist;[10] and even the attention liable to be paid to Walcott now that he is a Nobel Laureate will only be able to deal partially with this aspect of his work—for the simple reason that he is still alive and has, like us all, a right to privacy. After an author's death such materials as letters and diaries are regarded as fair game for critics, and some authors go to great lengths to destroy these materials, or to

[10] There is as yet no literary biography, but the interested reader may begin with the verse autobiography, *Another Life*, and continue with Walcott's astonishing and beautiful Nobel address, *The Antilles: Fragments of Epic Memory* (New York and London: Farrar, Straus & Giroux/Faber and Faber, 1992). See also the Further Reading.

interdict their use for a specified period by leaving them to libraries under binding legal conditions. These wishes should by and large be respected: but it is equally natural, if an author's work has been moving or of real importance to a reader, to want to know more about the person behind the words, and to try to deepen an understanding of how the words relate to the life that prompted them and the mind that arranged them in that way.

Chapter Glossary

Expressionist: of criticism, believing the meaning of a text to express and to be determined by the author's intentions. (The term has other meanings in art history and theatre studies.)

Persona: an alternative for 'poet'.

Poet: as distinct from 'poet', the actual historical person; the author.

'Poet': as distinct from poet (without single inverted commas), the supposed writer or speaker of a given text; the rhetorical construct designated by 'I' or 'me'. Also referred to as the 'persona'.

Gender

As biography is one aspect of history, so gender is of biography: but it is also much more than that, and while historically and biographically oriented criticisms have been strongly challenged, gender studies have been of growing importance. *Feminist* critics have pointed to the inequalities and iniquities of the traditional canon, overwhelmingly dominated by male writers selected by male critics; to the suppression and exclusion of female voices, experience and history by the use of male-forged criteria of excellence; and to the need both for the positive, separate consideration of women's writing, and for the inclusion of that writing in general teaching and research.

These allegations cannot be denied: to examine the contents page of any non-feminist anthology, or scan the poetry shelves in a library or bookshop, is to see how persistently and systematically the work of women is underrepresented. The *Oxford Anthology* is particularly weak in its representation of women: in total there are no women in volume 1 (in 128 selections) and six in volume 2 (in 94 selections); after Dorothy Wordsworth, the only female writers included are Christina Rossetti (7 poems; O2.1426), Elizabeth Barrett Browning (1 poem; O2.1477), Emily Brontë (2 poems; O2.1482), Edith Sitwell (1 poem; O2.2117), and Stevie Smith (1 poem; O2.2171). The *Norton*'s brief is wider, in that it includes American writers, but the editors, two of whom are women (itself a cogent testimony to Norton's sensibilities), also clearly have a completely different and positive approach to the importance of representing women. Seventy-nine female poets are included, ranging from Anne Askew (N128) in the sixteenth century to Cynthia Zarin (N1880) in the twentieth; and no century is allowed to seem a male preserve. It is true that a significant number of these women are nineteenth- or twentieth-century, and many are American or Canadian born, but one might have thought that Plath, at least, would pass the *Oxford* editors' criteria (they included Ted Hughes, Plath's husband); and even granting that the *Oxford* (1973) is earlier than the *Norton* (1996), and so less influenced by feminist debates, one may well ask why the *Oxford* wholly omits the British poets Felicia Hemans, Charlotte Mew, Mary Coleridge, Vita Sackville-West, Mina Loy, Sylvia Townsend Warner, Kathleen Raine, Elizabeth Jennings, and Karen Gershon.

Less prejudiced anthologization is one answer to *phallocracy*, the rule of the *phallus*,[1] and an important one, but as many women who might have written were either prevented or discouraged from doing so, and much never-published work written by women has been lost, it will never be possible wholly to redress the balance for past centuries; yet there is a great deal of work by women which can be recovered, from libraries, periodicals, and private collections. A start has been made, and there are now fascinating anthologies of women's writing from the seventeenth and eighteenth centuries, which challenge critical orthodoxies and platitudes, and greatly enrich the understanding of literary history and of the suffering to which women have been subjected. More anthologies and individual studies will follow, and as more women fight for and gain access to the power structures of society and academia the balance should begin to be redressed.

On this ground almost all can agree; and there is fairly widespread acceptance of the need to find alternatives to the once ubiquitous use of 'men' and 'his' as equivalents of 'people' and 'her'; but some of the theories which feminist critics have advanced about the nature of female and male writing are much more controversial, and as hotly disputed by women as by men. In particular, critics such as Julia Kristeva and Luce Irigaray, who have founded their work upon Freudian or Lacanian theories of language and gender acquisition, and Mary Daly, the American feminist theologian best known for her book *Gyn/Ecology* (1978),[2] have raised radical questions about gendered language. That women and men write about different subjects, have differing emotional concerns, and analyse with differing priorities is plain enough; and very recent magnetic resonance images of electrical patterns in the brains of men and women simultaneously doing the same task suggest that some of these differences may become neuroanatomically mappable: but do men and women write differently in the sense of employing language in a fundamentally different way? are there such

[1] To a Freudian or Lacanian the phallus is not identical with the penis, but its ideological counterpart. The proverbial phrase 'She wears the trousers' does in effect credit the female partner in a relationship with a phallus, but it does not imply that she has a penis.

[2] Mary Daly, *Gyn/Ecology: The Metaethics of Radical Feminism* (Boston: Beacon Press, 1978).

things as male and female language? and is it the case that in order to end patriarchal oppression women must develop a new language, because the old language, English as it now is, is in fact a male creation saturated with an inalienable maleness that has encoded within it misogynistic and oppressive structures? On these issues there is very little consensus, and the views which different feminists take on them often relate closely to their wider political and gender-political views, to whether, for example, they are *liberal* or *separatist* feminists, seeking co-operation with and from men or spurning such co-operation as compromise and betrayal.

What is worth noting, though, is the extent to which these kinds of questions assume a binary opposition of 'men vs women', the opposition of anatomical *sex* rather than of cultural *gender*. Almost everybody is, genetically and anatomically, either *male* or *female* at birth; but almost everybody acquires as they grow up both *masculine* and *feminine* characteristics, and the individual's combination of masculinity and femininity in their being—personal, sexual, vocational, and professional—constitutes their gender. In consequence, although the oppression of women and women's writing is the single largest concern of gender studies, the power and importance of the discipline is not identical with the power and interest of feminism: the oppression and writings of gays and lesbians are also beginning to be recovered, and explored, and the representation or concealment of homoeroticism within canonical works re-examined. The legacies of Freud and the early sexologists, particularly Havelock Ellis, and the later work of Michel Foucault on the histories of sexuality, have opened up to literary debate an enormous area of the human psyche, awareness of which presents a substantial challenge to traditional reading to complement and sometimes to qualify the challenge of feminism. What <u>are</u> the consequences for reading of the simple but bizarre fact that while (in Britain as elsewhere) the practice of male homosexuality has until recently been both a statutory crime and a moral sin, lesbianism has never been criminalized[3] and so rarely fulminated against as to have been ignored? What if any particular qualities are typical of male characters created by lesbian authors, or female characters by gay authors? What can study of the writings of oppressed, and of liberated, women and homosexuals teach us about how and why they continue to be oppressed or became liberated, and about how other groups are likely

[3] Queen Victoria was supposedly so incredulous at the inclusion of a paragraph on lesbianism in an 1885 bill criminalizing private homosexual acts that she refused to sign the bill into law until the paragraph was deleted.

to be persecuted? And what can we learn about the persecutors, who as much as the persecuted are all among us? There are some signs of an emergent *masculinism*, a movement focusing on the oppression of men, often by men: the commonest theme of first plays by men is school bullying, undoubtedly a problem as endemic in Britain as the binge alcoholism that puts a million young male drunks on the street in competitive groups every Friday and Saturday night. This saturating male–male violence will not be lessened by any masculinism less powerful and resilient than feminism has proved itself, and it will have to reach a long way beyond the study of poetry; but as a man who desires the reform of maleness I have found literature, and especially the poetry uncovered by feminist and gender studies, a necessary study.

As the wide range of these issues would suggest, literary gender criticism is complex and variable, but one point worth noting is that it remains very hard to escape dealing with the issues in highly polarized terms. The shift from 'male vs female' to 'feminine and masculine' is a move away from a rigid binary polarity (black/white) towards a fluid scale (greys): but the old polarity often creeps back into gender criticism in other ways (rigid/fluid; straight/gay; butch/femme; anal/oral; and so on). These oppositions may often be useful prompts to thinking, but the more sharply they are polarized the less helpful they are likely to be; and in reading gender studies it is usually worth examining how flexibly (or otherwise) the critic's categories are conceived and applied. The discipline is recent, and still very much in its early and exploratory stages, so it is no surprise that there is as yet little consensus; and with so many ideas in the air this flexibility test is a helpful rule-of-thumb.

Problematically, the mode of technical analytical thinking in which practical criticism is grounded is felt by some feminists to be itself patriarchal. The most obvious target is the use of the words *feminine* and *masculine* to describe different rhymes and metrical line-endings; and there is a correspondence, readily imaginable in the terms of sexist stereotypes, between the heavy tread of a masculine ending or rhyme, and the pittering pat of a feminine one.[4] This is sexist, but it is also changing—I have preferred to write of stressed and unstressed hyperbeats or rhyme—and it is not (as it would be in French, or any language

[4] Cf. Sir John Suckling, 'A Ballad upon a Wedding', 43–45: "Her feet beneath her petticoat, / Like little mice, stole in and out / As if they feared the light": N410.

with a full-blown system of grammatical gender) obviously a part of a large-scale and systematic sexism inscribed through the technical terminology of the discipline. A spondee is in English neither masculine nor feminine, the spondee not *le* or *la* spondee, and in and of itself the term may be applied as neutrally by a man as a woman, and to the word 'female' as much as to the word 'macho'; but the force of the accusation that practical criticism is intrinsically patriarchal lies less in specifics than in the contrast of a supposedly male analytical, divisive mode with a supposedly female fluid and unifying mode. There is some truth in that contrast, particularly in its development by French feminists into an *écriture feminine*, a mode of writing that finds new ways of writing femininity and the female body into texts; but when I encounter it used as a critical (rather than as a creative[5]) tool it often produces what strike me as very limited results. Applying the flexibility test suggests this is at least partly because it tends to be applied very rigidly, and so to drift away from the idea of masculine and feminine aspects or forms of writing (which is interesting) towards the predetermined opposition of the writings of male and female authors (which usually isn't).

One specific argument with which I know I disagree is the idea of gendered punctuation—specifically, that Emily Dickinson's use of dashes is in some way feminine, and that the popularity of the dash among more recent female poets confirms this. As an argument this simply does not stand up: not only because Dickinson's dashes may have been falsely transcribed and standardized (see p. 69 above); nor even because there is every likelihood that the more recent poets are imitating Dickinson rather than simply demonstrating their femininity; but because the facts that Dickinson is far and away the best-known poet to rely so heavily on the dash, and that she is of the greatest importance as a female and as a feminist poet, do not add up to anything. Until and unless other probable influences on Dickinson's punctuation—such as who taught her, her religious life and education (unexpectedly but consistently an influence on the practice of punctuation), and the mores of her culture and times—can be discounted, it is foolish to conclude that her dashes and her femininity are causally related.

[5] The best *écritures feminines* I know are the brilliant essays by Hélène Cixous, particularly 'The Laugh of the Medusa' and 'Coming to Writing', but it does not seem to me chance that her primary subject is her own experience rather than a pre-existing literary text. For the best translations (and the only ones to try to preserve Cixous's wonderful puns, *d'hommicile fixe* becoming 'perMANent address') see Hélène Cixous, *Coming to Writing & Other Essays*, ed. Deborah Jensen (Cambridge, Mass. and London: Harvard University Press, 1991).

It is of course true that a poem may seem overtly by a male writer or overtly by a female writer, in ways that may have to do with the sex and gender of the reader as well as of the poet. But that seeming is usually an effect of the poem as a whole, and commonly lost in the analytical dismemberment of the poem essential to other aspects of practical criticism. As a result, it is difficult to point to specific features of the poem which make it seem male or female; rather, one winds up discussing the content, the subject and the approach to that subject, as it is embodied in the whole work. There is, of course, nothing wrong with that—but it is easy for discussions of that kind to lose their analytical edge and become impressionistic. An instructive example for me was a question in a 1993 Cambridge examination paper, which asked candidates to compare an anonymous poem of 1740, 'Epitaph on a Child Killed by a Procured Abortion', with Gwendolin Brooks's 1945 poem 'The Mother', beginning "Abortions will not let you forget.". The sixty or seventy answers that I marked showed two pronounced traits: the assumption that both poems were honestly autobiographical[6] (involving the assumptions that the anonymous author was the woman who had the abortion, and that Brooks was writing of her own multiple abortions), and an absolute refusal to express any personal moral opinion, 'pro-life', 'pro-choice', or uncertain, about the actual abortions which were assumed to be honestly reported. The assumption of autobiography, the identification of 'poet' with poet, though emotionally understandable, is naïve, and in their answers to other questions most candidates showed themselves fully aware of the need not to make such an identification carelessly, and to beware of rhetorical manipulation and deception; but the refusal to express personal opinions is a different matter. Many undergraduates have told me that they were instructed at school never to use the word 'I' in practical criticism: it is not a word to be used often, and as a teacher I can understand what prompts the prohibition—but that prohibition is nonsense all the same. The emotional and critical response to those poems of any candidate, male or female, who has from experience or belief acquired strong views about abortion, will be affected by those views; and while exam discipline requires that candidates respond to the poems without writing a polemic, the attempt to construct a written response from which personal morality and emotion have been excluded is futile and limiting. To point to a poetic intensity created by metre or rhyme does

[6] In other words, the 'poet' (writer-speaker) was wholly identified with the poet (author).

not require the critic to identify themselves, but a written answer as a whole is a personal as well as a critical document, and much the best answers that I marked were those in which the candidate-critic had been willing to *inscribe* themselves, to write themselves as individuals into their answers, and to acknowledge that these poems drew from them passionate as well as watchful reactions. Some of these more forthright candidates were men, some women, but all had to acknowledge that their own sex was one ground of their response, in that only women can have abortions, and that their personal experiences of abortion (or, as it happened in all cases, lack of experience) and gendered views on abortion were other grounds. In these (and perhaps in all) matters the *politics of representation*, the ways in which each gender writes and reads itself and other genders, are inescapable, and best acknowledged.

In the same way I believe that the notion of the study of gender in literature should include the study of how gender affects the reading of literature, which foregrounds the identity (including the sex and gender) of the reader as much as that of the author; and I also believe that the way forward for the gender-conscious study of poetry is the inclusion within practical critical responses of the critic's gender as well as the continued search for the ways in which texts and language may be intrinsically or intentionally gendered.

Amidst all this debate and uncertainty it would be nice to find some truly common ground, and such statistical and linguistic facts as are known are set out by David Crystal in *The Cambridge Encyclopedia of Language*. Having discussed Japanese, where there are clearly differentiated male, female, and sex-neutral forms of speech, Crystal says:

> In English, the situation is less clear. There are no grammatical forms, lexical items, or patterns of pronunciation that are used exclusively by one sex, but there are several differences in frequency. For example, among the words and phrases that women are supposed to use more often are such emotive adjectives as *super* and *lovely*, exclamations such as *Goodness me* and *Oh dear*, and intensifiers such as *so* or *such* (e.g. *It was so busy*). This use of intensifiers has been noted in several languages, including German, French, and Russian.
>
> More important are the strategies adopted by the two sexes in cross-sex conversation. Women have been found to ask more questions, make more use of positive and encouraging 'noises' (such as *mhm*), use a wider intonational range and a more marked rhythmic-

al stress, and make greater use of the pronouns *you* and *we*. By contrast, men are much more likely to interrupt (more than three times as much, in some studies), to dispute what has been said, to ignore or respond poorly to what has been said, to introduce more new topics into the conversation, and to make more declarations of fact or opinion.

Most interpretations of these differences refer to the contrasting social rôles of the sexes in modern society. Men are seen to reflect in their conversational dominance the power they have traditionally received from society; women, likewise, exercise the supporting rôle that they have been taught to adopt—in this case, helping the conversation along and providing men with opportunities to express this dominance. The situation is undoubtedly more complex than this, as neither sex is linguistically homogenous, and considerable variation exists when real contexts of use are studied. The danger, as some commentators have pointed out, is that in the process of criticizing old sexual stereotypes, researchers are in danger of creating new ones.[7]

The very factors which sustain such linguistic differences in speech, and in cross-sex conversation, may inhibit them in poetry, often an uniquely intense and private mode of engagement with language; but it is reasonable to expect some relationship between the characteristic patterns of an individual's social speech and poetry, so it is worth asking whether any of the features Crystal identifies are reflected in male and female poetries. This is something the reader must decide for themselves; but my own belief is that there is evidence in the work of Dickinson (N1010), Elizabeth Bishop (N1409), Josephine Miles, Gwendolyn Brooks (N1479), Denise Levertov (N1571), Adrienne Rich (N1679), Sylvia Plath (N1728), and Amy Clampitt (N1503), of a quality of uninterrupted good listening (and good looking), unexpectedly and pleasingly free of opinionated assertion, which is a significant factor in generating the readerly sense that one is reading the work of a woman and not that of a man.

There is also, patently, a differentiation of subject-matter and points of view which reflects the common gender-differences in male and female biographies, and is probably clearest in the relations of the poetic voice to the domestic *roomscape* (the indoor 'landscape') and the public sphere. Patriarchal and misogynistic constructions of the female body in poetry often involve architecture, imagining women as

[7] Crystal, *The Cambridge Encyclopedia of Language*, 21.

temples for worship, fortresses for conquest, or palaces for decoration, and extreme political misogynies seek to control women by domestic and functional imprisonment, as the Nazis did in asserting that women's 'proper' concerns were "*Kinder, Küche, Kirche*" (children, kitchen, and church). One consequence of such oppression is that the common female experience of domesticity is very different from the male, as much imprisonment as shelter; and in the same way female entry into the public spheres of society, and especially of authority and political power, has to be fought for and negotiated in ways that few men experience. These pressures influence characteristically feminine conceptions of space, and drawing power from the traditional male imaginations and representations of virginity as determinative of moral value, of sexual intercourse as penetration and conquest, and of the womb as a space within the female body which men seek to occupy and control, such pressures make the issue of space as present for many women in their most private self-imagining as in their daily lives and political consciousness. Domestic and architectural imagery in the poems of Emily Dickinson or Sylvia Plath is closely related to their self-images and presentations of women, to threats of claustrophobic entrapment within their bodies, dress, rôles, and dwellings, and of agoraphobic or suicidal liberation from such traps. The same themes are equally keyed to the individual elements of their craft as poets—Dickinson's dashes and quatrains, Plath's rhyme and metre—and the possibilities of understanding how their femininity and their poetry co-operate are among the great enrichments of reading that gender studies has begun to offer. It also offers consideration of how Eliot's or Hardy's heterosexual masculinity, or Auden's or Hart Crane's homosexual masculinity, exists in <u>their</u> poetries; and it has posed some fascinating questions about (for example) the sexual orientation of Marvell, while equally demanding to know who put the curse on Tennyson's 'Lady of Shalott' (O2.1184/N888). As a reader of poetry I find issues here which can disrupt poems I thought I knew as thoroughly as a cow in a china shop; and as a teacher of practical criticism I can certainly report that there is no detectable gender bias in the enthusiasm, comprehension, or ability of students to perform the close reading and writing that is required to begin to answer those questions.

'Nearing Forty'

A majority (of both sexes) of the people to whom I have shown 'Nearing Forty' without ascription have felt that it is a masculine poem, one unlikely to be the work of a woman; but there has been little consensus about which if any features of the poem may be singled out as productive of this conviction.

At the broadest level is the suggestion that the *donné* of the poem (the basic idea upon which it rests, or from which it takes off), the notion of self-assessment as one approaches the age of forty, is far more a male preoccupation and habit than a female one, perhaps as a result of such factors as the exclusion of women from professional careers, in which forty is a traditional watershed, or the imposition upon women of a social value based on biological status rather than age-hierarchized achievement: but there are obvious points to be made in rebuttal. Forty is also traditionally associated with female menopause and the loss of youthfulness, and nearing forty may (especially for women who have been taught that their value depends on their sexual allure and reproductive capacity) provoke acute anxiety as well as sometimes painful and distressing physical changes. Similarly, forty-something husbands notoriously feel the need to demonstrate that they can still attract and satisfy a woman younger than their wives or themselves, to bolster a virility they fear to be waning with age; and one reader[8] found 'Nearing Forty' humorously to express deeply-felt anxieties about paternity, reproduction, and ageing in a specifically male body. The imagery of water and its forceful cyclical movement, drumming down and convecting up, contrast sharply with the 'poet's' anxieties about the false dawns and dry wheezings that signal <u>his</u> entrapment in the failing lifelines of <u>his</u> poetry. The force that symbolically attends the poem's resolution and self-comfort is the moon, traditionally female and here specifically associated with renewal: the lunar cycle becomes the paradigm of all the poem's cycles, and its traditional menstrual connotations identify the course of the poem as from the linear male anxiety attending men's inability to bear children and fear of death to a cyclical female comfort promising continued creativity.

In the middle ground is a case that the sparsity of domestic detail,

---

[8] Dr Hugh Stevens of York University (and formerly of Trinity Hall), a colleague to whom I am greatly indebted.

the 'poet's' (and by presumption the poet's) relations to the bedsheet and the kettle, and the exclusion from the poem of detailed observation and of other people by self-preoccupied rhetoric, are indicative of a masculine (and presumably male) author. Without exact knowledge of Walcott's domesticity, this can be neither confirmed nor refuted: this particular poem does not for me suffer from the absence of the details it lacks, but I would accept that there may be, as some critics have alleged,[9] evidence in Walcott's work as a whole of a masculinity that reflects his age and date of birth (1930) in domestic chauvinism as much as in the celebration of West Indian independence. The literary origins of the phrase "household truth" in Johnson's philosophically "domestick wisdom" lessen the extent to which the words can concretely place the idea of truth in a specifically domestic setting, implicitly feminine in contrast to a masculine public sphere. In conjunction with the bedsheet, the kettle, the blinds, and the water clerk, "household truth" does rebuke with simple domesticity and commerce an adolescent fantasy of "ambition as a searing meteor", which seems much more masculine than feminine; but neither the 'poet's' present nor memories seem to include any women, nor overtly to acknowledge any female influence. I am not myself persuaded by these arguments, because I find it perfectly possible to read 'Nearing Forty' as a love poem, and the "you" to whom it is addressed as a feminine (or feminized) figure, perhaps the poet's lover. (Try it.) I don't particularly read it like that, but the willingness of the poem to co-operate with such a reading makes me cautious about believing it to be narrowly masculine.

And most precisely, there is the contention that the phrase "as greenhorns at school" (23) is not one which a woman would use: as I find the 'poet' clearly masculine, and know of no female use to cite in refutation, I must agree that the contention is possible, but I am not impressed. "greenhorns" is more an American than a British term (though "school", unless Walcott means 'university', is British), and while American society is very conservative about gender rôles, I find it hard to believe that there has recently been any pressure on women not to say "greenhorns", or employ it in phrases. "greenhorns at school" also seems to me as much a poetic phrase as a colloquial one, and any female poet who wanted to use it would surely do so.

The technical features of the poem also do not seem to me much

9 See particularly Elaine Savory Fido, 'Macho Attitudes and Derek Walcott', in Walder (ed.), *Literature in the Modern World*.

influenced by Walcott's maleness, or even masculinity. More men than women have written heroic lines, but far more men's poetry has been recorded in all forms. The epigraph invokes the very masculine Samuel Johnson, but he has been widely influential, and there are certainly female poets who have engaged with his legacy—not perhaps as deeply as Walcott, but then Walcott's engagement with his canonical precursors is a primary cause of his greatness as a poet, so the standard is high. The layout is essentially conventional, the punctuation supple, and the delicacy of rhyme a tribute to West Indian culture rather than to either sex or gender. Skills of craft, once learned, are instruments of creative expression, and the pain of ageing is common to us all.

Chapter Glossary

Donné: the given image, fact etc. from which a poem or other work proceeds.

Écriture feminine: in some feminist theory, language that is gendered feminine and is written from the female body.

Female: of the female sex.

Feminine: here, the aspect of gender rôles reflecting cultural definitions of women.

Feminism: collective term for beliefs and action intended to assert the rights of women, and to liberate them from oppression by men and the patriarchy.

Gender: cultural femininity and masculinity, as distinct from biological femaleness and maleness.

Inscribe, inscription: here, the process by which the critic includes him- or herself as an individual within his or her writing. In this sense inscription used to be proscribed in practical criticism, but (used judiciously) it is now widely encouraged.

Liberal: of feminisms, here used to designate those which are in theory willing to co-operate with men.

Male: of the male sex.

Masculine: here, the aspect of gender rôles reflecting cultural definitions of men.

Masculinism: an emergent set of beliefs and actions intended to liberate men from oppression by other men, particularly peer pressure, bullying, and the patriarchal imposition of emotionally repressive gender stereotyping.

Phallocracy: the rule of the phallus, by the phallus, for those with phalloi. The French term *phallocrat* translates as '(male) chauvinist pig'.

Phallus: the representation of abstract patriarchal power (which may be wielded by masculinized women) as distinct from the anatomical penis.

Politics of representation: how women and men, and femininity and masculinity, are represented by an author, or in a text, and how those representations are received by (a) reader(s).

Roomscape: my coinage for the domestic 'landscape', to which responses are often gendered.

Separatist: of feminisms, desiring and recommending the isolation of women from men.

Sex: biological, anatomical, and chromosomal maleness or femaleness, as distinct from culturally acquired gender.

Exams

The school and undergraduate students for whom this book is primarily intended have all chosen to study literature, and I hope for their sakes that the practical criticism of poetry is for them a pleasure as well as study, exercise, and preparation—for if not they have chosen amiss. Writing it has been for me a pleasure as well as a job, and I hope that I have managed to convey something of my pleasure in poetry, rather than simply providing an introduction, and a revision crammer: but the book must be those things as well, which is why I am ending with a chapter on exams; for the hardest-working student is ill-prepared if they have not thought about the nature, and the structure, of the test which an exam represents.

This is particularly true of exams in practical criticism, for there is at one level a fundamental contradiction between different things which those exams require. On one hand candidates are asked to read a text, on its own or against other texts, with the greatest sensitivity, and in the greatest detail; on the other to write an account of their reading which reveals the sensitivity and detail cogently, and amounts to an argument; and there is a time-limit, usually of one hour (in a three-hour, three-question paper). The reading and writing compete for the available time: and it is patently true that if the writing is to be done adequately, the reading must be restricted; that if the reading is to be done adequately, the writing must be restricted: and the steel of the test is neither 'Can you read?' nor 'Can you write?', but 'How well can you combine the two?'. It is this that makes the results of a practical criticism exam relevant beyond the world of English studies, for the balancing act that a successful candidate will have managed is of use in many callings.

The need for such balancing is one good reason for mastering the technical vocabulary: however off-putting it seems, it is very compact and will enable you to say far more in the time available than is otherwise possible. Try to paraphrase 'the poem is in blank verse'; or 'in the sonnet's third line the fourth foot is inverted', without using any of the technical terms and you will see what I mean. And the technicalities are also a means of focusing your attention: they are not exhaustive, but they cover many of the things which can be done, and by knowing them you are alerted to what may be being done.[1] But this will not happen automatically, and one way of beginning your analytical reading within an exam (and your critical writing) is to make as complete, and as short, a technical description of a poem as you can: faced, for example, with 'Leda and the Swan' (O2.1704/N1095) you need only get as far as 'a Petrarchan sonnet', and far from being faced with a blank page to fill you have an embarrassment of things to remark: metrical conformity and deviation, exploitations of rhyme and layout, the tension of form and content, manipulation of syntax and diction, and so on. Some of these may be relatively isolated technical matters—the stress afforded to an individual word by a distinguishing foot, for example—but many of them are connected with, and underpin, the largest moral issues which the poem raises. Yeats's choice of the sonnet form, invoking its traditional associations with courtship and frustrated love, is connected to the questions of Leda's complicity and Zeus's responsibility: and that in turn reconnects to the smaller details, such as the questioning stress on "Did" in the inverted first foot of the penultimate line, "Did she put on his knowledge with his power / Before the indifferent beak could let her drop?".

It is far better to have more things to say than time allows than to be groping for material—to be blunt, waffle always reads like waffle—but it poses a problem of its own: what should you use the available time to say? The right determination of that question is fundamental to the balance which structures a good answer; and while there is no universal, abstract 'right determination', there are solid guidelines which will set you on your way. Different people behave very differently in exams, and need different sorts of routines and methods to enable them to do their best: this is only one method—but it is a method I can vouch for.

As best you can, clear your mind of preconceptions, and let the poem come to you. Read it carefully, and don't hesitate to mouth the words, so that you can mentally hear the sounds: one reading at that pace may well enable you to notice more than three swifter but unvocalized readings. Be able to review in your head the possible technical elements represented by my chapter titles (invent a mnemonic for them if that helps), and ask yourself which elements are most striking or doing most work in this particular poem. If something appears to be

[1] For readers who also write poetry, the elements may prompt thoughts during composition, but may prove more useful as a way of learning to revise and polish your own work, and as a troubleshooting kit.

of little importance—the layout is wholly conventional, for example—eliminate it from consideration, and move on. If something is clearly very complex, and would take a great deal of time to sort out—a highly disturbed metre, or a sprawlingly open form—note it as something that could be mentioned in one sentence ('The metre, like the layout, is disturbed and unsettling.') and move on. Take care in your judgements—if every line is end-stopped it may mean that lineation does not matter much, or it may be a carefully contrived effect of lineation—but judge nevertheless; and within a few minutes you will have a list of three or four elements which are, in this poem, hard at work, and must therefore be partly responsible for the poem's totality, its content and effects. It is worth spending another minute or two pondering the relations between those elements, and then decide in which order your written work should tackle them.

You now have a plan, which might note: a specific form, unusual punctuation, a succession of half-rhymes, and a particular subject-matter of historical importance; or, blank verse with several words stressed by metrical oddities, a layout which splits a line into two half-lines, and a sequence of words with related secondary meanings. As you begin to write about what you can see and hear in the poem, and how you respond, the technical identification, explanation, and relation of these elements will serve to structure what you write; it will peg down your responses to the text of the poem (essential for preventing waffle); and it will mean that when you end one paragraph you know what is due up in the next one, so that you don't have to stare into space for ten minutes while you think about it. It should also enable you to judge your timing, so that you can measure the time you have left against the matters that remain to be written.

A few other points. Plans are important, but stay flexible: if, halfway through writing, you realize that you have missed something that matters, readjust and include it, acknowledging if necessary (because you're going to contradict something you've already written, for example) that the process of writing has affected and changed your earlier reading. This is an occasion when the word 'I' can properly be used, and pretty much every examiner will be more impressed by clear evidence that you are thinking and responding, than they would be by your completing a neat plan that strove to be anonymous and ignored something important. It is also an occasion when you might risk a rueful joke, acknowledging your change of mind: humour is tricky, and flippancy is always to be avoided, but too many scripts show the handicaps of a candidate checking their sense of humour at the exam-room door; and an earnest response to a comic passage—which examiners may well set <u>because</u> it is comic—can easily commit howlers or become painful to read. Be careful: but if something strikes you as funny (or sad, or offensive, or . . .) do not be afraid to acknowledge your response, to assess it, and to put it to critical use.

Remember that no plan is good enough if it doesn't go somewhere, and support an argument which has a conclusion—for without that the technical points become simply unjoined dots which you are in effect asking the examiner to join up for you. The examiner won't: so make sure that you do. Remember also that you are being asked for a critical response founded on technical analysis, not simply a technical description—an essay, not a blueprint.

And, as in all exams, do write legibly and with syntactic clarity—nothing is more irritating, when you have a large pile of scripts to get through, than words or sentences which have to be puzzled over. Think about this: if your writing is very large, with the descenders of 'g's and 'y's looping far below the line, write on alternate lines; if you are quoting more than a line, leave a line blank above and below the quotation, and indent it slightly; make sure full-stops, capital letters, and other punctuation are clear; and if you have any time left at the end, use it to proof-read your answers, rewriting illegible words above the line or in the margin, re-punctuating as needed (and remember that your hand worsens as you tire, so proof-read essays in the reverse order of writing).

Finally, a word about rubrics which require you to read two or more poems (or passages of prose), and to compare and contrast them. This clearly puts an even greater pressure on the available time, but the same basic technique will serve: save that instead of simply asking which technical elements are doing the most work in each poem, you must select instead those elements relatively doing the most work which are common to both poems. The discussion of each element will then offer you a point of contrast and comparison, a bridge between the poems; and as those points of comparison build up, your judgement of the poems in relation to one another will be enabled and strengthened. It follows that (unless it is a very straightforward comparison) you will probably not know what to say in the concluding paragraph of your argument until you reach it: or to put it another away, the judging time becomes incorporated into the writing time. This can make it frightening to begin to write, for you are setting off somewhat in the dark: but it is far better to do that than to tack a preconceived conclusion lamely onto an argument to which it is inappropriate or contradictory. If there is a technical element that is crucial in one poem, and absent or very minor in the other, give it a paragraph to itself, but remember to comment, at least briefly, on the absence as well as on the importance; and if you think the two poems have nothing in common, think again: examiners may be bloody-minded (though it's actually very rare) but they are not irresponsible.

Examiners also hate failing people (though very few students give them credit for this); but they cannot give marks for what is not actually there in the script in front of them. The commonest reason for low marks is a short script: and in practical criticism (unless you've blown the timing, which is your problem) it is one thing that is fairly unforgiveable, because every poem has some kind of metre, some kind of form, syntax, diction, and all the rest—and there is <u>always</u> something more that you can say.

On the following pages there are some timed (one hour) responses to 'Nearing Forty' produced by first-year students of mine (in 1994–5) at Trinity Hall. The essays were required without notice at the end of the year; they had encountered the poem in lectures and one class in their first term, and had been practising unseen timed pieces throughout the year. Obvious errors induced by haste (such as misspellings) and simple solecisms have been corrected, but the essays are otherwise as they were handed in. I am very grateful to these students for agreeing to have their work appear, and I believe it is important to this book: for you the reader are now effectively in a position to mark these essays for yourself, judging what their authors have included and what you can see them to have omitted, by choice or in haste or forgetfulness. It is rarely possible for students (or parents) to be able in this way to put themselves into their (childrens') examiners' shoes, and it can be a revelation. Enjoy!

Student Essays

One

The main body of the poem consists of a single sentence split into three *semi-cola*. Such a fundamental lack of heavy punctuational stops lends the piece great speed, and when this syntactical pace is combined with that created by the iambic pentameter, readers find themselves being swept up into the verse and not really pausing until the end. As a result the poem seems to mime the narrator's thought process, and he does not stop to consider the implications of his ideas before he moves on. The pace of the verse also serves to emphasize the narrator's preoccupation with the passing of time. On a microcosmic scale, the setting is cyclical, moving from night ("Insomniac since four") through to day ("false dawn", "watching your leaves thin") and then back to "the night when you can really sleep".

On a more macrocosmic scale, the poem deals with the passage of the narrator's life. However, in this sense the temporal aspect is neither cyclical, nor even linear; the poem starts in the present, moves to the past, and finishes with a hope for the future. This schema is complemented by the semi-colon dividers: in the first section the narrator is "hearing" the rain; in the second he speaks of 'recall[ing]"; and in the third he looks ahead to the time when "you <u>will</u> rise".

This contrast between day and night, past and present, is also evoked through the rhyme scheme. The first six lines do contain rhyme, but this appears to be somewhat haphazard, in contrast to what follows: lines 7–18 contain six couplets and thus the poet invokes the historical associations of that form, regularising the verse in the process. The couplet is often linked with narration, and Walcott perverts this fact for his own purpose: his is not a straightforward narrative, and hence the couplets themselves are not entirely regular. Some of them utilise printers' rhyme; one has differing stress patterns on the rhyming words; and the "gutter-" / "sputter" rhyme rolls uneasily off the tongue because of the enjambment of the former, which causes it to be less pronounced than the latter. However, when the poem nears its close and enters the realm of the hypothetical the rhyme scheme alters: it becomes irregular and retrospective as "rain" in lines 22 and 30 reminds the reader of line 2, and "work" in lines 25 and 31 does the same for line 6. This could be another example of Walcott's demonstration of the cyclicality of the microcosmic time scheme he uses in the poem.

Using the iambic pentameter as his prosodic template, Walcott is able to create a variety of effects by writing lines whose actual metre overrides that of the pentameter. For example, there is a sense of uncertainty to line 2 caused by the fact that the words "rigidly metred" are not rigidly metred, since the initial inverted foot causes the line to stutter in an unregimented manner. When this is taken together with the oxymoron of "early-rising rain", the reader starts to perceive a lack of confidence in the approach to "forty". Elsewhere the metre complements the language, which lends an extra dimension to the reader's understanding of the verse, as in the lines:

glad for the sputter
of occasional insight, you who foresaw
ambition as a searing meteor (ll. 14–16)

The first line-and-a-half contain an irregular metre, augmented by an extra syllable in line 15, and the effect is mimetic of the sputter described. In line 16, however, the metre reverts to a normal iambic pentameter, giving the line an injection of pace and consequently miming the "searing meteor" described.

The poem is dedicated to 'John Figueroa', in a phrase that Walcott isolates away from the main body of the poem. The crotchets surrounding his name imply that any links between this man and the poem are slight, and this prevents the reader from assuming that the "you" described is the dedicatee. The epigraph from a work of Johnson's provides a gentle introduction before the reader is swept into the poem. The tone of this epigraph seems more positive than that of the verse: Johnson admits that "that pleasures of sudden wonder are soon exhausted" but suggests that truth is a constant to which the mind can always return. Walcott denies any such stability by claiming that the human mind does not reach an imaginative plateau; instead, even the attainment of the "night when you can really sleep" leads to a measuring of how "imagination / ebbs".

As the narrator nears forty he accepts that his most productive days are past and that his situation is worsening, and the poem seems to describe the process of his coming to terms with this. He admits that he will examine his work with "bleak modesty", and explains one of the antitheses of his position when he describes how the "you" of the piece "will set your lines to work / with sadder joy but steadier elation". The oxymoronic nature of this line harks back to line 2 and suggests that the narrator appreciates the awkwardness of his situation, but is unable to alter it. The clarity of his perception of his condition is remarkable, a fact which makes his helplessness all the more pitiable.

Adam Barnes

Two

The suspension marks at the end of the epigraph to 'Nearing Forty' suggest that the accompanying poem is, in part, an expansion of the debate superficially resolved in Johnson's preference for the "stability of truth" over "fanciful invention". The poem, which is comprised of a single, circular sentence, returning to the initial image of falling rain at its close, swings like a pendulum across past, present and future, and a range of attitudes towards creativity and invention. Within this self-analysis the spectre of Johnson re-emerges in an attempted stylistic classicism, but involves a range of refractions—cultural and personal—in which the narrative competes with the individual.

The poem's syntactical fluidity is mirrored in its dominant aqueous imagery. In the opening lines the "rigidly metred, early-rising rain", metrically insistent and evoked in professional poetic vocabulary, is an image of oppressive tedium and imaginative solipsism. Its corollary at the poem's close is the "lightly falling rain, / which . . . does its work / even when it seems to weep." The personal pathetic fallacy remains, and the truncated last line suggests an interrogatory lilt which may undermine the impression of circularity and closure; but the poet, reminded still of his mortality, sees beyond his own reflection to a broader perspective of regeneration.

The poem begins wearily in the present tense with a series of claustrophobic participles, which suggest the interminability of its anguish: "hearing", "nearing", "thickening". The last of these introduces the poem's other dominant motifs, those of light and vision. Its numerous images of light and incandescence are submerged in its presiding, nocturnal darkness: the "false dawn" is "fireless", the "searing meteor" replaced by a "damp match"; until in the closing lines the softer, feminine luminary—"the new moon"—sheds its light and facilitates sleep. This resolution is the second of the prognoses Walcott offers for his future. The first involves an anticipated retrospection in which he "will judge [his] work / by the bleak modesty of middle age"; in the assertion that "your life bled for / the household truth, the style past metaphor" it is evident that life and poetry have become intertwined. In this reaching back into the past, the poet, however, reaches beyond his own past towards Johnson. As he modulates into the second person, the subject of "your" is ambiguous; the poem's construction suggests a quasi-Latinate classicism, and in lines 7 and following, the poet attempts to assume a Johnsonian Augustanism of style and attitude. He purports to criticise the romanticism of his youth as naïf and adolescent, opposing the vocabulary of lyricism with the material vocabulary of the "bleaching bedsheet under a gutter- / ing rainspout" and the "dry wheezing of a dented kettle". The prognosis, and the *semi-colon,* closes with a recollection of days as "greenhorns at school"—redolent with maleness, stability, and cultural certainty. The affection of the recollection, and the returning image of the rain, herald the replacement of this dark prognosis with another; throughout, however, its incompleteness has been subtly signalled. When the projected Johnsonian judgement begins, the verse is almost formalised into the stability of rhyming couplets. Their momentum and confidence eventually dissolve, but throughout it is evident that this confidence—cultural and ideological—has been imitated rather than genuine. The couplets persistently avoid pentametric normality, and the tidiness of end-stopping; their rhymes are consistently imperfect: "age"/"average" is an eye-rhyme; "wretched"/"stretched" is metrically disrupted; and "gutter-"/"sputter" is achieved only by prosodic dislocation.

After this attitude has exhausted itself it is replaced with an alternative vision, which gathers momentum with its hopeful assonance: "you will rise and set your lines to work / with sadder joy but steadier elation". Walcott expects to "measur[e] how imagination / ebbs", as the verb ebbs prosodically onto the succeeding line; here, however, there is no bathetic juxtaposition of styles. The discussion has devolved from the portentous judgements of classicism to a plane of greater humility, where the less formalised rhyming ("elation"/"imagination", "work"/"clerk"/"work", and "sleep" stretching forward to "weep") suggests a more reticent confidence. Creativity is commodified, but the conventionality of the water clerk, the averageness and humility upon which the rain perpetually insists, are now reassuring rather than oppressive, sympathetic and regenerative rather than judgemental. The poet achieves a variation on Johnson's realism which is his own, and there is a sense that the expectation of the "night when you can really sleep" contains in its alleviation of insomnia the alleviation of the need for imitation, of historical inferiority; the putting to sleep of the past. The poem has been structured around antitheses—romance and classicism, past and future; but as the "new moon" sheds its light, the poem's nocturnal debate achieves a resolution as the poet finds his own "novelty" in the "stability of truth".

Andy Miller

Three

By invoking Samuel Johnson for his epigraph, Walcott immediately creates a tension between his own cultural background and that of the dead, white, English male who appears to be describing the transitional time of life being experienced by the speaker in the poem. By Johnson's description, the speaker is close to exhausting "the pleasures of sudden wonder", and he seems to relate a fear of artistic impotence with the loss of sight: he is afraid of the "weak / vision thickening to a frosted pane", and in associating the loss of "fanciful invention" with the physical disabilities of age, the speaker expresses the dichotomy implied by Johnson in such a manner as to justify any fear of age.

A sense of transition and urgency is generated by the repeated use of "nearing" and "nearer" three times within three lines, and this helps to compound the driving force of the poetry. The first lines are not quite as "rigidly metred" as the rain, nor are the rhymes as regular; but once the voice is established in the second quarter of the poem, it is pushed along by the rhyming couplets at the line-ends, and by the central cæsurae. The enjambed lines are thereby distinguished by rhyme, and ignored by the rocking rhythm which, together with the fact that the poem is a single sentence (a point which itself is insisted upon by the lower-case letters at the beginning of each line), insists upon the urgency and impotence of the speaker.

The inevitability of time is almost made apparent by the way so much in the first part of the poem can be associated with it. For a start, it is difficult for the reader to know simply from the text whether the speaker's "Insomniac since four" is referring to a time or an age; "day", "night", "seasons", and even "weak" (a pun enforced by the line ending) are all mentioned as the speaker ponders the loss of his youth.

It is of course the rain which recounts how he is "nearing forty", and this device is interesting because it allows the poet to create the idea of change and flux out of the same metaphor for repetition *ad infinitum*. This repetition is why "as greenhorns at school, we'd / call [the rain] conventional for convectional"; its regularity is why it is "rigidly metred". The reminiscence takes the speaker back to the youthful days to which the first half of the epigraph refers, and it is this youth which he fears he will look back on and judge with "the bleak modesty of middle age / as a false dawn, fireless and average".

The other character in the monologue, however, would seem to be no older than the speaker if they were "greenhorns at school" together. This character, "who foresaw / ambition as a searing meteor", provides the hope for the speaker because he appears to illustrate a mind which never succumbed to "fanciful invention". This mind, however, which appears to disprove Johnson's dictum, is not bleakly modest, but can "smiling, settle / for the dry wheezing of a dented kettle". But 'he' also has the option to "rise and set [his] lines to work / with sadder joy but steadier elation".

Because the poem is constructed within a single sentence there is a more complex syntax. This exaggerates the ambiguities of the poetry which, in particular, has the result of making it difficult (or impossible) to decide whether the character referred to as "you" is always the person the speaker went to school with. If one assumes that this is not always the case then there is evidence to suggest that the speaker is actually addressing Johnson as "you who foresaw / ambition as a searing meteor". This can be found when he refers to the peculiar figure of "measuring how imagination / ebbs, conventional as any water clerk / who weighs the force of lightly falling rain", which is what Johnson is doing.

While there is hope allowed in the poem for the joys of "the sputter / of occasional insight", one cannot really say that it is hope from which the speaker can take much joy. He seems to be cut off from the "sadder joy but steadier elation", unless one argues that by recognising the possibility he provides his own salvation. There is a sense of impotence about him though, which is expressed in his inability to subdue himself with sleep, and in the onward march of time, best expressed by the way the poem ends as it begins. Like the poet himself, the rain "does its work / even when it seems to weep.", and is manipulated by a force beyond its control or understanding, and the poem ends with an irresolution sounded to the ear by the final, catalectic line as it rhymes "weep" back five lines into the poem with "sleep".

Simon Oastler

Glossary and Index of Technical Terms

Page references follow the glossary entry or sub-entry in parenthesis.

Accent: the emphasis or stress placed on a beat. (1)

Accentual-syllabic: the kind of prosody principally used in English. (1)

Accusative: in grammar the case for the object of a verb. (68)

Active: of an individual's vocabulary, that part which is actually used. (103)

Alcaic: of an ode, of a particular and highly prescribed form; largely dactylic, alcaics are very rare in English. (39)

Aldine: of type, designed by Aldus Manutius (*c.*1450–1515).

Alexandrine: an iambic hexameter. (24)

***Alinéa*:** the convention by which, in prose dialogue, each new speaker begins on a new line. (67)

Alliteration: the repeated use of the same consonant(s) in two or more proximate words. (94)

Amphibrach: a foot of three beats, the first and last unstressed, the middle stressed (uxu). (3, 4, 90)

Amphimacer: a foot of three beats, the first and last stressed, the middle unstressed (xux). (3, 4)

Analytical: of a language, dependent on prepositions and word-order, having no inflections etc. (1)

Anapæst, anapæstic: a foot of three beats, two unstressed and the last stressed (uux); the metre produced by such feet. (3, 4)

Angled brackets: marked "< >"; used in maths but rare in poetry. (65)

Antibacchius: a foot of three beats, the first and second stressed, the last unstressed (xxu). (3)

Antispast: a foot of four beats, the first and fourth unstressed, the second and third stressed (uxxu). (3)

Antistrophe: (or *counterturn*), the second stanza of a Pindaric ode. (39)

Apostrophe: used with or without an 's' to indicate possession (the genitive case), or the elision of a letter; in either case marked ' or '. (3, 68)

Arch-rhyme: a rhyme scheme with mirror symmetry, as *abba*. (32, 161–2)

Assonance: the repeated use of the same vowel(s) in two or more proximate words. (94)

Asterisk: a *signe de renvoi*, marked "*". (70)

Augustan: of poetry, that of the later-seventeenth and first half of the eighteenth centuries. The boundaries are ragged and variable, but in schemata 'Augustan' follows 'Restoration' and is followed (after a gap) by 'Romantic'. The term derives from the Roman age of the Emperor Augustus, and hence is self-consciously imperialistic; the most obvious formal feature of Augustan poetry is the prevalence of closed heroic couplets. (143–4)

Autorhyme: occurs when a word is rhymed with itself (my coinage). (91–2)

Bacchius: a foot of three beats, the first unstressed and the last two stressed (uxx). (3)

Ballad: a narrative poem, commonly of traditional origin, often in quatrains with refrain; *literary* and *folk* ballads are now distinguished (40); of a stanza, or of metre, an iambic quatrain of the form *a8b6a8b6* (also called *common metre*). (31)

Bardolatry: the worship of Shakespeare. (140)

BBC English: used to denote a combination of Queen's (or King's) English with a plummy or Home Counties accent, such as BBC newsreaders used to have, particularly on the radio. (91)

BCE: or Before Common Era, a non-denominational equivalent of B[efore] C[hrist]. (39)

Beat: a word or syllable(s) bearing one stress (x) or unstress (u). (1–2)

Bembine: of type, designed by Pietro Bembo (1470–1547). (62)

Blackletter: the proper name of the old, gothic-style fount of type; replaced as a basic fount by roman and italic in the late sixteenth century, it is now used mostly for formal invitations and for mock-antique commercialism. (48)

Blank verse: unrhymed iambic pentameter. (23, 27, 76–81, 123–5, 126, 129–32)

Bob-lines/bobs: in a given stanza form, a line or lines which are markedly shorter than the others. (33)

Bowdlerize: to cut from a text, or to replace with euphemisms, anything thought 'improper'; an eponym from Thomas Bowdler (1754–1825), editor of the *Family Shakespeare* (10 volumes, 1818). (108)

Braces: curly brackets, marked "{ }"; a single brace is conventionally used to indicate a triplet within couplet-rhyme. (65, 30)

Brackets: a generic term covering braces, crotchets, and lunulæ; all may be used singly, but crotchets and lunulæ are normally used in pairs, to create parentheses to isolate (for subordination <u>or</u> emphasis) a word or phrase. (65–6)

Burden: an alternative term for a *refrain*, a line or lines that are repeated. (39)

Cadence: a fall, in tone, pitch etc. (9)

Cæsura, cæsurae: the medial pause(s) in a line; if there is no punctuation it will tend not to occur in lines shorter than a tetrameter, and to occur approximately centrally in tetrametric or longer lines; it may be forced towards the beginning or the end of a line by punctuation. (77–81)

Catalectic: of a line, missing one or more beats. (7)

CE: or Common Era, a non-denominational equivalent of A[nno] D[omini]. (39)

Glossary and Index of Technical Terms

Chiasmus, chiasmic: a 'diagonal', or mirror-symmetrical, arrangement of words, clauses etc.; of rhyme, arch-rhymed. (32)

Choriamb: a foot of four beats, the first and fourth stressed, the second and third unstressed (xuux). (3)

Clause: a word with no fully agreed definition, but used to mean units of syntax larger than a word or phrase, but smaller than a sentence. It is possible however for a sentence to have only one clause. Sub-, relative, and main clauses are (among others) distinguished. (121)

Clerihew: a quatrain of two couplets (*aabb*), preferably with the couplets of unequal length, and possibly with each line of a different length; the first line is usually someone's name; so-called after its inventor, Edmund Clerihew Bentley (1875–1956). (29–30)

Closed: of a couplet, with the second line end-stopped (28); of form, prescribed.

Coinage: of a word, a neologism or nonce-word; often used possessively, to indicate the coiner. Implicitly, new words are 'struck', or 'minted', rather than 'made' or 'invented'. (xvi, 104)

Colon(s): the second-heaviest stop, marked ":"; conventionally implies a completion of the immediate sense and a logical or dependent relationship between *cola*. (61–2)

Colon, cola: the part(s) of a sentence between colons, and/or between a colon and a full-stop. (61–2, 122–5)

Comedy, comic: one of the five classical genres, comedies dealt with ordinary people, social life, and marriage; applied to poetry, 'comic' has tended to the much broader meaning of 'humorous'. (41)

Comma(s): the fourth and lightest stop, marked ","; conventionally implies the completion of a sub-clause or clause; used in pairs to create parentheses. (63–4)

Comma(ta): the part(s) into which a period (or smaller unit of syntax) is divided by commas. (64)

Common metre: also *ballad metre*, or *ballad stanza*; an iambic quatrain of the form *a8b6c8b6*. (31)

Composition: in hand-press printing the process of assembling the individual pieces of type, including inter-word spaces, in the correct order. (54)

Concrete poem/poetry: a less satisfactory alternative for *shape poem/poetry*. (52)

Counter turn: another name for the antistrophe of a Pindaric ode. (39)

Couplet: a unit of two lines, usually rhyming, often used terminally to summarize or moralize; a very popular form in the eighteenth century. (28–30)

Couplet enjambment: or *external enjambment*; that between successive couplets. (28)

Couplet-rhyme: a rhyme scheme in couplets, as *aabb*. (32)

Cross-rhyme: a rhyme scheme with alternating rhymes, as *abab*. (32)

Crotchets: square brackets, marked "[ ]"; conventionally used to distinguish editorial comments and emendations from authorial prose. (65–6)

Curly: of brackets, a common term for braces. (65)

Dactyl, dactylic: a foot of three beats, the first stressed, the second and third unstressed (xuu); the metre produced by such feet. (3)

Dagger: also *obelus*; a *signe de renvoi*, marked "†". (70)

Dash: a variety of comma, marked "—"; conventionally used, in script, typescript, and word-processing (though not in print) with a space on either side, simultaneously to distinguish and to link a sequence of clauses, and in pairs to create parentheses. (68–9)

Degree-sign: here, a *signe de renvoi*, marked "°". (70)

Deictic: of punctuation, used to emphasize a word or phrase; distinguished from 'elocutionary' and 'syntactic' punctuation. (59)

Diamb: a foot of four beats, the first and third unstressed, the second and forth stressed (uxux). (3)

Diction: the choice of words (including the reasons for, and the consequences of, that choice). (103)

Dimeter: a line of two feet. (3)

Diple: a mediæval nota from which inverted commas and *guillemets* subsequently developed. (67)

Discourse: here, the diction of a particular poem, the relations between the words it actually uses. (A specialized use of an ambiguous and polysemic term). (103)

Dispondee: a foot of four beats, all stressed (xxxx). (3)

Distinguishing: of a foot, type-face, or fount, different from that normally used. (5)

Ditrochee: a foot of four beats, the first and third stressed, the second and fourth unstressed (xuxu). (3)

Donné: the given image, fact etc. from which a poem or other work proceeds. (179)

Dramatic monologue: a poem cast as a speech by a particular (historical or imaginary) person, often to a specific auditor. The form is particularly associated with Browning and Tennyson, and has remained popular in the twentieth century. (27, 40, 76–7, 131–2)

Duple: of a foot, having two beats; the rhythm produced by such feet. (7)

Écriture feminine: in some feminist theory, language that is gendered feminine and is written from the female body. (174)

Effusion: a form wholly without prescription, ideally spontaneous. (40)

Eisthesis: the indentation of a line or lines by one or more spaces from the left margin. (48)

Ekthesis: the setting of a line or lines hard to the left margin. (48)

Elision: the omission of one or more letters from a word, usually indicated with an apostrophe. (2)

Ellipsis: the omission of a word or words, and the indication of such omission with three suspension-marks, ". . .". (61, 149)

Glossary and Index of Technical Terms

Elocutionary: of punctuation, indicating speech-derived pauses; distinguished from 'deictic' and 'syntactic' punctuation. (59)

Emblem: a small picture, usually a woodcut, with an accompanying poem; often moral or allegorical, emblems were in vogue, and collected in *emblem books* between the later sixteenth century and the civil war. (53)

Emphatic: of punctuation, deictic. (59)

End-rhyme: occurs between words ending lines. (86)

End-stopped: of a line or stanza, having a terminal mark of punctuation. (24, 75)

Enjamb(+ed/ment): of lines, couplets, or stanzas, not end-stopped, with the sense (and/or syntax) continuing into the next line, couplet, or stanza. (24, 28, 75)

Epic: one of the five classical genres, epics are long narrative poems usually dealing with the heroic or martial exploits of a person or race. (41)

Epigraph: a short motto or quotation prefixed to a text. (48, 55, 148–9)

Epitrite: a foot of four beats, only one unstressed; called first (uxxx), second (xuxx), third (xxux), and fourth (xxxu) epitrites according to the position of the unstressed beat. (3)

Epode: (or *stand*) the third and final stanza of a Pindaric Ode. (39)

Etymology: the derivation and history of a particular word, or the general study of how words evolve. (103)

Exclamation-mark: used (instead of a full-stop) to indicate exclamations, marked "!"; also a tonal indicator, usually of rising pitch and volume; may be used both medially and terminally; invented in the 1360s by Iacopo Alpoleio da Urbisaglia, an Italian humanist. (65)

Expressionist: of criticism, believing the meaning of a text to express and be determined by the author's intentions. (The term has other meanings in art history and theatre studies.) (158)

External: of enjambment, between successive couplets. (28)

Eye-rhyme: (or *printers' rhyme*) occurs between words which, having endings spelt identically, look as if they rhyme, but are not pronounced as a rhyme. (91)

Face: of a type, a particular appearance of the letters and numbers, as roman or *italic*; thus any given fount of type will have many faces. (5)

Falling rhythm: that produced by feet with unstressed beats following stressed beats. (6–7)

Female: of the female sex. (172)

Feminine: the aspect of gender rôles reflecting cultural definitions of women (172); of an ending, with one or more unstressed hypermetrical beats (7, 173); of a rhyme, unstressed (87).

Feminism: collective term for beliefs and action intended to assert the rights of women, and to liberate them from oppression by men and the patriarchy. (170–4)

Folk: of a ballad, traditional and of popular origin. (40)

Font: the standard US spelling of 'fount'. (5)

Foot: a prosodic unit of stressed and/or unstressed beats, the component of a line. (2)

Fount: (or in the USA, 'font') of type, a particular design of the letters and numbers; each fount will comprise designs for each character in a number of faces. (5)

Fourteeners: couplets in iambic heptameter. (29)

Free verse: poetry in which the metre varies. (9–10)

Full-rhyme: (or *perfect rhyme*) occurs when the last stressed vowel and all following sounds of two or more words or phrases are identical. (87)

Full-stop: (or in the USA, *period*) the heaviest stop, marked "."; conventionally required at the end of each sentence. (61)

Gender: cultural femininity and masculinity, as distinct from biological femaleness and maleness. (172)

Genitive: in grammar the case for possession and origin. (68)

Genre: a classical method of distinguishing and grouping literary forms; the sets of conventional expectations readers learn to have. (40–1)

Germanic: of languages, belonging to a particular group of Indo-European languages, including modern German and Dutch, and Old English (Anglo-Saxon); of modern English words, deriving from one of these languages. (104)

Grammar: the rules governing the cases of words and the 'permissible' syntax of any given language. (120)

Guillemets: the French equivalent of inverted commas, marked "« »". (67)

Haiku: a Japanese form, of three lines, the first and last of five syllables, the second of seven, ideally with a turn between the first and second, or second and third lines. (31)

Half-rhyme: (or *near* or *slant rhyme*) occurs when <u>either</u> the last stressed vowel <u>or</u> all following sounds of two or more words or phrases are identical, but not both; includes vowel- and pararhyme. (90–1)

Heptameter: a line of seven feet. (3)

Heroic: of a form, in iambic pentameter. (27, 36)

Hexameter: a line of six feet. (3)

Historikerstreit: German, literally 'the battle of historians'; a sharp debate beginning in 1986–7 initially about whether it was acceptable to argue that the story of the Wehrmacht's defence of Germany's Eastern Front in 1944–5 deserved to be told as a tragedy. The principal figures involved were Ernst Nolte, Andreas Hillgruber, and Jürgen Habermas. (141)

Homographs: words with different meanings spelt identically. (87)

Homophones: words with different meanings pronounced identically. (87)

Horatian: of an ode, in a shortish but repeated unit of form. (39)

House style: the set of printing conventions observed by a given publishing house. (68)

Hudibrastic: of rhyme, comically strained or foolish, often because mosaic; the term derives from Samuel Butler's (1613–80) long comic poem *Hudibras* (1663–80). (87)

Hyperbeats: those beats in a line which are surplus to the beats allowed by the metre; *stressed* and *unstressed* hyperbeats are politically corrected *masculine* and *feminine* endings. (7)

Hypermetric: of a line in a given metre, with one or more hyperbeats. (7)

Hyphen: used to join two words into a single one, or to join the two parts of a word split between lines, marked "-". (69)

Iamb, iambic: a foot of two beats, an unstressed followed by a stressed (ux); the metre produced by such feet. (2–3, 4)

Identical rhyme: *rime riche*. (87)

Imagists: a school of poetry in the 1910s and 1920s, advocating that poetry be written in short lines each containing a clear image; Ezra Pound and H.D. were leading members. (81)

Imperfect rhyme: half-rhyme. (90–1)

Imposition: in hand-press printing the process of arranging the composed type on the bed of the press; decisions about leading, ornaments, running-heads etc. are involved, and two or more pages will have to be imposed together in any book or pamphlet format. (54)

In-house style: an alternative for 'house-style'. (68)

Indentation: the setting of a line or lines in from the left margin by one or more spaces. (48)

Index: in printing (as well as the usual sense of a listing of subjects in a book with page references), a numeral or other *signe de renvoi* used to indicate a footnote. (70)

Inscribe, inscription: here, the process by which the writer includes him- or herself as an individual within his or her writing. In this sense inscription used to be proscribed in practical criticism, but (used judiciously) it is now widely encouraged. (175–6)

Internal: of rhyme, that which occurs within a line between a medial and the end-word, or between medial words in different lines; includes leonine rhyme (44, 88, 94); of enjambment, between the first and second lines of a couplet. (28)

Intertextuality: generally, the relations between texts; more specifically, the aspects of a given text which derive meaning from relations with another text or texts. (145)

Intransitive: of a verb, not requiring an object. (60)

Inverted: of a foot, the reverse of that normally used in a given line. (5)

Inverted commas: used to indicate direct speech and quotations, marked " and ", or " and "; may also be single (' ', ‘ ’), often to indicate a slight suspension of the sense, or a distrust of the word; developed from a mediæval nota, the modern conventions of use date only from 1857. (67–8)

Ionic (a) majore: a foot of four beats, the first two stressed, the last two unstressed (xxuu). (3)

Ionic (a) minore: a foot of four beats, the first two unstressed, the last two stressed (uuxx). (3)

Italic: of a fount, with angled characters (such as *these*). (xvi, 5, 48)

Justified: of text and margins, aligned straight up and down. (48)

King's English: see *Queen's English*.

Leading: the amount of white space left between lines, stanzas, or other units of form, and in the margins. (50–1)

Leonine rhyme: occurs between the word preceding the cæsura and the end-word of the same line. (94)

Lexical set: any set of words specified by a given criterion. (104)

Lexicon: the vocabulary of a particular trade, activity, or profession. (xvi)

Liberal: of feminisms, here used to designate those which are in theory willing to co-operate with men. (172)

Limerick: an anapæstic pentain, of the form *a9a9b6b6a9*; one or more lines are commonly catalectic. (7–8, 33)

Line: a single sequence of characters read from left to right. (2)

Lineation: the organization of a poem into lines. (48, 75)

Line-break: the turn of one line into the next; notated as "/". (75)

Literary: of a ballad, composed by a known author, often of recent date. (40)

Litterae notabiliores: 'more noticeable letters', often capitals.

Long five: an iambic pentain, of the form *a8b8a8b8b10*. (33)

Long metre: a single-rhymed quatrain (*abcb*) in iambic tetrameter. (31)

Lower-case: of letters, not capitals or small capitals, small. (5)

Lunula, lunulæ: round brackets, marked "( )"; historically used in many conventions, including the indication of stage directions, attributions of speech, metaphors and similes, quotations, and the cruxes of argument; commonly used to indicate both subordination and emphasis; invented by Colluccio Salutati (1331–1406) in *c.*1399. (66)

Lyric: one of the five classical genres, lyrics were at first musically accompanied; the term now covers most short, non-narrative, non-dramatic verse. (41)

Main clause(s): those clauses which deal directly with or continue the principal action of a sentence; distinguished from sub-clauses. (125)

Male: of the male sex. (172)

Masculine: the aspect of gender rôles reflecting cultural definitions of men (172); of an ending, with one or more stressed hypermetrical beats (7, 173); of a rhyme, stressed (87).

Masculinism: an emergent set of beliefs and actions intended to liberate men from oppression by other men, particularly peer pressure, bullying, and the patriarchal imposition of emotionally repressive gender stereotyping. (173)

Meredithean: of sonnets, having sixteen lines in the rhyme scheme *abab cdcd efef ghgh*. (37)

Metaphysical: of poetry, that of the later sixteenth and first half of the seventeenth centuries; characterized by complex stanza forms and arguments, and by elaborate comparisons (or *conceits*). (143–4)

Metre: the rhythmic pattern of beats. (2)

Mise-en-page: the actual layout of a given poem (or prose text) on a given page. (48, 51)

Mock-epic: a poem comically or satirically dressed in epic conventions for which its subject and/or manner are inappropriate. (28, 111–12)

Molossus: a foot of three beats, all stressed (xxx). (3)

Monorhyme: a rhyme scheme in which all lines rhyme, as *aaaa*. (31, 32)

Mosaic rhyme: occurs when a phrase is rhymed with a single polysyllabic word or with another phrase. (87)

Near rhyme: half-rhyme. (90)

Neoclassical: Of prosody, etc., derived from Greek and/or Latin writings. (2)

Neologism: a new word. (104, 106)

Nominative: in grammar the case for the subject of a verb. (68)

Nonce-word: a word invented for a particular occasion or purpose. (106)

Nota, notæ: any mark(s) placed in the margins of a text; distinguished from 'punctuation', which is within the text. (67)

Obelus: also dagger; a *signe de renvoi*, marked "†"; may also be double, when marked "‡". (70)

Octave: (or *octet*) an unit of eight lines, usually the first eight of a sonnet. (36)

Ode: a formal poem of some dignity and length; *Alcaic, Sapphic, Pindaric*, and *Horatian* odes are formally distinguished. (39)

Onegin stanza: of fourteen lines, in iambic tetrameter, having the rhyme scheme *ababccddeffegg*; further prescription about stressed and unstressed rhymes may be made. (38–9)

Open: of form, variable (23); of couplets, with the second line enjambed to the first line of the next couplet (or other component unit of form) (28).

Ottava rima: a stanza of eight lines, in iambic pentameter, having the rhyme scheme *abababcc*. (34–5)

Paeon: a foot of four beats, only one stressed; called first (xuuu), second (uxuu), third (uuxu), and fourth (uuux) paeons according to the position of the stressed beat. (3)

Paragraph: the basic division of prose or verse into groups of lines, marked by the indentation of the first line; a unit of argument, and of emotion; the oldest form of punctuation in the West. (60)

Paragraphus: also section-mark; used to indicate a paragraph or section, marked "§". (60, 70)

Paraph: used to indicate a paragraph or section, marked "¢", "¶", or "||". (60, 70)

Pararhyme: occurs when the last stressed vowel of two or more words or phrases differ, but the sounds following the vowel are identical. (90–1)

Parenthesis: in rhetoric, one clause intercluded within another; such clauses may in written texts be marked with paired commas, dashes, or lunulæ. In the criticism of printed texts a parenthesis comprises the opening mark, the alphanumeric contents, and the closing mark. (66, 162)

Passive: of an individual's vocabulary, the whole range of words that is known. (103)

Pentain: an unit of five lines. (33)

Pentameter: a line of five feet. (3)

Perfect rhyme: full-rhyme. (87)

Period: a classical, rhetorically defined unit of syntax and argument, composed of *cola* and *commata*; closer to the modern paragraph than the modern sentence (122–5); also, latterly and in the USA, a full-stop (61).

Persona: an alternative for 'poet'. (159–60)

Petrarchan: of a sonnet, having the octave rhyme scheme *abbaabba*, and the sestet rhyme scheme *cdecde* (or a variant thereof). (36)

Phallocracy: the rule of the phallus, by the phallus, for those with phalloi. The French term *phallocrat* translates as '(male) chauvinist pig'. (171)

Phallus: the representation of abstract patriarchal power (which may be wielded by masculinized women) as distinct from the anatomical penis. (171)

Pindaric: of an ode, having three stanzas of a specified form, called the *strophe* and *antistrophe* (which are metrically and formally identical), and the *epode* (which is metrically and formally distinct). (39)

Pitch contour: the movement in pitch from one note to a higher or lower note; the curve(s) of sound in the voice, or required by a text. (90)

Plosive: of letters, requiring for their pronunciation that the vocal tract be closed and then opened, producing a small explosion of breath/sound. (136)

Poet: as distinct from 'poet', the actual historical person; the author. (159–60)

'Poet': as distinct from poet (without single inverted commas), the supposed writer or speaker of a given text; the rhetorical construct designated by 'I' or 'me'. Also referred to as the 'persona'. (116, 155, 159–60)

Politics of representation: how women and men, and femininity and masculinity, are represented by an author, or in a text, and how those representations are received by (a) reader(s). (176)

Polysemic: of words, having many senses and/or distinct meanings. (112)

Portmanteau: a word created by merging two or more existing words. (106)

Poulter's measure: an iambic rhyming couplet of the form *a12a14*.

Printers' rhyme: eye-rhyme. (91)

Proceleusmatic: a foot of four beats, all unstressed (uuuu). (3)

Prose poem: one written and printed as prose, without the use of metrical lineation and often with a justified right margin; commoner in French literature, it was attempted by T. S. Eliot, and used by Geoffrey Hill for *Mercian Hymns* (1971); also used in modern American poetry. (75, 81–2)

Glossary and Index of Technical Terms

Prosody: the study and notation of metre. (1)

Punctuation: a variety of marks, spaces, and other signs (such as distinguishing type-faces or founts) placed within the text to indicate pauses, emphases, and the sense. (58)

Pyrrhic: a foot of two unstressed beats (uu). (3, 4, 11–12)

Quadruple: of a foot, having four beats; the rhythm produced by such feet. (3)

Quatrain: a unit of four lines; often used for narrative. (25, 31–3)

Queen's English: or *King's English*: terms used since the sixteenth century to denote an ideologically and grammatically desirable standard of speech and writing, English 'as it should be spoken'. Compare 'BBC English', and the German equivalent, *Hochdeutsch* (or 'high German'). (91)

Question-mark: used (instead of a full-stop) to indicate questions, marked "?"; also a tonal indicator, usually of rising pitch; may be used medially or terminally. (64–5)

Quintain: used by some for a unit of five lines of identical length. (33)

Quintet: used by some for a unit of five lines where one or more differs in length from the others.

Ragged: of texts and margins, not justified. (48)

Raw syntax: my coinage to describe sequences of words which lack one or more of the elements (such as prepositions, pronouns, conjunctions, and punctuation) which conventionally indicate clausal hierarchy and other aspects of syntactical construction. (132–3)

Refrain: (or *burden*) a line or lines that are repeated. (39)

Relative clause: one which gives additional but syntactically inessential information about a subject, verb, or object; commonly signalled by 'who', 'which', or 'that'. (125)

Rhetoric: originally, the formal rhetorical devices used in any text, such as rhetorical questions, repetition, and so on, but the term now (and especially in the USA) usually has the looser sense of 'the persuasiveness of a text'. (61)

Rhyme: the coincidence of sounds. (87)

Rhyme royal: a stanza of seven lines, in iambic pentameter, having the rhyme scheme *ababbcc*. (34)

Rhyme scheme: a method of notating the pattern of rhymes in a stanza or poem using the alphabet. The first line, and all subsequent lines that rhyme with it, are *a*; the next line that does not rhyme, and all subsequent lines that rhyme with it, are *b*; and so on. Line-lengths may also be indicated, by placing the number of beats after the letter denoting the line. (23, 86)

Rime riche: (or *identical rhyme*) occurs when the sounds both before and after the last stressed vowel of two or more words or phrases are identical; principally the rhyming of homographs and homophones. (87)

Rising rhythm: that produced by feet with stressed beats following unstressed beats. (5)

Rocking lineation: the effect of counterpointed (cæsura-to-cæsura) lines created by placing a cæsura in the same position in two or more successive lines. (78–81)

Roman: of a fount, with ordinary upright characters (such as these). (5)

Romance: of languages, deriving from Latin; of modern English words, deriving from Latin or a Romance language. (104)

Romantic: of poetry, that of the later eighteenth and first half of the nineteenth centuries; a part of the general Romantic movement, a reaction against the Enlightenment, such poetry is characteristically vigorous, formally innovative, and concerned with nature and subjective emotion. (143–4)

Roomscape: my coinage for the domestic 'landscape', to which responses are often gendered. (177)

Round: of brackets, a common term for lunulæ. (66)

Roundelay: a simple Elizabethan song, usually with a burden. (94)

Rules: in printing, horizontal lines longer than a dash, such as those separating footnotes from the main text. (69)

Sapphic: of an ode, of a particular and highly prescribed form; largely dactylic, sapphics are very rare in English. (39)

Satire, satiric: one of the five classical genres, satires were (and are) complex forms (or sequences) unified by the intention to ridicule. (40)

Scanning: the process of working out the scansion. (10)

Scansion: the individual metrical pattern of a particular line or poem. (10)

Scriptio continua: text without word-separation, standard until the late seventh century CE, thereafter passing into disuse. (60–1)

Semi-colon(s): the third heaviest (or second lightest) stop, marked ";"; conventionally implies completion of the immediate sense, and either a change or development in the sense between *semi-cola*, or the itemization of each *semi-colon*; invented by Pietro Bembo (1470–1547) in Venice in the 1490s explicitly as a stop intermediate between the colon and the comma. (62–3)

Semi-colon, semi-cola: the part(s) of a sentence between semi-colons, and/or between a semi-colon and a heavier stop. (62–3)

Sentence: in modern use, the largest unit of syntax, composed of one or more clauses, and normally containing at least one grammatical subject, one transitive or intransitive verb, and if appropriate an object; typographically, sentences begin with a capital letter and end with a full-stop. (60, 122)

Separatist: of feminisms, desiring and recommending the isolation of women from men. (172)

Sestet: a unit of six lines. (33–4)

Sestina: a poem of thirty-nine lines, each ending with one of six words in the sequence *abcdef faebdc cfdabe ecbfad deacfb bdfeca eca* (or *ace*), all six terminal words to be used in the final three lines. (34)

Sex: biological, anatomical, and chromosomal maleness or femaleness, as distinct from culturally acquired gender. (172)

Shakespearean: of a sonnet, having the rhyme scheme *ababcdcdefefgg*. (36–7)

Shape poems: or *concrete* poems, those whose text is organized on the page to depict a shape, or otherwise to involve pictorial as well as verbal representation. (52–3)

Sho'ah: The Hebrew word for what is usually referred to in English as 'the Holocaust'. (108, 141)

Short metre: an iambic quatrain of the form *a6b6c8b6*. (31)

Signe(s) de renvoi: any mark(s) used to associate matter in the text with material added in the margin (including foot- and endnotes). (69–70)

Single-rhyme: a rhyme scheme with only one set of rhyming lines, as *abcb* or *abac*. (31–2)

Singleton: a unit of one line. (33, 27)

Slant rhyme: half-rhyme. (90)

Slash: (or *solidus*), used to indicate alternatives, marked "/", as in he/she; and to indicate line-breaks (/) and stanza breaks (//) in transcribed verse. (64)

Small capitals: smaller upper-case letters, such as THESE. (48)

Solidus: another name for the slash. (64)

Sonnet: until the early seventeenth century, any short lyric poem; thereafter specifically a poem of fourteen lines in iambic pentameter. As a form its traditional use is for poems of (frustrated) love and courtship. (23, 25–6, 36–8)

Special sorts: in a fount of type, the non-alphanumeric characters which are rarely used. (70)

Spenserian: of a sonnet, having the rhyme scheme *ababbcbccdcdee* (37); of a stanza, in iambic pentameter and having the rhyme scheme *ababbcbcc12* (24, 35).

Spondee: a foot of two stressed beats (xx). (3, 4)

Square: of brackets, a common term for crotchets. (65)

Stand: another name for the epode of a Pindaric ode. (39)

Stanza: a group of lines with a specified rhyme scheme, pattern of line-lengths, etc.; used as a unit of form; usually shown on the page by blank lines above and below. (24)

Stanza break: the physical (and syntactical) space (and pause) between stanzas, marked in transcription with a double slash, "//". (75)

Stichic: of verse, not stanzaic; a sequence of individual lines. (24)

Stops: a collective term once covering all punctuation, but now usually restricted to the four marks (comma, semi-colon, colon, and full-stop) which, analysed syntactically, indicate some degree of completion of the sense, or, analysed as elocutionary, require the reader to pause. Though imprecise the term can be particularly useful in the analysis of long verse periods. (61–4)

Stressed: of a beat, spoken emphatically, often with the voice pitched slightly higher than for an unstressed beat (1); of an ending, with one or more stressed hypermetrical beats (7); of a rhyme, with the stressed vowel in the last beat (87, 89).

Strophe: (or *turn*), the first stanza of a Pindaric Ode. (39)

Style: here, the verbal manner in which an argument is conducted. (61)

Sub-clause: any clause that is not a main clause, including all relative clauses, parenthetical clauses, etc. (121)

Substitute foot: any foot used as a replacement for one of the regular feet in a given line; includes inverted and distinguishing feet. (5)

Suspension-mark(s): full-stops used singly to indicate the abbreviation of a word by the suspension of terminal letters, and used in threes to indicate an ellipsis. (61)

Syllabic: of verse, with a prescribed number of syllables per line. (31)

Synonyms: different words with the same meaning. (104)

Syntactic: of punctuation, indicating the sense; distinguished from 'elocutionary' and 'deictic' punctuation. (59)

Syntax: the relations between words and clauses (of whatever kind) within a period or sentence. (120)

Synthetic: of a language, having inflected endings, prefixes etc. (1)

Tennysonian stanza: an arch-rhymed quatrain in iambic tetrameter, so-called for its use by Tennyson in *In Memoriam A.H.H.* (33, 161–2)

Tercet: a unit of three lines in which one or more does not rhyme with the others. (30–1)

Terza rima: successive tercets rhyming *aba bcb cdc ded* etc. (30–1, 89–90)

Tetrameter: a line of four feet. (3)

Teutonic: of languages or words, Germanic. (104)

Thematic puns: those connected to the subject or theme of a work. (97, 110–11)

Tragedy, tragic: on the of the five classical genres, tragedies dealt with the lives and fates of individuals, usually of high social or political rank; long-regarded as the highest or noblest genre. (41–2)

Transitive: of a verb, requiring an object. (60)

Tribrach: a foot of three beats, all unstressed (uuu). (3)

Trimeter: a line of three feet. (3)

Triple: of a foot, having three beats; the rhythm produced by such feet. (3, 7–8)

Triplet: a unit of three lines which all rhyme together. (30)

Trochee, trochaic: a foot of two beats, a stressed followed by an unstressed (xu); the metre produced by such feet. (3, 4, 6–7)

Turn: a moment of disjunction and/or renewal, creating a shift or development of the sense at a specified point in a form (31, 37–8); in relation to the Pindaric ode, another name for the strophe (39).

u: notation for an unstressed beat. (3)

Unstressed: of a beat, spoken unemphatically, often more rapidly and with the voice pitched slightly lower than for a stressed beat (1); of an ending, with one or more unstressed hypermetrical beats (7); of a rhyme, with one or more unstressed beats following the last stressed vowel (87, 89).

Upper-case: of letters, capitals. (5)

'Value-free' history: history supposedly written objectively, without ideological selection or emphasis of material; presently regarded as a chimæra. (141)

Verse paragraphs: the divisions of a long poem in a constant non-stanzaic (or *stichic*) form, indicated (like prose paragraphs) by indenting the first line of each. (27)

Victorian: of poetry, literally that written during the reign of Victoria (1837–1901), but used in schemata of literary history to fill the gap between 'Romantic' and 'Modernist' poetry. (143–4)

Villanelle: nineteen lines in iambic pentameter, of the form *aba aba aba aba aba abaa*, with lines 1, 6, 12, and 18 a refrain, and lines 3, 9, 15, and 19 a second refrain. (39)

Virgula plana: mediæval term for the dash. (68)

Virgula suspensiva: mediæval form of the comma, marked "/"; never common in print, it survived in manuscript at least until the early nineteenth century (Coleridge). (64, 68)

Vowel-rhyme: occurs when the last stressed vowel of two or more words or phrases is identical, but the sounds following the shared vowel differ. (90)

Word: a single unit of sense. (60–1)

Word-separation: the practice of using spaces between words, invented in Ireland in the late seventh century CE. (60–1)

Wrenched accent: occurs when the requirements of metrical stress prevail over the natural stress of a word or words. (10)

Wrenched monorhyme: my coinage to describe the rhyming of unstressed participle endings. (87–9)

x: notation for a stressed beat. (3)

Index of Poems and Poets Quoted and Cited

Initial definite and indefinite articles are omitted in English titles.

I BY POEM

Index of Poems and Poets Cited

II BY POET

Select Bibliography and Further Reading

A: General

Brogan, T. V. F. (ed.), *The New Princeton Handbook of Poetic Terms* (Princeton: Princeton University Press, 1994); ISBN 0–691–03672–1.

Brower, Reuben A., 'The Discovery of Design', in *The Fields of Light: An Experiment in Critical Reading* (1951; repr. London, Oxford, and New York: Oxford University Press, 1962); ISBN 0–31–322653–9.

Chisholm, Alison, *A Practical Poetry Course* (London: Allison & Busby, 1994); ISBN 0–7490–0114–3.

Ciardi, John, *How Does A Poem Mean?* (Boston: Houghton Mifflin, 1959); ISBN 0–39–518605–6.

Cuddon, J. A., *A Dictionary of Literary Terms* (revised edition, Harmondsworth: Penguin, 1982); ISBN 0–14-051112–1.

Hamilton, Ian (ed.), *The Oxford Companion to Twentieth-Century Poetry* (Oxford and New York: Oxford University Press, 1994); ISBN 0–19–866147–9.

Hyland, Paul, *Getting into Poetry* (Newcastle-upon-Tyne: Bloodaxe Books, 1992 [Bloodaxe Poetry Handbooks: 1]); ISBN 1–85224–118–7.

Parrott, E. O. (ed.), *How to be Well-Versed in Poetry* (Harmondsworth: Penguin, 1991); ISBN 0–14–011275–8.

Perrine, Laurence, *Sound and Sense: An Introduction to Poetry* (5th edition, New York: Harcourt Brace Jovanovich, 1977); ISBN 0–15–582604–2.

Preminger, Alex, *et al.* (eds), *The New Princeton Encyclopedia of Poetry and Poetics* (Princeton: Princeton University Press, 1993); ISBN 0–691–02123–6.

B: Metre and Form

Attridge, Derek, *Well-Weighed Syllables: Elizabethan Verse in Classical Metres* (Cambridge: Cambridge University Press, 1974); ISBN 0–521–20530–1.

—— *The Rhythms of English Poetry* (London: Longman, 1982); ISBN 0–582–55105–6.

Bibby, Cyril, *The Art of the Limerick* (Hamden, Conn.: Archon Books, 1978); ISBN 0–208–01761–5.

Fussell, Paul, *Poetic Meter and Poetic Form* (New York: McGraw-Hill, 1979); ISBN 0–07–553606–4.

Nabokov, Vladimir, *Notes on Prosody & Abram Ganibal* (Princeton: Princeton University Press, 1964 [Bollingen Series]); ISBN 0–691–01760–3.

Read, Herbert, *Form in Modern Poetry* (1932; repr. London: Vision Press, 1989); ISBN 0–85478–336–9.

Roethke, Theodore, 'Some Remarks on Rhythm', in Ralph J. Mills, Jr. (ed.), *On the Poet and his Craft: Selected Prose of Theodore Roethke* (Seattle and London: University of Washington Press, 1966); ISBN 0–295–74003–5.

Spiller, Michael R. G., *The Development of the Sonnet: An Introduction* (London: Routledge, 1992); ISBN 0–415–08741–4.

Taylor, Dennis, *Hardy's Metres and Victorian Prosody* (Oxford: Clarendon Press, 1988); ISBN 0–19–812967–X.

Thompson, John, *The Founding of English Metre* (1966; repr. New York: Columbia University Press, 1989); ISBN 0–231–06755–0.

C: Layout and Lineation

Cook, Elizabeth, *Seeing Through Words: The Scope of Late Renaissance Poetry* (New Haven and London: Yale University Press, 1986); ISBN 0–300–03675–2.

Gray, Alasdair, *1982 Janine* (Harmondsworth: Penguin, 1985); ISBN 0–14–007110–5.

—— *Poor Things* (Harmondsworth: Penguin, 1993); ISBN 0–14–017554–7.

Griffiths, Eric, *The Printed Voice of Victorian Poetry* (Oxford: Clarendon Press, 1989); ISBN–0–19–812989–0.

Hollander, John, Introduction to *Types of Shape* (new edition, New Haven and London: Yale University Press, 1991); ISBN 0–300–04925–0.

Levertov, Denise, 'On the Function of the Line', in *Chicago Review*, 30: 3 (1979), 30–6.

McCloud, Scott, *Understanding Comics: The Invisible Art* (New York: Harper Perennial, 1994); ISBN 0–06–097625–X.

McGann, Jerome, *The Textual Condition* (Princeton: Princeton University Press, 1991); ISBN 0–691–01518–X.

—— *Black Riders: The Visible Language of Modernism* (Princeton: Princeton University Press, 1993); ISBN 0–691–01544–9.

D: Punctuation

Graham-White, Anthony, *Punctuation and Its Dramatic Value in Shakespearean Drama* (Newark, NJ, and London: University of Delaware Press/Associated University Presses, 1995); ISBN 0–87413–542–7.

Honan, Park, *Browning's Characters: A Study in Poetic Technique* (New Haven: Yale University Press, 1961).

Lennard, John, *But I Digress: The Exploitation of Parentheses in English Printed Verse* (Oxford: Clarendon Press, 1991); ISBN 0–19–811247–5.

—— "Punctuation—and: 'Pragmatics' ", in A. H. Jucker (ed.), *Historical Pragmatics* (Amsterdam and Philadelphia: John Benjamins, 1995); ISBN 90–272–5047–2 (Hb; Eur.)/1–55619–328–9 (Hb; USA).

Parkes, Malcolm B., *Pause and Effect: An Introduction to the History of Punctuation in the West* (Aldershot: Scolar Press, 1992); ISBN 0–85976–742–7.

E: Rhyme

Bradford, Richard, 'Rhyme', in *Silence and Sound: Theories of Poetics from the Eighteenth Century* (Rutherford/Madison/Teaneck, NJ and London: Fairleigh Dickinson University Press/Associated University Presses, 1992); ISBN 0–8386–3435–4.

Daniel, Samuel, 'A Defence of Ryme' (1603), in e.g. A. C. Sprague (ed.), *Samuel Daniel: Poems & A Defence of Ryme* (Chicago and London: University of Chicago Press, 1965); ISBN 0–226–13609–4.

Milton, John, 'The Verse', a note prefixed to the second edition of *Paradise Lost*, in e.g. Alastair Fowler (ed.), *Paradise Lost* (London: Longman, 1976); ISBN 0–582–48455–3.

Ricks, Christopher, 'John Milton: Sound and Sense in *Paradise Lost*', in *The Force of Poetry* (Oxford: Clarendon Press, 1984); ISBN 0–19–811722–1.

—— 'Frustration at a Recalcitrant World', in *T. S. Eliot and Prejudice* (London: Faber and Faber, 1988); ISBN 0–571–15254–6.

Stillman, Frances, *The Poet's Manual and Rhyming Dictionary* (London: Thames & Hudson, 1966); ISBN 0–500–27030–9.

F: Diction and Syntax

Baugh, Albert C., and **Cable, Thomas**, *A History of the English Language* (4th edition, London: Routledge & Kegan Paul, 1993); ISBN 0–415–09379–1.

Coetzee, J. M., 'The Rhetoric of the Passive in English', in David Attwell (ed.), *J. M. Coetzee: Doubling the Point: Essays & Interviews* (Cambridge, Mass. and London: Harvard University Press, 1992); ISBN 0–674–21518–4.

Crystal, David, *The Cambridge Encyclopedia of Language* (Cambridge: Cambridge University Press, 1987); ISBN 0–521–42443–7.

—— *The Cambridge Encyclopedia of the English Language* (Cambridge: Cambridge University Press, 1995); ISBN 0–521–40179–8.

Empson, William, *Seven Types of Ambiguity* (1930; repr. London: Hogarth Press, 1984); ISBN 0–7012–0556–3.

—— *The Structure of Complex Words* (1951; repr. London: Hogarth Press, 1985); ISBN 0–7012–1006–0.

Lewis, C. S., *Studies in Words* (2nd edition, repr. Cambridge: Cambridge University Press, 1990) [Canto]); ISBN 0–521–39831–2.

Nash, Walter, *Jargon: Its Uses and Abuses* (Oxford: Blackwell, 1993); ISBN 0–631–18063–X.

Nowottny, Winifred, *The Language Poets Use* (with corrections, London: Athlone Press, 1965); ISBN 0–485–12009–7.

Robinson, Ian, *The Foundations of English Prose: The Art of Prose Writing from the Middle Ages to the Enlightenment* (Cambridge: Cambridge University Press, 1996); ISBN 0–521–48088–4.

Sacks, Shelson (ed.), *On Metaphor* (Chicago and London: University of Chicago Press, 1979); ISBN 0–226–73334–3.

Williams, Raymond, *Keywords: A Vocabulary of Culture and Society* (revised edition, London: Fontana, 1988); ISBN 0–00–686150–4.

G: History and Biography

Appleby, Joyce, Hunt, Lynn, and Jacob, Margaret, *Telling the Truth about History* (New York and London: Norton, 1994); ISBN 0–393–03615–4.

Cunningham, Val, *British Writers of the Thirties* (Oxford: Oxford University Press, 1989); ISBN 0–19–282655–7.

Davenport, Guy, 'Ozymandias', in *The Geography of the Imagination: Forty Essays by Guy Davenport* (London: Picador, 1984); ISBN 0–330–28415–0.

Empson, William, *Using Biography* (London: Chatto & Windus/Hogarth Press, 1984); ISBN 0–7011–2889–5.

Everett, Barbara, *Poets in Their Time* (Oxford: Oxford University Press, 1991); ISBN 0–19–811281–5.

Friedlander, Saul (ed.), *Probing the Limits of Representation: Nazism and the "Final Solution"* (Cambridge, Mass. and London: Harvard University Press, 1992); ISBN 0–674–70766–4.

Hartman, Geoffrey H. (ed.), *Holocaust Remembrance: The Shapes of Memory* (Oxford and Cambridge, Mass.: Blackwell, 1994); ISBN 1–55786–367–9.

Lowes, John Livingston, *The Road to Xanadu: A Study in the Ways of the Imagination* (1927; repr. London: Picador, 1978); ISBN 0–330–25270–4.

Maier, Charles S., *The Unmasterable Past: History, Holocaust, and German National Identity* (Cambridge, Mass. and London: Harvard University Press, 1988); ISBN 0–674–92975–6.

Walcott, Derek, *The Antilles: Fragments of Epic Memory* (New York: Farrar, Straus & Giroux, 1992/London: Faber and Faber, 1993); ISBN 0–374–10530–8/0–571–17080–3.

—— *Derek Walcott reads a selection of his work* [from] Collected Poems 1948–84 *and* Omeros (Argo/Polygram, 1994; catalogue no. 522–222–4).

Wilmer, Clive (ed.), *Poets Talking:* Poet of the Month *Interviews from BBC Radio 3* (Manchester: Carcanet, 1994); ISBN 1–85754–075–1.

Young, James E., *Writing and Rewriting the Holocaust: Narrative and the Consequences of Interpretation* (Bloomington and Indianapolis: Indiana University Press, 1990); ISBN 0–253–36716–6.

H: Gender

de Beauvoir, Simone, *The Second Sex* (1949; translated and edited by H. M. Parshley, London: Picador, 1988); ISBN 0–330–30338–4.

Cameron, Deborah (ed.), *The Feminist Critique of Language: A Reader* (London: Routledge, 1990); ISBN 0–415–04260–7.

Cixous, Hélène, *Coming to Writing & Other Essays* (edited by Deborah Jensen, Cambridge, Mass. and London: Harvard University Press, 1991); ISBN 0–674–14437–6.

Epstein, Julia, and Straub, Kristina (eds), *Body Guards: The Cultural Politics of Gender Ambiguity* (New York and London: Routledge, 1991); ISBN 0–415–90389–0.

Flynn, Elizabeth A., and Schweickart, Patrocinio P. (eds), *Gender and Reading: Essays on Readers, Texts, and Contexts* (Baltimore and London: Johns Hopkins University Press, 1986); ISBN 0–8018–2907–0.

Kramarae, Cheris, and Treichler, Paula A. (eds), *Amazons, Bluestockings and Crones: A Feminist Dictionary* (London: Pandora, 1992); ISBN 0–04–440863–3.

Montefiore, Jan, *Feminism and Poetry: Language, Experience, Identity in Women's Writing* (2nd edition, London: Pandora, 1994); ISBN 0–04–440893–5.

Yorke, Liz, *Impertinent Voices: Subversive Strategies in Contemporary Women's Poetry* (London: Routledge, 1991); ISBN 0–415–05204–1.

I: Writing Poetry

Brownjohn, Sandy, *To Rhyme Or Not to Rhyme: Teaching Children To Write Poetry* (new edition, London: Hodder & Stoughton, 1994); ISBN 0–340–61148–0.

Bugeja, Michael J., *The Art and Craft of Poetry* (Cincinatti: Writer's Digest Books, 1994); ISBN 0–89879–633–4.

Hart, David (ed.), *Border Country: Poems in Process* (Birmingham: Wood Wind Publications, 1991); ISBN 1–871320–01–1.

Sansom, Peter, *Writing Poems* (Newcastle-upon-Tyne: Bloodaxe Books, 1994 [Bloodaxe Poetry Handbooks: 2]); ISBN 1–85224–204–3.

Singleton, John, and Luckhurst, Mary (eds), *The Creative Writing Handbook: Techniques for New Writers* (London: Macmillan, 1996); ISBN 0–333–64226–0.

Turner, Barry (ed.), *The Writer's Handbook* (London: Macmillan/PEN, annual editions from 1987).

J. Anthologies and Volumes of Poetry

Adcock, Fleur (ed.), *The Faber Book of 20th Century Women's Poetry* (London: Faber and Faber, 1987); ISBN 0–571–13693–1.

Coote, Stephen (ed.), *The Penguin Book of Homosexual Verse* (with revisions, Harmondsworth: Penguin, 1986); ISBN 0–14–058551–6.

cummings, e.e., *Poems 1913–62* (New York: Harcourt Brace Jovanovich, 1972); ISBN 0–15–121060–8.

Ferguson, Margaret *et al.* (eds), *The Norton Anthology of Poetry* (4th edition, New York and London: Norton, 1996); ISBN 0–393–96820–0.

Greer, Germaine *et al.* (eds), *Kissing the Rod: An Anthology of 17th Century Women's Verse* (London: Virago, 1988); ISBN 0–86068–851–8.

Harold, John (ed.), *How Can You Write a Poem When You're Dying of AIDS?* (London: Cassell, 1993); ISBN 0–304–32904–5.

Harrison, Tony, *Selected Poems* (2nd edition, Harmondsworth: Penguin, 1987); ISBN 0–14–010563–8.

—— *v.* (2nd edition, Newcastle-upon-Tyne: Bloodaxe, 1989); ISBN 0–906427–97–5.

—— *The Shadow of Hiroshima and other film/poems* (London: Faber and Faber, 1995); ISBN 0–571–17675–5.

Heaney, Seamus, *New Selected Poems 1966–1987* (London & Boston: Faber and Faber, 1990); ISBN 0–571–14372–5.

Hill, Geoffrey, *Collected Poems* (Harmondsworth: Penguin, 1985); ISBN 0–14–008383–9.

——, *New & Collected Poems 1952–1992* (Boston and New York: Houghton Mifflin, 1994); ISBN 0–395–68086–7.

Kermode, Frank, *et al.* (eds), *The Oxford Anthology of English Literature* (2 vols; New York: Oxford University Press, 1973); ISBN 0–19–501657–2/501658–0.

Lonsdale, Roger (ed.), *The New Oxford Book of Eighteenth-Century Verse* (with corrections, Oxford: Oxford University Press, 1987); ISBN 0–19–282054–0.

—— *Eighteenth-Century Women Poets* (with corrections, Oxford: Oxford University Press, 1990); ISBN 0–19–282775–8.

Morris, John N., *A Schedule of Benefits* (New York: Atheneum, 1987); ISBN 0–689–11950–X.

Morrison, Blake, *The Ballad of the Yorkshire Ripper and other poems* (London: Chatto & Windus, 1987); ISBN 0–7011–3227–2.

O'Siadhail, Micheal, *Hail! Madam Jazz: New & Selected Poems* (Newcastle-upon-Tyne: Bloodaxe, 1992); ISBN 1–85224–208–6.

—— *A Fragile City* (Newcastle-upon-Tyne: Bloodaxe, 1995); ISBN 1–85224–334–1.

Powell, Jim, *It was Fever that Made the World* (Chicago: Chicago University Press, 1989); ISBN 0–226–67707–9.

Reilly, Catherine (ed.), *Scars Upon My Heart: Women's Poetry and Verse of the First World War* (London: Virago, 1981); ISBN 0–86068–226–9.

Seth, Vikram, *The Golden Gate* (London: Faber and Faber, 1986); ISBN 0–571–13967–1.

Soyinka, Wole, *Mandela's Earth and other poems* (London: Methuen, 1990); ISBN 0–413–61610–X.

Walcott, Derek, *The Gulf and Other Poems* (London: Jonathan Cape, 1969); ISBN 0–224–01057–3.

—— *Collected Poems 1948–84* (New York: Farrar, Straus & Giroux/London: Faber and Faber, 1986); ISBN 0–374–12626–7/0–571–16291–6.